Monogram Monarch Series

DORNIER 335
ARROW

Monogram Monarch Series

OTHER FINE BOOKS FROM MONOGRAM

The Luftwaffe in Sweden 1939-1945
By Bo Widfeldt
ISBN: 0-914144-28-6

The Vanishing Paperclips,
America's Aerospace Secret
By Hans H. Amtmann
ISBN: 0-914144-33-2

Monarch-1, Arado 234 Blitz
By J.R. Smith & E.J. Creek
ISBN: 0-914144-51-0

V-Missiles of the Third Reich
By Dieter Hölsken
ISBN: 0-914144-42-1

Jet Planes of the Third Reich;
The Secret Projects, Vol. 1
By Manfred Griehl
ISBN: 0-914144-36-7

German Aircraft Interiors 1935-1945, Vol. 1
By Kenneth A. Merrick
ISBN: 0-914144-41-3

The Official Monogram US Navy &
Marine Corps Aircraft Color Guide
1950-1959, Vol. 3
By Maj. John M. Elliott, USMC ret.
ISBN: 0-914144-33-2

The Official Monogram US Navy &
Marine Corps Aircraft Color Guide
1960-1993, Vol. 4
By Maj. John M. Elliott, USMC ret.
ISBN: 0-914144-34-0

The Official Monogram US Army
Air Service & Air Corps Aircraft
Color Guide 1908-1941, Vol. 1
By R.D. Archer
ISBN: 0-914144-46-4

DORNIER 335 ARROW

J. Richard Smith, Eddie J. Creek

&

Thomas H. Hitchcock

Monogram Aviation Publications, Sturbridge, Massachusetts

Monogram Monarch Series

Library of Congress Card Number
96-75250
ISBN 0-914144-52-9
Printed in Hong Kong

Published by Monogram Aviation Publications
Post Office Box 223, Sturbridge, Massachusetts 01566 USA

CONTENTS

Introduction

In 1983, Monogram Aviation Publications published *Monogram Close-Up 21, Dornier 335*, which was widely acclaimed as the foremost survey of one of the most interesting warplanes to emerge from the Second World War. Unfortunately, *Close-Up 21* went out of stock in 1988. Recognizing that interest in the history of this remarkable aircraft design had not waned over the intervening years, Monogram is pleased to bring this expanded story back to active circulation. Chapters 1 and 4 are completely new, as are most of the illustrations, photographs, and appendices. Chapters 2 and 3 formed the bases for our text within *Close-Up 21*.

Of all the aircraft that emanated from the drawing boards of German designers during the Second World War, it was the Dornier 335 that was perhaps the most intriguing. Seemingly unique in its push-pull layout, it could have been the predictor of what was to come, had it not been for the advent of the turbojet. The jet engine offered so much more power for its weight, that it was understandable this form of propulsion overshadowed the whole Dornier 335 program.

However unusual the tandem-engine layout was, the Dornier 335 was *not* the first aircraft to employ this engine arrangement. Several designers of other nations adopted the tandem- engine concept but *always* in conjunction with a tailplane supported by twin booms. Dornier was the first to stretch the fuselage long enough, enabling it to support not only the wings, but also the entire tailplane assembly.

Officially known as the *Pfeil* (Arrow), Dornier 335 production was authorized at a time when many military planners questioned the wisdom of allocating valuable and finite resources to a new and unproven aircraft type no matter how promising the design appeared on paper. They reasoned, not without good cause, that there were already other aircraft in production that fulfilled the mission of the Do 335 Arrow. They argued that it was ill advised to waste so much material and manpower on a brand new aircraft, no matter how spectacular its performance, at a time when the *Luftwaffe* (German Air Force) desperately needed more of those aircraft already committed to battle. Furthermore, they reasoned that two single-engined fighter-bombers could be built for one Do 335. Although this assertion was not altogether correct, it certainly had merit by the time the Do 335 was ready to enter full-scale production. Nevertheless, these viepoints were academic by late 1944, for no amount of Arrows could have altered the final outcome of the war in Europe.

What then was the significance of the Dornier 335 Arrow? On a purely technical level, its design was based on proven engineering principles. But on a conceptual level it was, for its day, a brilliant and unique achievement. Designed from the beginning to meet more than one mission requirement, the basic design was so sound that it easily lent itself to further development. In addition, it was undoubtedly the fastest propeller-driven aircraft to enter production during the war. It was a pilot's aircraft. For its size (slightly larger and heavier than the American P-47 Thunderbolt) it was fast, remarkably agile, and a steady gun platform. It was rugged but not

Opposite: *Professor Dr.* Claudius Dornier, born on May 14, 1884, in Kempten, Bavaria, was the son of a foreign language instructor from France. Field Marshal Erhard Milch, the second most powerful man in the German Air Force, described Claude (a familiar form of Claudius) Dornier as a man who kept his promises. Therefore, when the Technical Office of the Air Ministry initially rejected Dornier's submission for the new twin-engined heavy fighter and high speed bomber, it was Milch who overruled his own staff and sanctioned development of what would become the Do 335. *Prof.* Dornier lived and worked through two world wars, and each time he rebuilt his company better than before. The tradition endures into the 21st Century. Claude Dornier died at the age of 85 on December 5, 1969. His son, *Prof.* Claudius Dornier, Jr., carried forth his father's ideals as a designer and chief executive officer of Dornier GmbH until his retirement in the early 1980s.

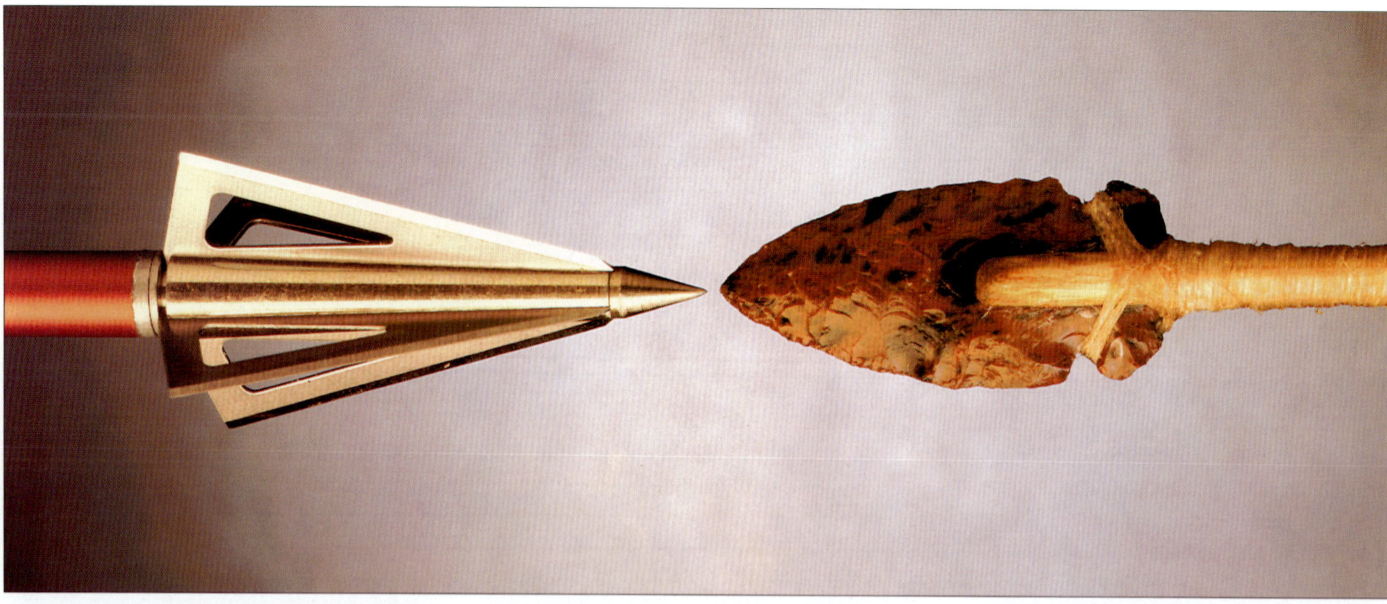

impervious. Had a sufficient number of Arrows entered operational service with the *Luftwaffe*, there is no doubt it would have lived up to its designer's expectations.

The reader may find it helpful to understand the German system of aircraft designations from the earliest forms, through the end of the war. To the casual historian, these designations do not, by themselves, enlighten or detract from the narrative, they are simply a means of identification. Yet it is often beneficial to see beyond the obvious, to better grasp the complexity of German aircraft nomenclature as it existed through approximately thirty years, from 1915 to 1945.

In the early days of aviation, the German state did not have a universal system of allocating aircraft designations or aircraft names. Instead, individual aircraft manufacturers evolved an internal system tailored to each firm for establishing order and model identification. In 1910 when Claudius Dornier began his career in aviation, while employed at the *Luftschiffbau* Zeppelin, aircraft designations were devised by the various manufacturers without any central control. However, by the summer of 1914, the German Army foresaw the need for classifying aircraft according to their characteristics in the following manner:

A - Unarmed two-seat, single-engined monoplanes (training aircraft).
B - Unarmed two-seat, single-engined biplanes (training aircraft).
C - Armed two-seat, single-engine biplanes (observation aircraft).
D - Armed single-seat, single-engined biplanes (fighter aircraft).
E - Single-seat, single-engined monoplanes (observation aircraft).
F - Multi-engined, multi-seat flying boats.
G - Twin-engined, multi-seat biplane (bomber aircraft).
R - Multi-engined, multi-seat biplane (*Riesenflugzeug*-Giant aircraft)

All other aircraft designations from the period were created by the individual aircraft manufacturers.

From 1915 to a period shortly after the Armistice of 1918, most German aircraft firms employed the system described above but sometimes with certain modifications to suit the circumstance. For example, the Zeppelin-Lindau (Do.) Cl-1 of 1918 was a single-engined, two-seat observation or reconnaissance biplane, while the Do.CsI (the lowercase "s" indicated *see* - sea) also of 1918, was a single-engined, two-seat observation monoplane with twin floats. Note that in this instance, since there was no classification matching the aircraft's description and role, the Cl-1 was classified within the primary group, which in this case was the C-class. The C-classification was further expanded by the Roman numeral I, which indicated that this aircraft was the first design within the C-class. The hyphen followed by the number 1 designated that more than one variant of this design existed, namely the Do. CI-2.

However, by 1922, when the Zeppelin-Lindau name was officially changed to the Dornier *Metallbauten* GmbH, Dornier took this opportunity to introduce a new system of identifying his aircraft. Gone was the old system of listing an aircraft by its design and role. The new system instead employed letters, beginning with the first letter of the alphabet and, occasionally, in conjunction with descriptive names. For example, the Do A was a small flying boat known as the *Libelle* I (Dragon-fly I). The firm's name was abbreviated in the same way as before, but with the period in Do. deleted. The *Libelle* II, although an entirely new aircraft, was also known as the Do A. This system is summarized within the listing at the base of page 9.

The three unknown letters (M, W, and Z), that were apparently never assigned, possibly were at one time intended for three racing seaplane projects dating from 1924 to 1931. This supposition is purely speculation, as no confirming evidence is known to exist.

By 1930, aviation in Germany was expanding at a phenomenal rate, fueled by optimism and the astonishing advances made in civil aviation during this remarkable period. Recognizing the necessity to simplify and bring order to a maze of private and government systems, the Weimar Republic's Communications Ministry (*Reichsverkehrsministerium - RVM*) instituted a new universal system applicable to all powered aircraft built from 1931 onward. This system was simple, calling for the issuance of sequential blocks of numbers to the principal manufacturers of aircraft within Germany. This system did not pertain to the type, role, or description of the aircraft. However, the Ministry's system had an additional feature intended to standardize the nomenclature between airframes and engines: all airframe numbers were preceded by the number 8 (e.g., 8-217 was the Do 217 twin-engined bomber), while aero-engine numbers were preceded by the number 9 (e.g., 9-211 was the Junkers Jumo 211 water-cooled engine). It must be stressed that these "8" and "9" prefixes were seldom used except for aircraft and engine parts lists and other miscellaneous company internal communications. Duplicate numbers were avoided. Each number was preceded by a two or three-letter aircraft manufacturer abbreviation. The RVM's aircraft manufacturers' system began with the number 10 and progressively moved forward to higher numbers. Initially, whole blocks of numbers were allocated to specific aircraft manufacturers. The honor of being the first recipient of the new numbering system was Dornier. This firm received the first thirty-one numbers: 10 through 30 inclusive. For the most part, the issuance of specific numbers to specific aircraft was left to the discretion of the manufacturer. Once assigned to a manufacturer, these Ministry numbers were almost never reassigned. There were a few isolated exceptions, however. In changing over to the new system, some manufacturers, including Dornier, elected to allocate their preassigned block numbers to an already existing aircraft. For example the Do 10 was really the Do C 4 and the Do 11 was originally known as the Do F under the old system. There was some confusion at first, but the short-term use of dual designations easily corrected the situation.

To give the new system stability, it was decided that only those designs sanctioned for construction should be given a government number. All firms were free to institute their own internal project identification systems; but, once approved for construction, the firm's internal number was replaced with one of the preassigned ministry block numbers. In the case of the Dornier 335, it was originally conceived as Dornier *Projekt* P 231. When this project was approved for construction, it received its government air ministry number 335, and henceforth would always be identified as the Do 335.

In 1933 Adolf Hitler came to power in Germany and in 1935 he announced the creation of the *Reichsluftfahrtministerium,* State Ministry of Aviation, or RLM, which took over those activities formerly associated with the old RVM Communications Ministry. The new RLM embraced the established alpha-numeric aircraft designation system controlled by the *Generalluftzeugmeisters* C- *amt* (GL/C), or General Chief of Aircraft/ Office C. On the whole, this system worked remarkably well, though there were privately funded single-engined sport aircraft that were flown exclusively with their maker's low-digit identification number (e.g., the Erla 6 and the Fieseler Fi 5) and had no relationship to the GL/C list.

Chapter 1 describes all of the known Dornier aircraft, except the Do 335 family, which were allocated RLM GL/C numbers from the Do 10 up to the Do 417. It is notable that some of these aircraft, although designed and approved for construction, were never built. Dornier inexplicably, elected not to use or assign certain low numbers within the GL/C list until the end of the war. The first batch allocated to Dornier, including numbers 21, 25, 27, 28, 29, and 30 could have been held in abeyance pending the possible continued production of older aircraft previously identified within the so-called letter system.

Although outside the scope of this book, it is worth noting that the first batch of post World War Two aircraft designed by Dornier were, on his own initiative, assigned the unused prewar numbers 25, 27, 28, 29, and 30.

Before leaving the subject of German aircraft designations, it is helpful to understand how an aircraft designation reflected its production status along the path from prototype to series manufacture. During the transition period between the RVM and the RLM, it was not uncommon for manufacturers to use lowercase letters as a suffix, and to identify aircraft prototypes (e.g., Do 11a). By 1935, this practice was abandoned and, in its place, the capital letter"V" (*Versuch* - experimental) followed by a number was standardized (e.g., the Do 17 V1 was the first prototype for the Do 17). This method of identifying experimental aircraft continued unchanged throughout the period of the Third *Reich,* however, by mid-1944, an additional prototype rating came into use which, although similar, embodied a broader application. This was the *Muster* (model) classification which had long been favored by the Austrians and was adopted by Dornier. The change over from V-numbers to M-numbers resulted in some Dornier 335 air-

DORNIER AIRCRAFT A - Z, 1921 TO 1933

Do A Libelle I (1921) and II (1922) single-engine small flying boat.
Do B Merkur I (1925) commercial single-engine aircraft.
Do C 1931 single-engine reconnaissance floatplane. Became the **Do 10.**
Do D 1924 single-engined torpedo and reconnaissance floatplane.
Do E 1924 single-engined reconnaissance flying boat.
Do F 1932 twin-engined cargo and mail aircraft (later as the **Do 11**).
Do G Greif (1920) twin-engined trans port aircraft project. Not built.
Do H Falke (1922) and Seefalke (1925) single-engined land and sea fighter.
Do I Letter not used to avoid confusion with Roman numeral one.
Do J Wal (1922) twin-engined flying boat (later as the **Do 16**).
Do K 1929 single-engined commercial utility aircraft.
Do L Delphin I (1920), II (1924) and III (1928) single-engined flying boats.
Do M Unknown assignment. Possibly a project design.
Do N 1925/26 twin-engined land plane military version of the Wal for Japan.
Do O Not used to avoid confusion with the number zero.
Do P 1928/29 four-engined land-based military version of the Superwal.
Do Q Reportedly a flying boat based on the Do A. Possibly the **Do 12** (1932).
Do R Superwal 1(1926) and 2 (1927) two and four-engined civil flying boats.
Do S 1930 four-engined large commercial flying boat.
Do T 1925 single-engined ambulance land or floatplane based on the *Komet* III.
Do U 1931 projected commercial version of the Do Y.
Do V Reportedly a special version of the *Komet* II (1922) for Russia.
Do W Unknown assignment. Possibly a project design.
Do X 1929/30 twelve-engined large civil flying boat.
Do Y 1931 three-engined bomber which became the **Do 15**.
Do Z Unknown assignment. Possibly a project design.

craft actually using both concurrently. These are summarized on page 166.

Once an aircraft was approved for quantity manufacture, the first series was the A-series. Subsequently, each new production variant took the next available letter *excluding* the letters I, O, Q, U, and V which, with the exception of the letter U, were never used. The sole example for the use of the letter U, as a series designator, was confined to the small number of Dornier Do 17 U-0 and U-1 pathfinder aircraft constructed during 1938. The problem with the letter U rested with the fact this letter became universally associated with modified (*Umbau*) aircraft, and as such, was used in conjunction with the modification of an existing aircraft series (e.g. the Do 217 N-1/U1). As recounted earlier, the letter V was always used in conjunction with experimental (*Versuch*) prototypes. In some instances, a particular letter was favored for reasons other than its being the next available. The aircraft-carrier version of the famous *Messerschmitt* 109, the Bf 109 T, used the letter T to identify its role (*Träger* - carrier). Occasionally, particularly when it came to single-seat fighters, there was a so-called preproduction series, such as the Do 335 A-0 (preproduction designated by the"0"). This"series" usually amounted to no more than ten aircraft which were set aside to serve as development aircraft for the testing of engines, weapons, and electronics for the planned A-1 series.

Aircraft which were modified at the factory, or in the field, to carry additional equipment, crew members, or to be fitted with a new engine or weapons system, had their designations amended to reflect these changes. Sometimes, these alphanumeric designations were quite extended due to the great number of non standard items. In the early days of the Second World War, designations were even amended to indicate an aircraft sub-type destined for export. This was accomplished by the insertion of the lowercase letter "a" (*ausland* - foreign) within the series letter designation as in the Fw 190 Aa-3. Lowercase letters could also be tacked onto a series designation for an alternative engine installation (e.g., Me 262 A-1a and Me 262 A-1b).

On the opposite page is a development flowchart for the Dornier 335, the projected Do 435, He 535 and the final production variant, the Junkers Ju 635. At the top is the RLM specification that resulted in the creation of the Do 335, calling for a twin-engined, single-seat warplane of the so-called *Zerstörer* class with a secondary mission of a *Schnellbomber* (high-speed bomber). The term *Zerstörer* was applied to a heavily armed, twin-engined day fighter capable of attacking heavily defended targets.

The Air Ministry had a change of mind on several occasions depending upon circumstances and the pressures of the day being exerted from higher authority. As a result, the development of the *Schnelbomber* was slowed, while increased interest was shown in the development and production of night fighter and reconnaissance variants.

This book describes in detail the protracted development program that attempted to bring the Do 335 to operational service with the *Luftwaffe* during the last year of the war in Europe.

ACKNOWLEDGMENTS

The authors and publisher are deeply appreciative for the kind assistance provided by Dana Bell, Arthur L. Bentley, Adrian P. Bishop, Helga Burgmaier, Philip Butler, Jean-Christophe Carbonel, Peter W. Cohausz, Philippe Couderchon, Mark Day, Manfred Griehl, Lee Gullick, Hans Kinzler, John H. Kuehnert, Alexander Kyd-Rebenburg, Richard P. Lutz, Jr., Peter Petrick, Philip Reed, Franz Selinger, Paula Smith, Konrad Soppa, Jay P. Spenser, Edward Tulley, Gen. Harold E. Watson (†), and *Dr. Ing.* Elmar Wilczek for their unselfish assistance in the preparation of this report.

Thomas H. Hitchcock

Sturbridge, MA

Below: The Do 335 A-02, photographed in Germany after restoration by the firm who built the aircraft some thirty-one years earlier.

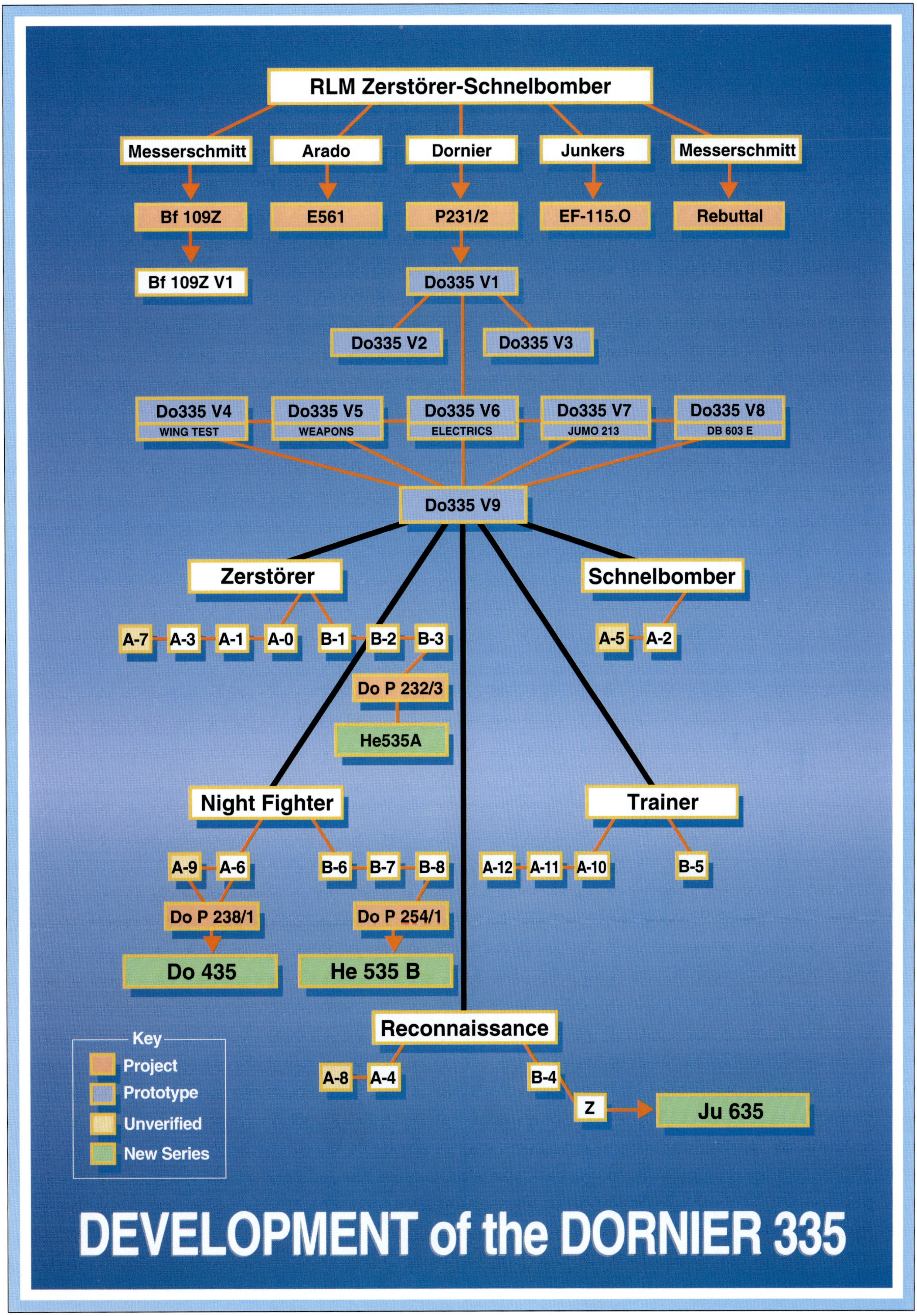
RLM Zerstörer-Schnelbomber
Messerschmitt
Arado
Dornier
Junkers
Messerschmitt
Bf 109Z
E561
P231/2
EF-115.O
Rebuttal
Bf 109Z V1
Do335 V1
Do335 V2
Do335 V3
Do335 V4
WING TEST
Do335 V5
WEAPONS
Do335 V6
ELECTRICS
Do335 V7
JUMO 213
Do335 V8
DB 603 E
Do335 V9
Zerstörer
Schnelbomber
A-7
A-3
A-1
A-0
B-1
B-2
B-3
A-5
A-2
Do P 232/3
He535A
Night Fighter
Trainer
A-9
A-6
B-6
B-7
B-8
A-12
A-11
A-10
B-5
Do P 238/1
Do P 254/1
Do 435
He 535 B
Reconnaissance
A-8
A-4
B-4
Z
Ju 635
Key
Project
Prototype
Unverified
New Series
DEVELOPMENT of the DORNIER 335

Foreword

Mit der Do 335 ist es durch die Tandemanordung der Triebwerk gegenüber allen anderen Flugzeugmustern mit Kolbenmotoren der gleichen Entwicklungsstufe gelungen wesentliche Vorteile zu erzielen, nämlich überlegene Geschwindigkeiten, uneingeschränkten Einmotorenflug und Lastenmitnahme ohne wesntlichen zusätzlichen Widerstand, durch Unterbringung im Rumpf. Das alles bei vorzüglichen Flugeigenschaften. Natürlich war dafür auch ein gewisser Aufwand erforderlich - z.B. für die zwei Triebwerke, für einen entsprechend geräumigen Rumpf und für den Einbau eines zuverlässigen Schleudersitzes bzw. einer entsprechenden Absprengeinrichtung an der hinteren Luftschraube. Allerdings waren die technischen Entwicklungsaussichten der Grundform - etwa durch Verwendung weiter fortgeschrittener Triebwerke, durch aufgesetzte Kabine (zur Sichtverbesserung), durch Zwillingsrumpf (635) u.s.w. beeinträchttigt durch die Konkurrenz der Flugzeug mit Strahltriebwerken (auch bei der Do 335 dachte man an solche Antriebe). Von entscheidendem Einflufl wasen dann selbstverständlich die geschichtlichen Ereignisse.

Due to the tandem arrangement of the Do 335's engines, substantial performance advantages could be achieved over all other piston-engined aircraft; namely, superior speed, unimpaired flight on one engine and an internal load carrying capability without a substantial increase in drag due to its engine placement. All this in an extraordinary handling aircraft.

However, these advantages came at a certain expense. For example, with two heavy tandem engines there had to be a correspondingly spacious fuselage plus a mandatory reliable ejection seat, or an appropriate explosive charge device to jettison the rear propeller. The development of the basic design, on the other hand, namely through the use of increasingly powerful engines, a raised cockpit (for improved vision), double fuselage (Ju 635) etc., was limited due to the competition by aircraft with jet engines (such engines were also envisaged for the Do 335). Naturally historic events were, in the end, of decisive influence.

Heinrich Beauvais

H. Beauvais

Opposite: A recent photograph of *Dipl.-Ing.* Heinrich Beauvais, born in 1908, was one of the *Luftwaffe's* most respected test pilots. He made five test flights in two Do 335 prototypes between May 9, 1944 and September 19, 1944 while stationed at the *Luftwaffe's* primary research station located at Rechlin. Today he lives in southern Germany and is a Honorary Fellow of the Society of Experimental Test Pilots.

Chapter I

A SURVEY of DIVERSITY

By Thomas H. Hitchcock

Opposite: Banking steeply is this newly completed Do 217 M-1 in night bomber matte black camouflage and outfitted with tubular exhaust flame suppressers attached to its two DB 603 A engines. Approximately 230 examples of this successful twin-engined bomber were built during 1943.

No history of the Dornier Do 335 would be complete without a survey of the company which produced this fascinating warplane. To understand and appreciate the engineering achievement which the Do 335 represented, we must travel back to 1913 to the shores of the Bodensee at Friedrichshafen in southern Germany. It was here that the gifted 29-year-old Claudius Dornier was beginning his long career in aviation. After three years of working as an engineer in their experimental division for the legendary pioneer of airships, *Graf von* Zeppelin (founder of *Luftschiffbau* Zeppelin), Dornier's talents were fully recognized. Appointed as chief scientific advisor to *Graf von* Zeppelin, Dornier was initially entrusted with the preliminary design of a very large all-metal rigid transatlantic airship. But, it was the idea of all-metal aircraft which fascinated young *Dipl. Ing.* Dornier. To better explore the possibilities of producing such aircraft, Dornier with a small support staff, headed the newly created Zeppelin-Werke Lindau GmbH located at Lindau-Reutin. During the summer of 1914, Claudius Dornier and his assistants completed the design of their first aircraft, a large 142.7 foot (43,5 m) span, all-metal flying boat.

When war erupted in Europe in August 1915, Dornier's design offices were relocated to a modest, single-level wooden barracks at Seemoos near Manzell and Friedrichshafen. By this time, construction of Dornier's first aircraft was nearing completion. Known as the **Rs I** (*Riesenflugboot* I - Giant Flying Boat I), this very large flying boat was completed in October 1915, and powered by three 240-hp Maybach engines driving wooden propellers, each with a diameter of 11.5 feet (3,5 m). The Rs I held the distinction of being the first German aircraft to be constructed entirely of stressed Duralumin. Although the Rs I was wrecked during a winter storm before she could fly, two months of extensive taxiing trials were nevertheless successfully concluded. Six months later, the next Dornier-designed aircraft, the slightly smaller **Rs IIa**, was flown for the first time on June 30, 1916. But the Rs IIa was not entirely satisfactory, due to the complexity of three engines mounted in the hull driving propellers via long extension shafts and gearboxes. After studying the problem, Claudius Dornier designed an alternative engine layout, which would become the hallmark of so many Dornier-designed aircraft; namely engines arranged in tandem. The **Rs IIb** featured four Maybach engines in two tandem pairs. Without stretching the imagination, it could also be said that the basic design concept of tandem engine placement would, twenty-seven years later, result in the Do 335.

From 1916 up to the end of the First World War in November 1918, an additional six aircraft types were completed and flown. These included not only seaplanes but land-based fighter and reconnaissance aircraft. Most of these aircraft were produced as prototypes and many featured unusual metal structural fabrications, which were clearly well ahead of their time. Thus, although none of Dornier's aircraft saw operational duty during the Great War, they paved the way for what was to follow.

What followed were several unusual commercial flying boat designs of varying size plus a number of commercial land-based utility aircraft.

At the end of the Great War, the German aviation industry was virtually intact. The Allies had not invaded Germany and her aviation industry

had not been destroyed through bombing. Moreover, the Zeppelin-Werke Lindau GmbH, believing the future lay in civil aviation, continued to design, build, and test large aircraft which were technically in violation of the terms of the Armistice imposed by the Allies. On April 25, 1920, the crew of the commercial flying boat known as the **Gs I** (the letter G denoted the type as a bomber while the small "s" indicated *see* - sea) scuttled their aircraft off Kiel in the Baltic rather than allow it to fall into the hands of the Allied Control Commission. Six months later, during the autumn of 1920, the large **Rs IV** floatplane had to be broken up in compliance with strict size limitations imposed by the Allies. By this time, Dornier was taking no chances with the Allies. When their single-engined commercial flying boat, known as the **Cs 2**, *Delphin I* (Dolphin I, later as the Do L1), took to the air for the first time on November 24, 1920, few knew that it had been transferred in sections and assembled across the Bodensee on the other side of the lake (known to the Swiss as Lake Constance) in neutral Switzerland at Rohrschach.

These were difficult times for the German aviation industry, including Zeppelin-Lindau and Claudius Dornier. During the summer of 1921, under the watchful eye of the Control Commission, the all-metal commercial land plane, the **C 3**, *Komet I* (Comet I), flew for the first time, followed in mid-August by the small all-metal flying boat, ***Libelle I*** (Dragon-fly I, later known as the Do A). Both of these designs were carefully tailored to fit within the Commission's strict weight and performance limits. In 1922, after the appearance of the slightly larger ***Komet II***, and the ***Libelle II***, the Seemoos facility closed after being briefly prohibited by the Commission from engaging in further aircraft production from this facility. At this time, *Dipl. Ing.* Dornier took this opportunity to divest himself of his association with Zeppelin, and changed the name of the business to Dornier *Metallbauten* GmbH while relocating his principal design offices to Friedrichshafen. In addition, be-

Above: The first prototype of the Do *J Wal* (Whale) is shown undergoing test during 1922 at Dornier's Italian facility at Marina di Pisa. It had accommodation for eight passengers within the bow and featured a tandem engine installation patterned after the earlier Do Gs II of 1919. The *Wal* proved very popular with over 260 being produced for customers in several countries including Argentina, Brazil, Chile, Japan, Netherlands, Soviet Union and Yugoslavia.

Left: This Do C III, *Komet III* (Comet III) was license built in Japan by Kawasaki during 1925. The *Komet III* was much larger than either the *Komet I* or *II* and successfully flown by Deutscher Aero Lloyd and Deutsche Lufthansa. It had a top speed of 104 mph (168 km/h) and a ceiling of 11,483 feet (3,500 m) and was piloted by a crew of two and had accommodation for up to six passengers.

Above: This photograph shows two of the 28 examples of the Do N produced for the Japanese in 1926. The Do N was essentially a land plane version of the *Wal* whose materials were fabricated in Germany and shipped to Japan for assembly by Kawasaki. Two tandem BMW VI engines enabled the Do N to attain a maximum speed of 112 mph (180 km/h).

cause the Swiss Rohrschach plant was too limited, *Dipl. Ing.* Dornier traveled to Italy where he established a satellite factory known as the *Societa di Construzioni Meccaniche di Pisa*, at the former Gallinari plant located at Marina di Pisa with the intention of freely building aircraft not permitted in Germany.

Although the sole prototype of Dornier's 1919 flying boat, the Gs I, was no more, it had proven its capabilities while being demonstrated in the Netherlands. Building on his experience with the Gs I, Dornier evolved the next generation flying boat, based on the **Gs II** (which was aborted after the Allies demanded the destruction of the Gs I). He hoped thereby to firmly establish his company's future. The resulting aircraft from the Italian factory was a sleek, three-seat all-metal parasol wing military flying boat with a wing span of 73.8 feet (22,5 m) known as the **Do J**, *Wal* (Whale). First flown on November 6, 1922, it proved an immediate success for Dornier. Soon plans were formalized to license and build the *Wal* in Japan, Netherlands, and Spain. It would be powered by a variety of engines from several countries. The *Wal* featured a number of advanced design concepts including a wide beam hull with sponsons (airfoil-shaped protrusions attached at the waterline for added stability), multiple water-tight bulkheads, and powered by two engines, arranged in tandem, atop the wing. It was so successful that no less than twenty world records were set by the *Wal,* and the type remained in production in Italy for ten years, up to 1932.

During 1922, Dornier produced a trim, single-seat parasol-wing fighter, at his Italian plant. Known as the **Do H** *Falke* (Falcon) powered by a 300 hp Hispano-Suiza engine, it was capable of reaching 155 mph (250 km/h) at 19,686 feet (6,000 m). This type was produced under license in Switzerland and the United States for the US Navy as the Curtiss-Wright WP-1. A floatplane version, known as the *Falke-See*, was also produced under license by the Japanese.

In 1923, the Dornier company purchased the Manzell plant of the Flugzeugbau Friedrichshafen after selling off the old Seemoos property. Dornier used the newly acquired Manzell facility for production of the Control Commission-approved commercial aircraft *Delphin I, Delphin II, Komet I* and *Komet II.*

Further production and expansion in 1924, introduced the sport flying boat known as the ***Spatz*** (Sparrow), the single-engined utility aircraft **Do C**, and the military version, the **Do D**, fitted with twin floats, intended for reconnaissance and torpedo bomber duties. The **Do E** also appeared in 1924 as a single-engined parasol-wing reconnaissance flying boat. On December 7, 1924, the new *Komet III* flew for the first time as an enlarged and improved commercial aircraft based on the earlier *Komet II.* Meanwhile, the Japanese were seeking to expand their air force as rapidly as possible and were keenly interested in several German aircraft manufacturers; especially Dornier. The Japanese firm of Kawasaki, applied for and was granted license rights to the Do L1, the Do J and the *Komet III.*

On February 10, 1925, the Dornier **Do B**, *Merkur I* (Mercury I), a six-passenger commercial aircraft powered by a 460 hp BMW VI engine, flew for the first time. Essentially a development of the company's highly successful *Komet III*, the *Merkur* set seven world records in June 1926. It was primarily manufactured as a land plane, but a seaplane version with two floats was also produced as the *Merkur Is.*

The Dornier **Do N** of 1926 was an interesting departure from the usual practice of building aircraft under license. The Do N was a *Wal* modified for use as a land plane for the Japanese. The materials were fabricated by Dornier and shipped to Kobe, Japan, for assembly and flew for the first time on February 19, 1926. A total of twenty-eight examples of the Do N were completed by the Japanese. During the summer of 1926, Dornier was attempting to shorten the long lines of production

Above: First flown in 1925, the Do B *Merkur I* (Mercury I) was essentially an enlarged development of the *Komet III*. It was powered by a 600 hp BMW VI engine without reduction gear and had provision for a crew of two plus accommodation for up to six passengers. It also had the luxury of a toilet directly behind the passenger compartment. Approximately 46 examples of the *Merkur I* were built with most serving with Deutsche Lufthansa although a number were also operated by the Soviet airline. **Left:** The Do B *Merkur I* See (Mercury I Sea) was a floatplane version of the landplane built for Walter Mittelholzer general manager of Ad Astra, the Swiss airline, for explorer flights over Africa. The aircraft logged over 12,428 miles (20,000 km) in 76 days when it reached Cape Town on February 20, 1927. **Below:** A view of the Japanese license built version of the *Merkur I* which was operated between major Japanese cities in the late 1920s.

Above: A Japanese operated Do J II Wal dating from 1931 showing certain improvements over the initial design. **Below:** A Do J II Bos *Wal* used on Lufthansa's South Atlantic airmail route. These *Wals*, the so-called 8,5 ton *Wals*, were reinforced for catapult launch.

which had been necessitated by the earlier imposition of strict rules by the Allied Control Commission, although by this time they were largely eliminated. He built a new factory in Switzerland at Alterheim near Rorschach, across from Manzell on Lake Constance, which was known as the *Aktiengessellschaft für* Dornier-*Flugzeuge* (Corporation for Dornier Aircraft). During this period the Italian factory produced the twin-engined **Do R2** *Superwal* 1 which flew for the first time on September 30, 1926, and the similar four-engined **Do R4** *Superwal* 2, which took to the air for the first time on September 15, 1928. Earlier, on

March 30, 1928, the eight-passenger **Do L3** *Delphin III* appeared. The **Do K 1** was a single-engined land plane capable of carrying eight passengers, which flew for the first time on May 7, 1929. A twin-engined version, known as the **Do K 2** was completed and flown in December 1929, but not built in series.

October 1929 will be remembered for the crash of the American stock market and the beginning of the Great Depression. But, some months prior to this calamity, on July 12, 1929, the largest aircraft ever was flown for the first time by Dornier's chief test pilot, Richard Wagner. The aircraft was the huge 12-engined Dornier **Do X**. Reportedly designed to a secret 1927 German Navy specification call-

Above: One of six Do R4 *Superwals* operated by the Italian airline SANA during 1928. Essentially similar to the twin-engined Do R2 *Superwal*, the R4s were powered by four engines such as the Siemens Jupiter radial. A crew of 4 and up to 19 passengers could be carried at a top speed of 130 mph (210 km/h).
Below: One of three Do L 3 *Delphin III* (Dolphin III) ten-passenger flying boats built in 1928 by the newly opened Dornier facility at Altenrheim on the Swiss side of the Bodensee.

Above and Below: The huge 12-engined prototype Do X of 1929 being outfitted at Dornier's Altenrheim facility prior to its maiden flight. With a height of 33.1 feet (10,1 m), it was impressive from any perspective. It was designed for a crew of 14 and accommodation for up to 66 passengers

ing for a large, long-range reconnaissance aircraft capable of carrying mines and torpedoes, the Do X was nevertheless built at Dornier's Altenrheim facility on Lake Constance as a 66-passenger commercial flying boat. Powered by twelve 525 hp Siemens Jupiter air-cooled engines and with an all-up weight of 53 tons (48,000 kg), the Do X was decidedly underpowered. Yet on October 21, 1929, the Do X took off with a crew of ten carrying 150 passengers plus 9 stowaways, for a record flight that was not bettered until 1949.

During August 1930, the twelve Jupiter engines, with their horizontal interconnecting airfoil supports, were removed and replaced by twelve American Curtiss Conqueror water-cooled engines, each developing 640 hp for takeoff. Like the Jupiter engines, the Conqueror powerplants were mounted in six tan-

Above and Below: Two views, taken in 1930, of the Do X re-engined with 12 American Conqueror water-cooled engines. The top photograph shows the Do X taking off from Lake Constance carrying the name Lufthansa on her bow in spite of the fact, Lufthansa never operated the giant flying boat. The lower view was taken during its long distance flight from Europe to Africa to South America to North America before returning to Germany in May 1932.

dem pairs above the wing. But unlike the first installation, which featured a single airfoil-shaped vertical support section, the Conquerors were supported by vertical struts while the horizontal bracing between engines had horizontal struts at the front and rear of each engine nacelle. In this configuration, the Do X left Germany on November 2, 1930, for an extended long-range flight to America by way of the Netherlands, England, Portugal, Portuguese Guinea, Brazil, the West Indies, and on to New York, creating a sensation when it arrived on August 27, 1931. Negotiations with potential American operators failed, and after visiting the United States for almost nine months, during which time it was in dry dock, on May 19, 1932, the Do X returned to Germany. In spite of the vast publicity bestowed upon the giant Dornier X, and the fact that the name of the German airline, Lufthansa, was painted on the bow, the airline declined to fly the aircraft because of economics. The world-wide Depression had spread to Europe and the German economy was in a precarious state.

It is interesting to note that two additional examples of the Do X were completed for the Italians during 1932. Powered by twelve Fiat A-22

Above: The sole example of the Do S, D-1967, which appeared in 1930. It was a 4-engined enlargement of the *Superwal* operated by a crew of 4 and capable of carrying up to 30 passengers.
Below: Powered by 4 Walter-Castor tandem radials, the prototype Do K3, D-2183, of 1931 was 10-passenger commercial aircraft which failed to enter production.

R water-cooled engines, each developing 580 hp, these aircraft were a disappointment and saw only limited service with the Italian Navy. The first example, Do X2, I-ABBN, Alessandro Guidoni, and the second aircraft, Do X3, I-REDI, Umberto Maddalena, were eventually scrapped in 1935.

On September 23, 1930, the four-engined flying boat Do S flew for the first time. Intended as a 22-passenger commercial flying boat, the **Do S** never carried paying passengers since the sole example completed was built at a time when the world was suffering the ravages of the Great Depression and political upheaval in Germany. It was fitted with four Spanish Hispano-Suiza 12 Lbr water-cooled engines, developing 600 hp in the now familiar Dornier arrangement of tandem placement in pairs above the 101.7 ft (13,0 m) wing. In 1933, it was delivered to the *Deutsche Verkehrsfliegerschule* (DVS) (German Commercial Flight School) on Sylt where it served as a training aircraft.

In 1931, the **Do K 3**, a four-engined

high-wing commercial transport designed to carry a crew of two plus ten passengers was built. It was broadly based on the Do K 2, but differed in several respects from the earlier 1929 model. First flown on August 17, 1931, it was powered by four 305 hp Walter-Castor air-cooled radials. These were mounted in tandem pairs under the graceful wing just outboard from the lower fuselage and attached to the main wheel supports. The Do K 3 type was evaluated by Deutsche Lufthansa, but because of financial constraints, they declined to invest in the aircraft. The sole example of the Do K 3, D-2183, was finally purchased by the DVS for pilot training. The **Do K 4** was supposed to feature retractable gear, but this projected design was never built. During this period, Claudius Dornier was able to purchase the remaining shares Dornier Metallbauten GmbH from the holding company of *Luftschiffbau* Zeppelin, thus consolidating his control over the firm. Additionally, one of the first steps for Dornier-Werke GmbH (as it was now known) was to centralize operations at Friedrichshafen and to expand facilities at Manzell while at the same time acquiring two new satellite operations at Löwenthal and Allmansweiser.

Further growth of the Dornier firm resulted in the creation of the Dornier-Werke-Wismar located between Rostock and Lubeck, on the Baltic coast at Wismar. This facility was jointly financed by the state.

Initially known as the **Do C4** and flown for the first time on July 25, 1931, this military aircraft was the

Above: One of only two Do C4 fighters built in 1931 which featured a variable incidence engine installation designed to improve rate of climb. In 1933 it was redesignated Do 10. This aircraft was only the third fighter design built by Dornier since 1918. **Below:** The Do F of 1932 was a twin-engined cargo and mail plane. This example, D-3029, was one of ten aircraft flown by the *Reichsbahn* on their *Reichsbahnstrecken* (State railroad extension) flights in conjunction with Deutsche Lufthansa. In 1933 the Do F was redesignated Do 11.

Above: The graceful Do 12 known as the *Libelle III,* was a light amphibian first flown in 1932. With a crew of two and accommodation for up to four passengers, the sole prototype was flown by Fr. Schulte, known as the Flying Priest of Africa. It had a maximum speed of 130 mph (210 km/h).
Below: Based on the Do 11, the Do 13 C of 1933 incorporated a fixed and spatted main gear. It was one of the early bomber aircraft of the *Luftwaffe* which was powered by two BMW VI engines, each developing 750 hp for take off.

first fighter created by Dornier since his all-metal single-seat *Falke* fighter of 1922. It also had the distinction of receiving the first number in the 1933 RLM GL/C list (see p. 9) officially becoming the **Do 10**. A highly unusual feature of this design was the variable incidence of the entire engine. It was powered by a 710 hp BMW VI liquid-cooled engine mounted in such a way as to allow the pilot to change the angle of attack of the entire nose, thus increasing the rate of climb.

The **Do 11** (originally built as the Do F), first flew on May 7, 1932, as a twin-engined all-metal cargo and mail aircraft powered by two Siemens Jupiter radials of 550 hp. With the formation of the new German Air Force, the Do 11 served as an interim bomber. On June 23, 1932, the sole prototype of the **Do 12**, known as the *Libelle III*, was first flown. This single-engined light amphibian, initially powered by a 220 hp Argus AS 10, was later re-engined with the 317 hp Gnône-Rhône Titan 5 Ke radial and used by the missionary Father Schulte, known as the *Fliegenden Pater* (Flying Priest).

First flown on February 13, 1933, the **Do 13** was designed from the beginning as a twin-engined bomber for the new *Luftwaffe*. Not an entirely new design, it was based on the earlier Do 11 but incorporated a number of differences. Instead of a retractable landing gear, the Do 13 had fixed and braced gear and was initially powered by two Siemens Jupiter radials, but later versions had 750 hp BMW VI engines which gave the bomber a top speed of 162 mph

(260 km/h). It carried a crew of four and featured machine gun positions in the nose and mid fuselage. The Do 13 had a number of serious structural deficiencies which Dornier attempted to correct. To the superstitious, the number 13 of this aircraft took on a very real significance. Therefore, when the final modifications were made, Dornier designated the "new" bomber as Do 23.

The **Do 14**, first flown on August 5, 1936, was an experimental transocean flying boat incorporating a highly innovative engine and cooling arrangement. Two 690 hp BMW VI engines, buried side-by-side within the hull, were joined by a gearbox that drove a large (16 ft - 5 m) wooden propeller mounted on pylons above the fuselage by means of a single hollow drive shaft. Cooling was accomplished by an unusual surface evaporation system located on the wing's upper surface. Testing continued for a year, but no further examples of the Do 14 were built.

On October 17, 1931, from the Do Y

Above: The experimental transocean flying boat Do 14, of 1936, featured a novel engine arrangement of two BMW VIs buried within the fuselage driving a pusher propeller through shafts and a gearbox. As an economy measure, it was intended to switch off one of the powerplants during cruise. **Below:** The three-engined Do Y was a 4-seat bomber of 1931 built in Switzerland, and demonstrated in Germany. In 1933 it was redesignated Do 15 but it failed to enter military service with the *Luftwaffe.*

Above: The Do 16 was a military version of the 8-ton Wal produced between 1933 and 1935. This example, 60+G12, operated by Kü.Fl.Gr. 106, a coastal reconnaissance unit, was one of about thirty produced.
Below: The Do 17 P-1, W.Nr. 4013,"M", produced in 1937, was a long-range reconnaissance aircraft.

had its maiden flight from Dornier's Alterheim facility. The aircraft was a three-engined bomber powered by 450 hp Bristol Jupiter VI radials. In 1933, it was redesignated **Do 15** and re-engined with the more powerful 625 hp Gnône-Rhône Jupiter 9 Kers engines driving three-bladed propellers. Only two examples of this aircraft were built.

The **Do 16** was perhaps better known as the Do *Militar Wal*. It was produced in 1935 as a coastal defense flying boat fitted with three gun positions and underwing bomb racks for up to four 110 lb (50 kg) bombs. It was viewed as an interim

aircraft pending availability of the new Do 18.

The **Do 17** which first flew on June 18, 1938, was a highly successful and well known military aircraft design. It was produced in a dozen different versions and fulfilled a multitude of combat missions with total production reaching almost 2,400 units before being phased out of production in June 1940. It was fast, easy to handle, dependable, and lent itself to numerous modifications during its service career.

Intended as a possible replacement for the Do Wal, the well-known **Do 18** was first flown on March 15, 1935, as a long-range flying boat with both civil and military applications. Approximately 200 were completed before production ceased in June 1940. It served as a long-range mail aircraft with Deutsche Lufthansa, as a military long-range reconnaissance, maritime patrol, and air-sea rescue flying boat. Like many previous Dornier designs, the Do 18 proved to be an exceptional aircraft. Although it's defensive armament was considered weak, it was nevertheless popular with the crews who flew the 11 ton (10,000 kg) flying boat.

The **Do 19** was Dornier's first attempt at a long-range heavy bomber. It was created to meet a 1934 RLM requirement and was first flown on October 26, 1936, powered by four Bramo 322 J2 radials developing 715 hp each at takeoff. Its capability involved hitting distant targets in the British Isles in the west and the vicinity of the Ural mountains in the east. Three prototypes were

Above: A Do 18 D-1, 60+A42, serving with Kü.Fl.Gr. 106, was one of about 80 examples built by Dornier and under license by Weserflug.
Below: The Do 19 V1, D-AGAI, of 1936 was Dornier's first attempt at a four-engined long-range bomber. It carried a crew of seven and was capable of reaching 195 mph (315 km/h) with a service ceiling of 18,372 feet (5600 m). Three were ordered, but only one was completed.

Above: An artist impression of the Do 20, a large long-range flying boat project of 1936. It was to have been powered by eight coupled 1000 hp diesel engines driving four large propellers, and was to have carried up to 60 passengers. Unfortunately, Lufthansa was not enthusiastic for the Do 20, and the design remained only a project.
Below: An interesting 1944 commemorative issue stamp celebrating 25 years of German airmail service showing a hypothetical float plane strongly influenced by Dornier aircraft. Compare this fictional design with that of the Do 26 shown on page 31.

ordered, but only the first was actually completed and flown before the whole project was canceled in April 1937. Considerable controversy surrounded the decision to drop the long-range heavy bomber, but most historians now view the reasons given as being entirely valid, given the political aims of the Nazi leadership during the late 1930s.

In 1936, Dornier participated in a design competition sponsored by Deutsche Lufthansa (DLH), to create a large transoceanic flying boat capable of carrying at least 20 passengers. Dornier, who had considerable experience with very large flying boats, designed a large aircraft with a wing span of 160 feet (49,0 m) and a length of 131 feet (40,0 m). Given the designation **Do 20**, the flying boat would be powered by eight 1,000 hp Diesel engines buried within the wing. Through gearboxes and extension shafts, two engines were paired to drive one large propeller housed in aerodynamically streamlined fairings. Dornier calculated that the 62 ton (56,000 kg) flying boat could carry up to 60 passengers, or 12 to 16 passengers with spacious lounges and sleeping compartments. Dornier further calculated the Do 20 would have a maximum speed of 211 mph (340 km/h) with a range of 3,107 miles (5,000 km). Unfortunately for Dornier, the DLH contract was given to the firm of Blohm & Voss for their less ambitious BV 222. As a consequence, the Do 20 went no further. A scale model of the Do 20 was exhibited at the 1936 International Aviation Exhibition held in Stockholm, Sweden.

Although the next GL/C number, 21, was previously assigned to Dornier, it appears that this number was never allocated to an aircraft project. Thus, the **Do 21** remains a complete mystery. It has been suggested that it may have been linked to one of Dornier's proposed racing plane designs of the early 1930s, but there is no evidence to support this assumption.

Flown for the first time on July 15, 1938, the **Do 22** was a single-engined military floatplane based upon the earlier Do C-2A but incorporating a number of improvements. It was to carry a crew of three and was intended to fulfill the roles of coastal reconnaissance, light bomber, and torpedo bomber. Since Dornier was unsuccessful in obtaining *Luftwaffe* interest in the Do 22, permission was obtained which allowed Dornier to offer the aircraft on the export market. Soon, orders were obtained for a small number to be sold to Greece (12), Latvia (4), and Yugoslavia (12). A

land-plane version was created and flown for the first time on March 10, 1939. It was similar to the floatplane and was powered by an 880 hp Hispano-Suiza 12 Y21 twelve-cylinder, liquid-cooled engine, driving a three-bladed, variable pitch VDM propeller.

The **Do 23**, produced in 1934, was a medium bomber evolved from the earlier Do 11 and Do 13. It was similar to the earlier bombers, but incorporated a number of features designed to remedy the more objectionable vices which characterized the earlier versions. Powered by two BMW VI engines, each developing 735 hp, the Do 23 had a maximum speed of 163 mph (262 km/h) for an all-up weight of 20,282 lb. (9,200 kg). Approximately 280 examples were completed and flown by the *Luftwaffe*.

Flown for the first time on July 3, 1937, the three-engined **Do 24** proved to be a highly successful reconnaissance and air-sea rescue flying boat. The aircraft was designed to meet a 1935 Royal Netherlands Air service requirement. The first eleven aircraft completed for the Dutch were built under license by Weser Flugzeugbau of Bremen while an

Above: The Do 22L, was a landplane version of the Do 22 floatplane, and was produced during 1939. The example shown above, was one of the 4 aircraft originally ordered by the Latvians, but before they could be delivered, the Soviets occupied that Baltic country.
Below: This Do 23 G, coded S13+D49, served with a *Flugzeugführerschule* (Aircraft pilots' school) after the type had been relegated to trainer duties.

Above: One of the most successful Dornier flying boats was the three-engined Do 24. It first appeared in 1937 but in its later versions, it served as air-sea rescue type. Shown here is Do 24 N-1, KD+GJ, which was one of the aircraft formerly flown by the Dutch, but which had been modified by the addition of rescue equipment and two gun positions.
Below: The newly completed Do 26 V2, D-AWDS, *Seefalke*, beginning its take-off run on the Bodensee in May 1939. The Dornier trademark of tandem engines is evident in this view.

additional 25 were to be assembled under license in the Netherlands. After the occupation of the Netherlands by German forces, all incomplete airframes were sent to Germany for modification and use by the *Luftwaffe.* During the service life of the Do 24, several subtypes were built, each with different engines and/or equipment. Approximately 320 examples of the Do 24 were manufactured before production ceased. However, the end of the war did not bring an end to the career of the Do 24. The type remained in service with the French Navy until 1953 and in the Spanish air-sea rescue service until 1970.

The GL/C number 25 was allocated to Dornier before the war, but not assigned to an aircraft until after the war. Although beyond the scope of this book, the postwar **Do 25** was first flown in Spain during June 1954, as a single-engined liaison aircraft.

Only six examples of the sleek **Do 26** were built and the initial flight took place on May 21, 1938. The aircraft was fast, dependable, and innovative in design. Designed as a transocean flying boat for use by DLH, the Do 26 was intended for transatlantic mail service, but only eighteen flights across the South Atlantic were made before World War II. Powered by four Jumo 205 Diesels mounted in

the wings, the Do 26 was capable of reaching 208 mph (335 km/h) with a range of almost 3,107 miles (5,000 km). During the war, armament was installed, and the flying boat was used by the *Luftwaffe* as a transport and reconnaissance aircraft. One of the most innovative aspects of the tandem-engine layout was the hinging of the rear-facing Diesels which could pivot upward through 10 degrees to clear the water spray for take off and landing.

The next four RLM GL/C numbers of the first batch assigned to Dornier (27, 28, 29, 30) were not taken up by Dornier prior to the end of the war. The **Do 27** (single-engined utility aircraft), **Do 28** (twin-engined utility aircraft), **Do 29** (experimental STOL aircraft), and **Do 30** (projected STOL transport) are postwar aircraft and beyond the scope of this book.

The next GL/C number allocated to Dornier, the **Do 212**, was assigned to

Above: The red and white flag of Switzerland adorns the vertical tailplane of the Do 212 V1, HB-GOG, built in Dornier's Swiss facility in 1942, as an experimental single-engined amphibian. **Below:** An artist impression of the projected Do 214 graphically illustrates the aircraft's size. Designed during 1938 as a transocean flying boat, both civilian and military versions were planned. A mock-up was completed, but by 1942 this promising project was shelved indefinitely.

Above: The Do 215 B-1, NO+TB, was used as a reconnaissance bomber by the *Luftwaffe.* **Below:** The projected six-engined Do 216 dating from 1939. Both civilian and military versions were planned but none were completed by 1942 when the RLM ordered all work stopped.

a single-engined amphibian built by Dornier in Switzerland and first flown on August 3, 1942. The sole prototype, registered HB-GOG and carrying Swiss insignia, was a four-seat aircraft powered by a Hirth HM 512 B-0 buried within the fuselage and driving a four-bladed aft-mounted propeller via a long extension shaft.

Designed in 1938 as a large transocean flying boat, the **Do 214** was planned both as a 40-passenger (plus a crew of 12) civilian airliner for use by DLH, and a military supply aircraft for the *Luftwaffe.* A full-size mock-up was completed during the summer of 1939, but with the beginning of hostilities in September of that year, the RLM advised Dornier to defer work on the civil airliner. A large flying boat, with a wingspan of 197 feet (60,0 m), a length of 169 feet (51,6 m) and an estimated all-up weight of 160 tons (145,000 kg) it would have been larger than a Lockheed C-141 Starlifter.

The aircraft featured large stabilizing floats attached to the lower hull and, in the military version, a sideways hinged nose section to facilitate the loading of trucks. It was to be initially

powered by eight DB 606 or Jumo 218 engines, but later variants were to employ the DB 613. In spite of the aircraft's great potential, in 1942 all work on the Do 214 was halted.

The **Do 215** was originally planned as an export version of the well-known Do 17 Z bomber. The initial prototype was flown for the first time on December 5, 1939, equipped with two DB 601A engines. But, because of the outbreak of war, the export license was canceled by the German government. Instead, the Do 215 was taken over by the *Luftwaffe.* A total of 105 examples of the Do 215 were completed as reconnaissance aircraft, light bomber, and night fighter variants.

The **Do 216** was conceived in 1939 as a medium-size, six-engined, transocean flying boat in both civil and military versions. Power was to be supplied by six DB 603 or Jumo 223 engines driving large four-bladed propellers. The civil airliner was designed to accommodate 24 (North Atlantic route) or 44 (South Atlantic route) passengers plus a crew of six. The military version was to be armed and used for long-range reconnaissance. With a wingspan of 158 feet (48,0 m), a length of 138 feet (42,0 m) and an all-up weight of 82 tons (75,000 kg) the Do 216 had an estimated maximum speed of 277 mph (446 km/h). As in the case of the larger Do 214, work continued slowly on the Do 216 until 1942, when the RLM stopped further development.

No survey of Dornier aircraft would be complete without inclusion of the firm's highly successful and well-known **Do 217**. Produced in many

Above: One of the most successful and well liked medium bombers employed by the *Luftwaffe* was the Do 217. This Do 217 E-3/R2, W.Nr. 1044, TC+KR, is shown fitted with special under wing racks to accommodate a 551 lb (250 kg) SC 250 bomb. **Below:** The Do 317 V1, VK+IY, was a special high altitude bomber development of the Do 217.

Above: An impression of the Do 318 shows the flying boat to have been based upon the Do 24. Built by Weser Flugzeugbau, to investigate a new wing using a boundary control system, it was scuttled in the Bodensee in 1945 to prevent its capture. **Below:** The Do 417 was the last of the "17s"and represented a simplified medium bomber base on the Do 217.

different versions from 1940 until 1943 as a dive and medium bomber, reconnaissance aircraft, night fighter, and high altitude bomber, as well as a developmental aircraft for a diversity of unusual propulsion systems and parasite aircraft.

Only one **Do 317** was built and first flown on September 8, 1943, as a high- altitude bomber development of the successful Do 217. It was powered by two DB 603 engines driving VDM four-bladed propellers. Because its performance was disappointing, and little advantage was found over the Do 217, it was decided to abandon further development of the design.

The **Do 318** was a 1943 flying boat development of the successful Do 24. Built by the Weser Flugzeugbau, it was very similar to the Do 24, but incorporating a novel wing boundary control system devised by Arado engineers. One prototype was under test on the Bodensee when it was purposely sunk in 1945 to prevent its capture.

The last Dornier bomber of the war, the **Do 417**, remained only a project in spite of the fact that some components were flight-tested in other aircraft. Designed in 1942, was a simplified medium bomber with heavy defensive armament, powered by two Jumo 222 or DB 603 engines. The characteristic twin tail of the Do 17 - Do 317 series was discarded for a single vertical fin and rudder, beneath which a tail gunner was positioned.

This concludes our survey of Dornier aircraft produced up to the end of the Second World War with the exception of the Do 335 and its various derivatives. These are covered in the chapters which follow.

Chapter II

THE A-SERIES

By J. Richard Smith

Opposite: **Opposite:** Close-up of the forward engine to the Do 335 M13 showing the large VDM metal three-bladed propeller and the muzzle to the engine-mounted MK 103 cannon extending through the spinner. This aircraft was the first prototype for the heavily armed *Zerstörer* aircraft classification; the Do 335 B-2 series.

"This was possibly the most fascinating aircraft I've seen anywhere. Certainly the Do 335 had a most astonishing history. It was developed as an all-weather fighter and there were also night fighter and trainer versions, and I think it had tremendous potential. At the time it was probably the fastest piston-engined aircraft in the world. It think I'm right in saying that the Germans claimed a speed of 472 mph at 21,000 ft, and we'd no reason to disbelieve this figure. From what little we saw, it showed that it was a remarkably speedy aeroplane"

So commented Captain Eric M. Brown of Britain's Royal Aircraft Establishment on the Do 335, one of the most remarkable German aircraft produced during the Second World War. Had it not been for the advent of the turbojet, the layout pioneered by this airplane could have become standard for future piston-engined fighters.

For many years *Professor Dr.* Claudius Dornier had been working on the design of aircraft with tandem engines arranged back-to-back in a single nacelle. Before the mid-1930s this arrangement had been applied solely to flying boats and a few experimental bombers, but toward the end of the decade some thought was given to the design of a twin-engined fighter with this layout. The first patent (No 728 044) for such an aircraft was filed on August 3, 1937. The advantages of the layout were, to quote the patent: "(1) an aircraft consisting of at least three separately built and interchangeable parts; a front section containing a propulsion unit with a tractor propeller; a center section protected by fire walls fore and aft containing the crew, instrumentation and possibly also the fuel; and a rear section carrying the tail unit and second engine with pusher propeller. (2) an aircraft as (1) above, with the center section provided with an outer skin having increased resistance to bullets in the usual manner, for instance by several millimeter thick steel plating."

Shortly after filing the patent, Dornier began work on a project to incorporate the features proposed within it. Designated Dornier P 59, the project was for a single-seat, low-wing monoplane powered by a pair of Daimler-Benz engines. The radiator intakes for the rear engine were positioned on either side of the fuselage, behind the cockpit, with this unit driving the pusher propeller via an extension shaft. Other unusual features of the design were cruciform tail surfaces, the lower fin incorporating a tail skid and a variable incidence wing.

To prove the feasibility of a rear-mounted engine driving a pusher propeller via a long extension shaft, Dornier commissioned *Dr.* Ulrich Hüter to design a flying test bed incorporating such a feature. Designated Göppingen Gö 9, the airplane was built by the large Schempp-Hirth glider factory at Wüsterburg. It was a tiny single-seat machine powered by a single 80 hp Hirth I M60 R air-cooled, in-line engine. Like the Dornier P59, the Gö 9 had a cruciform tail, but with a retractable tricycle undercarriage.

Considerable ground testing of the Gö 9 (registered D-EBYN) was carried out before it made its first flight early in 1940 from Mengen with Dornier test pilot *Flugkapitän* "Ivan" Quenzler at the controls. For the first flights the Gö 9 was towed into the air by a Do 17 bomber (coded CO+JB), but it later took off under its own power. By the end of the test program late in 1941, the airplane had attained 137 mph (220 km/h) in level flight and proved the feasibility of the rear-engined layout.

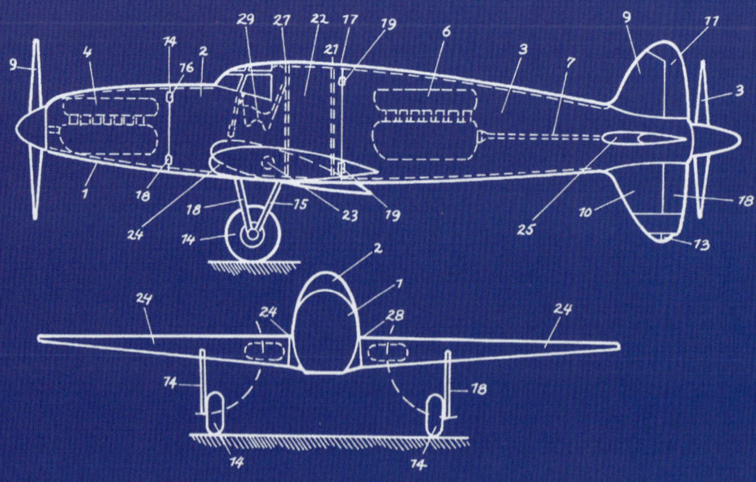

Airframe for Aircraft with Power Propulsion (Group 3-24)

b303 Pat. 728 044 of 3rd August 1937, published 18th Nov. 1942, Dornier Werke G.m.b.H. and Dr. Ing. e.h. Dornier, Friedrichshaven)*. Aircraft with 2 engines installed in tandem.

Patent Claim:

1. Aircraft consisting of at least three separately built and interchangeable parts, i.e. front section containing a propulsion unit with tractor propeller, a center section protected by fire walls fore and aft containing the crew, instrumentation and possibly also the fuel, and a rear section carrying the tail unit and a propulsion unit with a pusher propeller.
2. Aircraft as per Claim 1, characterized by the center section being provided by an outer skin having increased resistance against bullets in the usual manner, for instance by a several millimeter strong plating.

*) Inventor: Dr. Ing. e.h. Claude Dornier, Friedrichshafen

Despite the successful testing of the Gö 9, it appears that like many interesting projects of the early war period, the Dornier P 59 was delayed because the favorable progress of the conflict slowed the need for advanced aircraft of this type. By 1942 the course of the war had begun to change and in that year the German Air Ministry (RLM) issued a specification for a twin-engined fighter-bomber capable of carrying a 1,100 lb (500 kg) bomb at speeds in the order of 500 mph (800 km/h).

The specification was issued to Arado, Junkers and Dornier, the latter putting forward an improved version of its tandem-engined design under the designation P 231. Following an examination of the projects, the RLM issued a contract for the P 231 allocating its own designation, Dornier Do 335.

The Dornier P 231 /1 was similar to the original P 59 proposal, but without the complex variable incidence wing and retractable tricycle undercarriage. It was to be powered by two 1,500 hp Daimler-Benz DB 605 E engines, the improved P 231/2 having the more powerful 1,900 hp DB 603 Gs. A variation of the latter was proposed with twin fuselages each with an engine in the nose driving a conventional tractor propeller. This layout was eventually abandoned by Dornier in favor of the original single fuselage back-to-back idea. A third proposal was the P 231/3 in which the rear piston engine was to be replaced by a turbojet. All three projects had the radiators for the piston engines installed in the leading edges of the wing roots.

Prototypes

A development contract for three prototypes was initiated in January 1943. Little time was lost in developing the earlier two projects which led to construction beginning on the Dornier Do 335 VI , the first prototype of an aircraft intended for a large number of roles including those of interceptor fighter, fast bomber and reconnaissance. The prototype was similar to the P 231/2 but with an annular radiator for the forward engine and a large scoop under the rear fuselage feeding the after radiator. The Do 335 V1, W.Nr. 230001,CP+UA, made its first flight from the Dornier plant at Friedrichhafen on October 26, 1943. The pilot on this flight was *Flugkapitän* Hans Dieterle, who had previously gained the world speed record for Germany. This had occurred on March 30,1939, when the young 23 year old pilot had attained an average speed of 463.919 mph (746.606 km/h) in the He 100 V8 experimental fighter. He later left Heinkel to become Dornier's chief test pilot.

Top: A copy of the German patent drawing taken out on August 3, 1937. Interestingly, Dornier took out a similar patent in France, No. 840.203, on July 4, 1938. **Left:** Only one prototype of the Gö 9 was built by Schempp-Hirth to prove the feasibility of a pusher propeller mounted behind the tailplane - a key feature of the Do 335.

Above: The unusual Gö 9 presented an interesting sight in flight with its fully retractable tricycle landing gear stowed and the rear mounted propeller rotating as a blur. The Gö 9 was painted in RLM Color 05, cream overall with a black registration. Note the small tail-mounted wheel at the base of the ventral fin. This served as bumper to protect the tailplane and propeller from making contact with the runway.

Two further tests with the Do 335 V1 took place on November 2, 1943, the first with Werner Altrogge at the controls, the second with Quenzler. Diploma Engineer (*Dipl. Ing.*) Werner Altrogge had previously flown the high altitude Ju 86 R reconnaissance aircraft over the British Isles before joining the Dornier company as a test pilot. These two men, in company with Dieterle, conducted all early tests with the Do 335.

On the fourth flight of the prototype, the Do 335 VI attained a speed of 373 mph (600 km/h) at sea level and later tests were to prove that the prototype could fly quite handily on one engine without the asymmetric problems associated with normal twin-engined aircraft. In fact it was found that it could fly faster with the forward engine stopped than with the rear propeller feathered. A speed of 348 mph (560 km/h) was possible in the former condition in level flight. One problem did however manifest itself, one that was to plague the airplane throughout its life. This was that the rear engine tended to overheat because of the difficulty of providing adequate cooling.

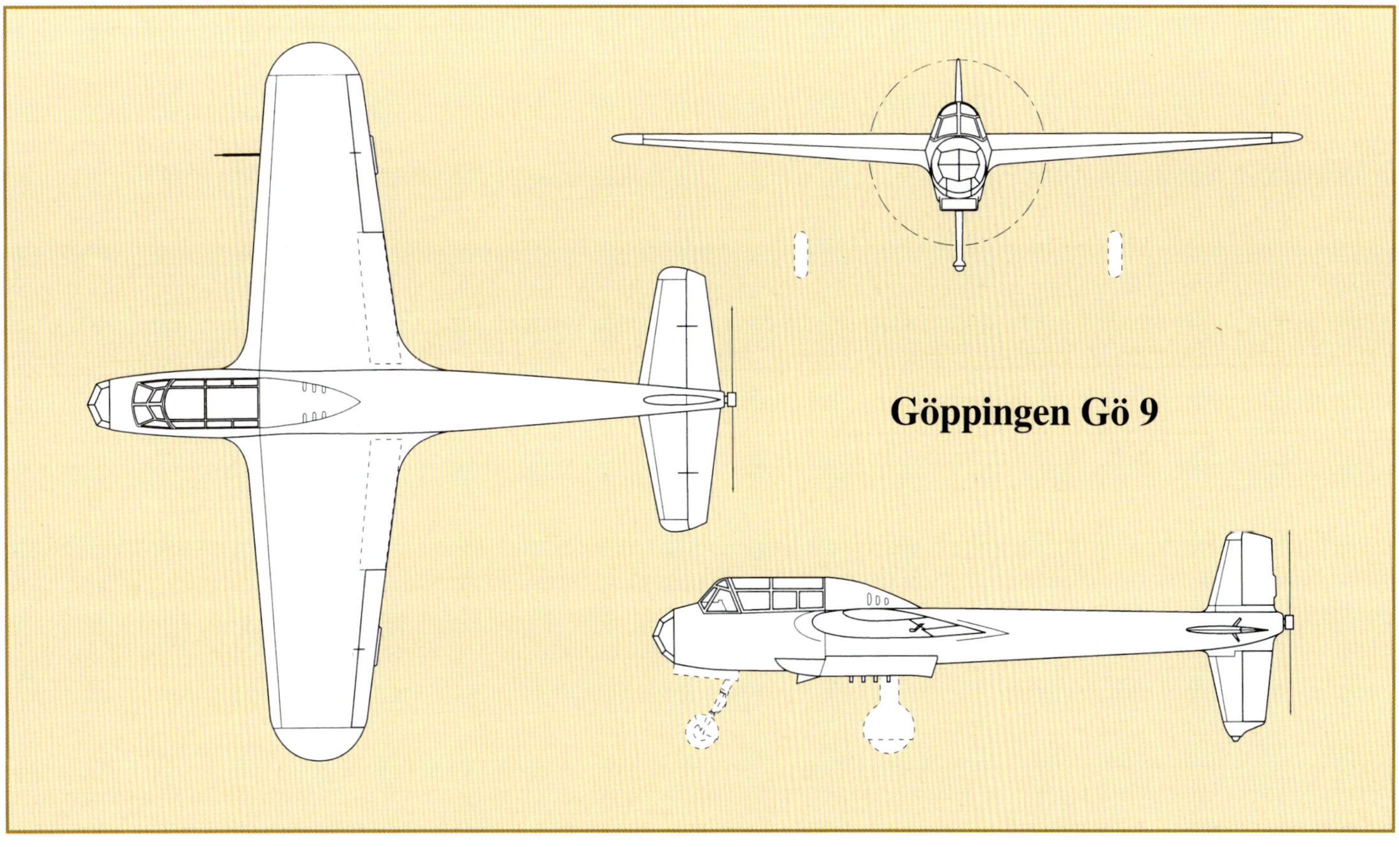

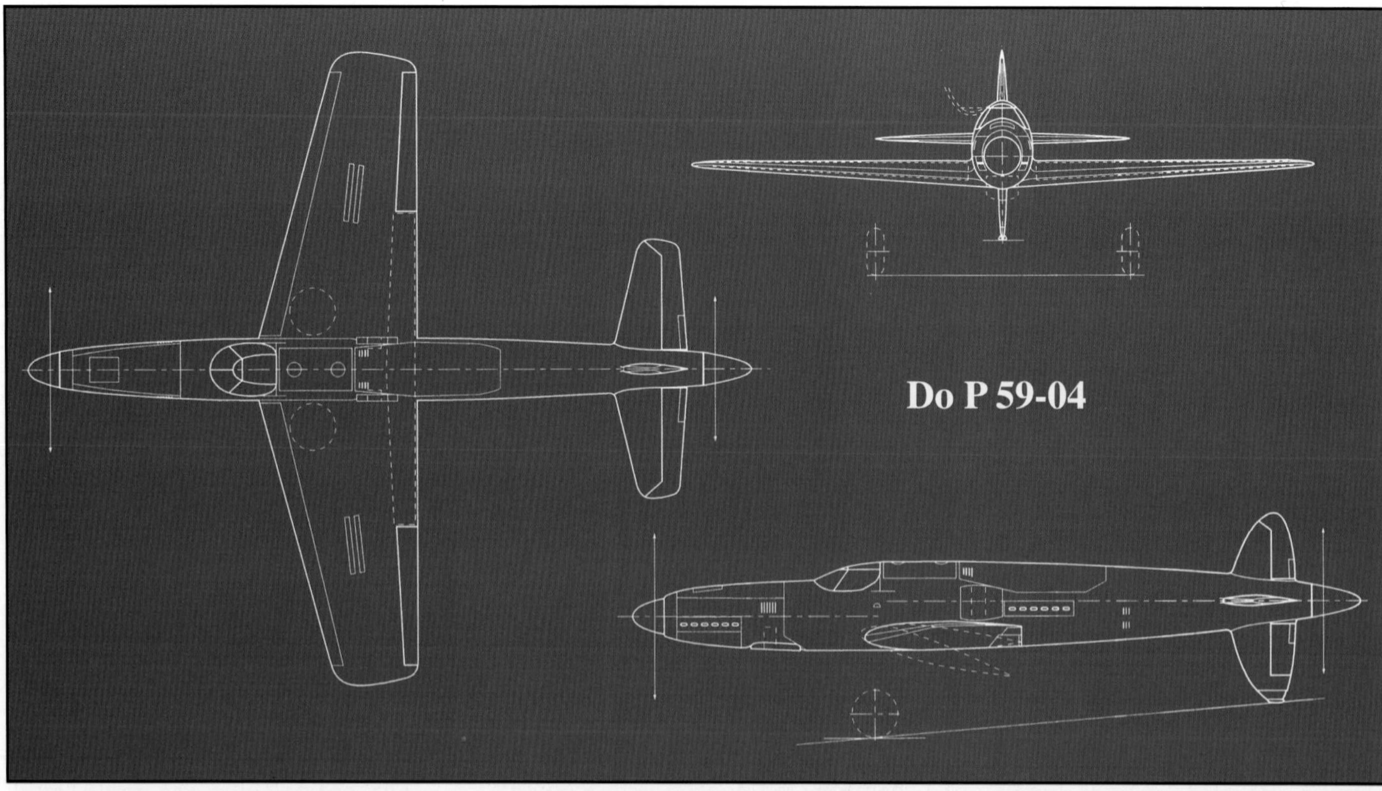

A second prototype, the Do 335 V2, W.Nr. 230002, CP+UB, joined the test program on December 31, 1943, the pilot on this first flight again being Dieterle. The aircraft differed in several respects, having a redesigned forward engine cowling with the air cooler intake incorporated, and modified mainwheel covers. The Do 335 V3, W.Nr. 230003, CP+UC, which made its first flight on January 20, 1944, was generally similar to the V2, but with modified exhausts wing root fairings and a canopy designed to slide up and rearward instead of being hinged to open to the right. Both aircraft had a transparent blister on both sides of the canopy, housing an interior mirror to improve rearward visibility.

The Do 335 V4, W.Nr. 230004, CP+UD, did not make its maiden flight until July 9, 1944, during which five additional prototypes had been completed and flown. The fourth prototype was allocated to test a high aspect ratio wing developed by Heinkel. This new wing with a wing span of 60 feet 4½ inches (18,4 m) was subsequently assigned to the Do 335 B-4 and Do 435 which are discussed in Chapters 3 and 4.

The next prototype, the Do 335 V5, W.Nr. 230005, CP+UE, was the first test aircraft fitted with armament. It had a long-barrelled 30 mm MK 103 cannon mounted between the cylinders of the DB 603 inverted "v" in-line engine, with two 20 mm MG

Continued on p. 45

Above and Below: Details of the Do P 59-05 of November 1939. Of particular interest to the P 59, was the variable incidence wing whose angle of attack could be adjusted through 20 degrees to improve landing characteristics and rate of climb. Opposite top: The Do P 231/1-02 design study for a high-speed bomber (wing area 376 ft² - 35 m²) powered by two DB 605 E engines from early 1940, would have carried either one SC 500 bomb in the fuselage bay beneath the forward portion of the rear engine, or two smaller SC 250 bombs. **Opposite bottom:** Dornier design study, Do P 231/2-01 dated June 6, 1943, was similar but equipped with two DB 603 G engines (wing area 387 ft² - 36 m²).

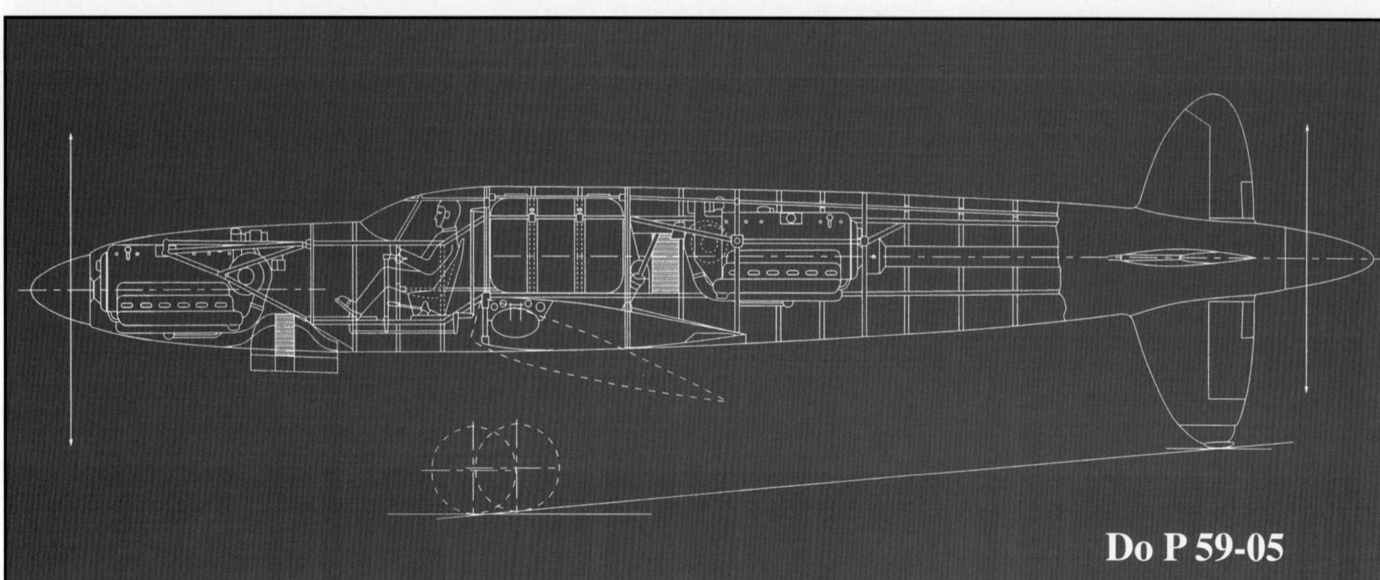

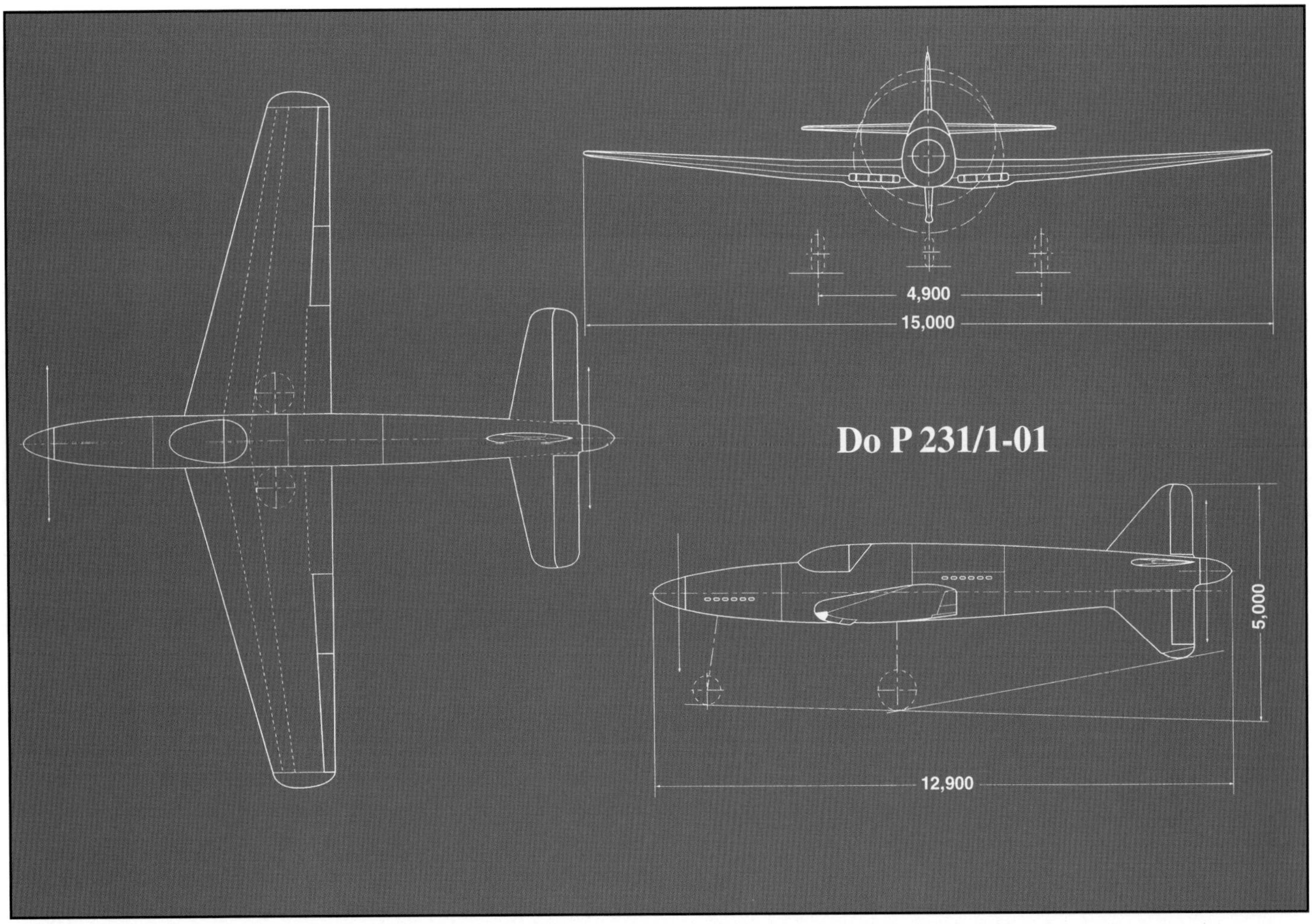
4,900
15,000
Do P 231/1-01
5,000
12,900

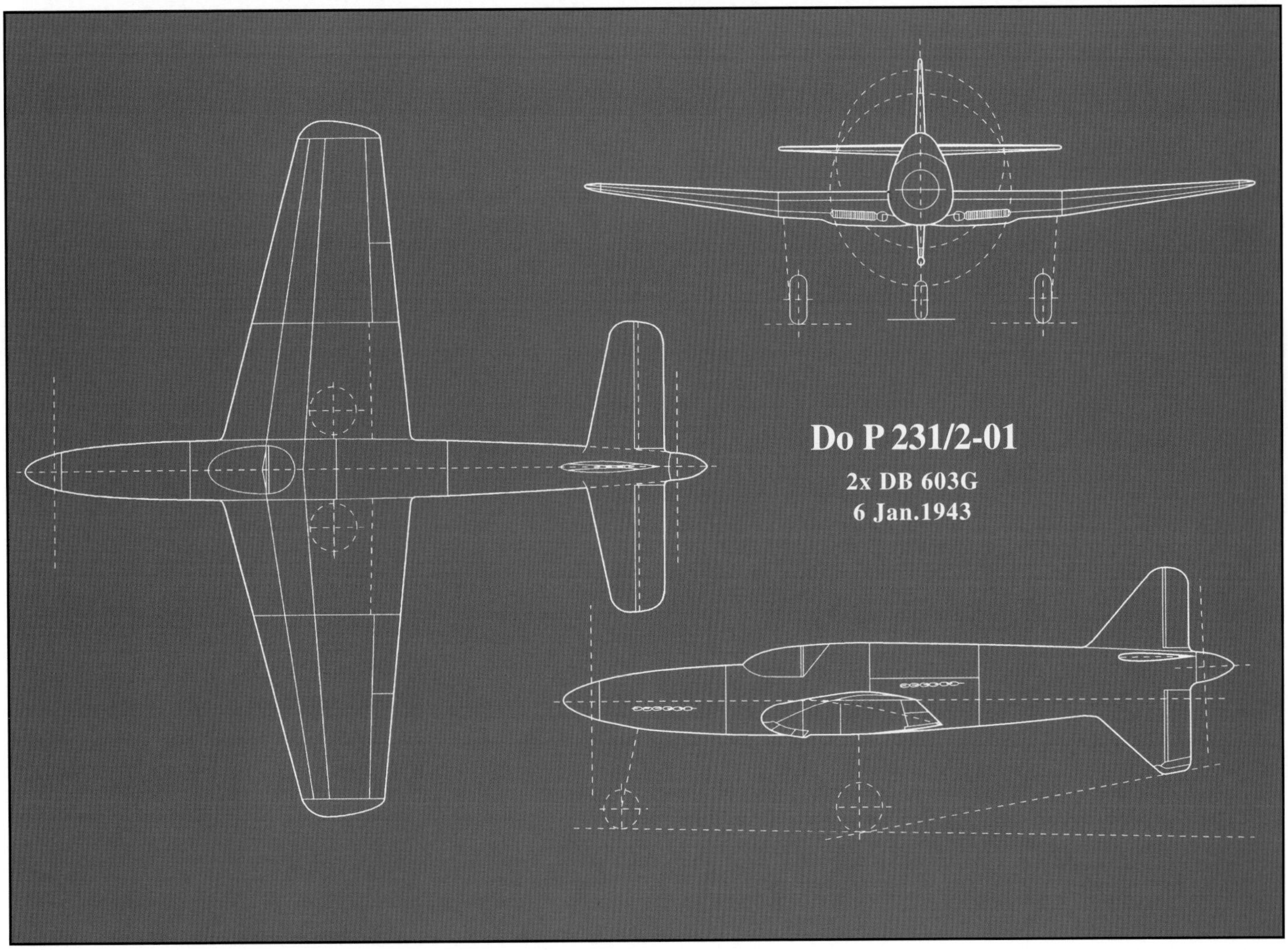
Do P 231/2-01
2x DB 603G
6 Jan.1943

BF 109 Z

THE CONTENDERS

The chart on page 11 graphically depicts the evolution of the Do 335 from the original RLM specification up to the Ju 635. The 1942 RLM specification for a *Zerstörer* (twin-engined heavy day fighter) and *Schnelbomber* (high speed bomber) was initially issued to three firms: Arado, Dornier and Junkers. Each of these firms developed design studies which were submitted to the RLM for consideration. Arado proposed project E-561, a design which gave the appearance of a conventional twin-engined aircraft, yet it featured a novel powerplant arrangement consisting of two liquid - cooled engines buried side-by-side within its broad fuselage which, in turn, drove twin propellers via long extension shafts connected through junction boxes. Armament was to consist of four weapons in the nose plus one hand-held machine gun in a ventral position which was to be fired by the third crewman. The Ar E (E - *Entwicklungs* / Development) 561 was a 1938 project which was too complex and really did not appear to fit the specification. While the concept of locating both engines within the fuselage may have appeared to offer less drag, the complexity associated with linking buried engines to their propellers would have been formidable.

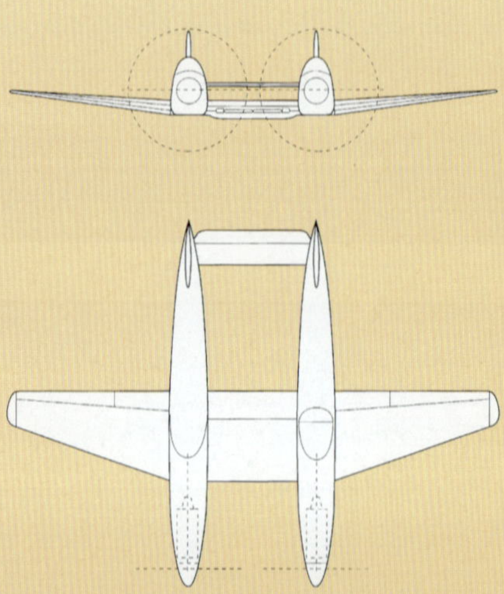

Do P 231/2-03 Proposal 2

The Dornier submission, *Projekt* P 231, was offered in several variations including a conventional twin fuselage arrangement (shown left). Do P 231/1 and Do P 231/2-01 both represented a bold step forward. Although the tricycle undercarriage was novel, it was not new. The forward engine arrangement was entirely conventional whereas the

Ar E 561

Ju EF 115.0

placement of the second engine and its pusher propeller with cruciform tail were radical departures. However, in contrast to the Arado entry, the complexity of the Dornier design appeared relatively simple.

The Junkers firm had several design studies in their stable but finalized their entry with the Ju EF 115.0, a twin-engined design featuring coaxial counter-rotating propellers, tricycle undercarriage and a clear vision canopy. The Ju EF (EF - *Entwicklungs Flugzeug* / Development Aircraft) 115.0 could have become a serious contender if it were not for the engineering challenge of delivering power from the rear engine past the front powerplant to the counter-rotating propeller assembly.

Although not officially involved in the competition, Messerschmitt advised the RLM late in 1942, that they *already had* an aircraft that could fulfill the requirement, in the form of his twin Bf 109, the Bf 109 Z. This statement was not entirely without merit since the basic concept was essentially bringing together two standard Bf 109s joined with a new center section and new horizontal tailplane. Nevertheless, even though the RLM was not favorably disposed toward the Bf 109 Z, it did sanction further development. It is reported that Messerschmitt succeeded in completing a single prototype of the Bf 109 Z by mid 1943, but was apparently damaged beyond repair in an Allied bombing attack prior to its first flight. By early 1943, the RLM was about to award a development contract to Dornier for their Do P 231, when Messerschmitt stepped forward with a new aircraft design not unlike the basic Dornier approach. Known as the *Gegenprojekt* (Rebuttal or counter project) to the Dornier entry, it was essentially a copy. Notwithstanding the question of patent infringement, it is unclear how the Messerschmitt design would have offered anything over the Dornier project. However, the RLM was not sufficiently impressed with this last-minute effort, and lost little time awarding the development contact to Dornier for their P 231, which was now given the official RLM CL/C list number 335, becoming the Do 335.

Me P Rebuttal

DAIMLER-BENZ DB 603 A

Standard engine for the Do 335 A-0 and A-11 series. This liquid-cooled, inverted V12, with a displacement of 44.5 Liters, had a bore of 162 mm and a stroke of 180 mm with a compression ratio of 7.5:1 for the left block and 7.3:1 for the right block and required B4 aviation fuel of 87 octane. It was a right hand rotation engine developing 1,750 hp at 2,700 rpm for take-off and war emergency power. The weight was 2,006 lb (910 kg).

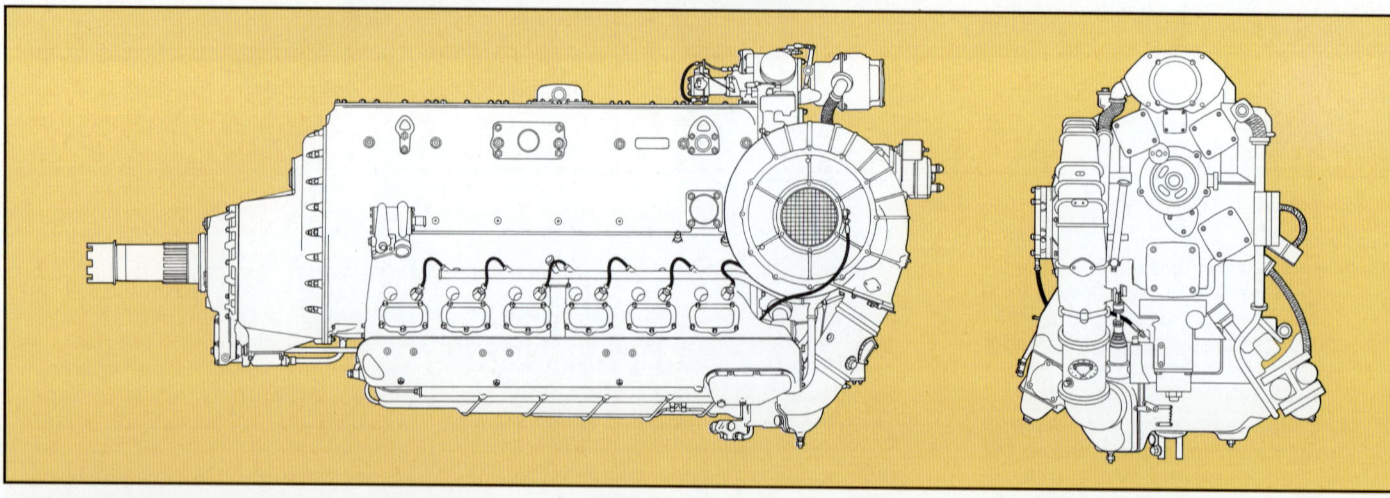

JUNKERS Jumo 213 A

Intended for the Do 335 A-5, A-7, A-8 and A-9 series, but owing to development delays, it was only installed in the Do 335 V6 and V7 prototypes. This liquid-cooled inverted V12 had a bore of 150 mm and a stroke of 165 mm with a compression ratio of 6.5:1 and required B4 aviation fuel of 87 octane. It was a right-hand rotation engine with a one-stage, two-speed supercharger and developed 1,776 hp at 3,250 rpm for take-off and war emergency power. Weight of the engine was 2,028 lb (920 kg). Overall length was 2437 mm while the height was 1095 mm and width was 776 mm.

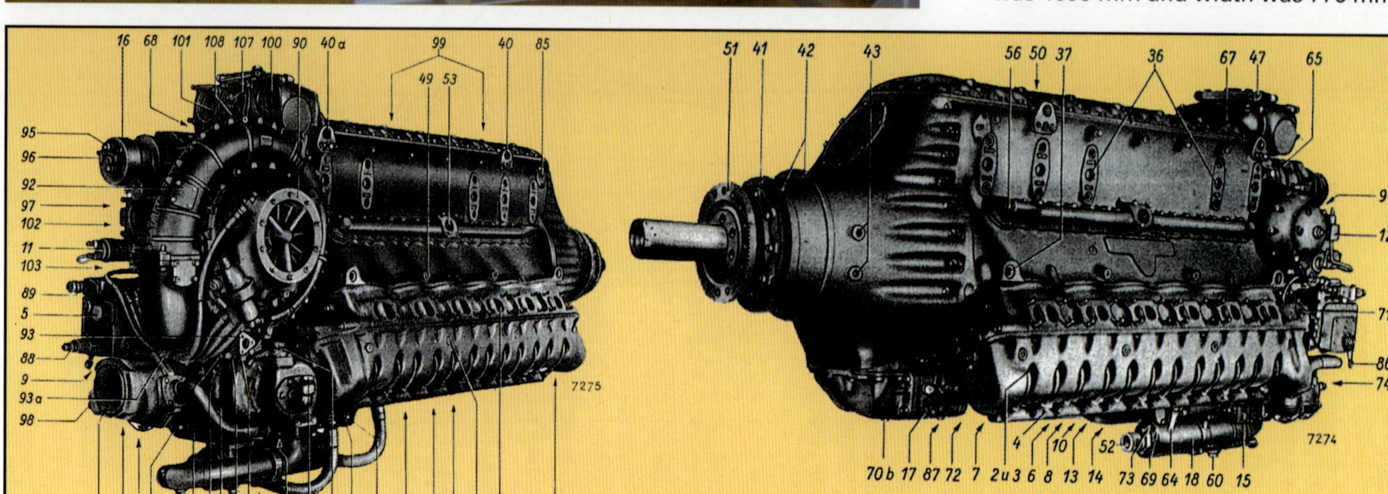

Abb. 1. JUMO 213 A-1. Ansicht auf linke Motorseite

Above: The newly completed Do 335 V1, W.Nr. 230001, CP+UA, with it distinctive circular mainwheel covers and separate oil cooler intake. This aircraft flew for the first time on October 26, 1943, piloted by *Flugkapitän* Hans Dieterle. Note that the upper surface camouflage consisted of only one overall color; color 71 Dark Green.

Continued from p. 40

151/20 cannon mounted above the forward engine. Although having a slower rate of fire than the more common MK 108 cannon, the MK 103 had almost twice the muzzle velocity and hence a much greater range. After making its first flight in February 1944, the Do 335 V5 was handed over to the armaments test center at Tarnewitz for weapon firing trials.

The fifth prototype to fly was the Do 335 V6, W.Nr. 230006, CP+UF, which tested various items of equipment including the FuG 101 radio altimeter. It made its first flight on March 25, 1944, with Altrogge at the controls. Shortly afterward, on April 15, this pilot was killed tragically when evaluating the roll characteristics of the Do 335 V2. The rear engine caught fire and this probably burnt through the elevator controls, causing the aircraft to dive vertically into the ground near Memmingen. Altrogge's place was later taken by *Flugkapitän* Karl-Heinz Appel.

Because of its unusual configuration a unique sequence of events had to be triggered before the pilot could escape safely from the cockpit of the Do 335. A row of three buttons was provided on the starboard side of the cockpit, the first of which blew off the rear propeller, the second the upper fin and rudder and the third armed the ejector seat. The Do 335 was only the second piston engined aircraft to be fitted with an ejector

Right: This front view of the Do 335 V1, taken at Dornier's Friedrichshafen facility, dramatizes the low drag character of the tandem engine arrangement, which significantly contributed to the aircraft's outstanding high speed capabilities.

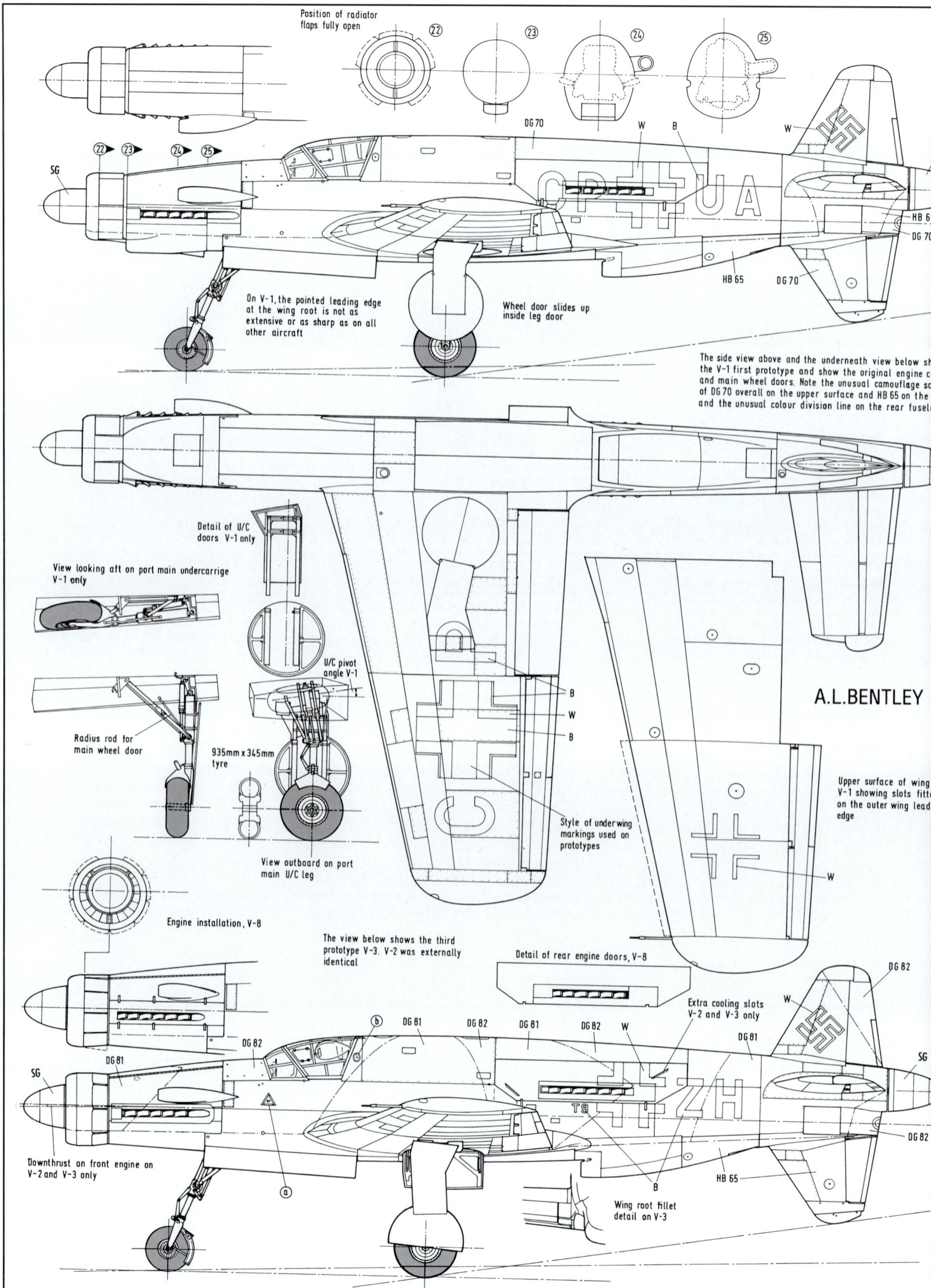

Position of radiator flaps fully open
22
23
24
25
SG
DG 70
W
B
CP UA
HB 65
DG 70
HB 65
DG 70
On V-1, the pointed leading edge at the wing root is not as extensive or as sharp as on all other aircraft
Wheel door slides up inside leg door
The side view above and the underneath view below sh
the V-1 first prototype and show the original engine c
and main wheel doors. Note the unusual camouflage sc
of DG 70 overall on the upper surface and HB 65 on the
and the unusual colour division line on the rear fusel
Detail of U/C doors V-1 only
View looking aft on port main undercarriage V-1 only
U/C pivot angle V-1
Radius rod for main wheel door
935mm x 345mm tyre
View outboard on port main U/C leg
Style of underwing markings used on prototypes
A.L.BENTLEY
Upper surface of wing
V-1 showing slots fitt
on the outer wing lead
edge
Engine installation, V-8
The view below shows the third prototype V-3. V-2 was externally identical
Detail of rear engine doors, V-8
Extra cooling slots V-2 and V-3 only
DG 81
DG 82
T9
ZH
Downthrust on front engine on V-2 and V-3 only
Wing root fillet detail on V-3

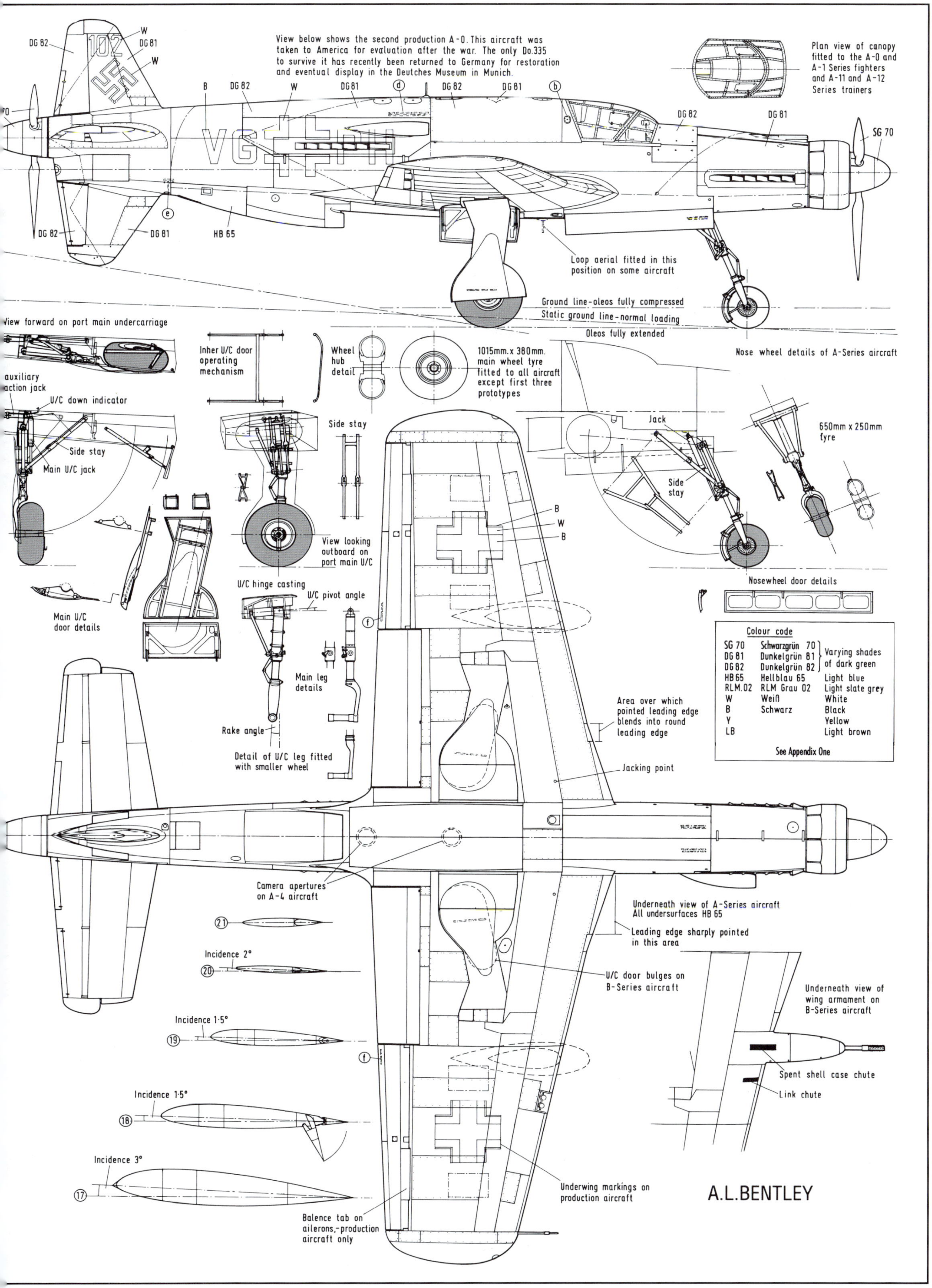
View below shows the second production A-0. This aircraft was taken to America for evaluation after the war. The only Do.335 to survive it has recently been returned to Germany for restoration and eventual display in the Deutches Museum in Munich.
Plan view of canopy fitted to the A-0 and A-1 Series fighters and A-11 and A-12 Series trainers
DG 82
DG 81
W
B
SG 70
HB 65
VG
102
Loop aerial fitted in this position on some aircraft
Ground line-oleos fully compressed
Static ground line-normal loading
Oleos fully extended
Nose wheel details of A-Series aircraft
View forward on port main undercarriage
auxiliary action jack
U/C down indicator
Side stay
Main U/C jack
Inner U/C door operating mechanism
Wheel hub detail
1015mm.x 380mm. main wheel tyre fitted to all aircraft except first three prototypes
Side stay
View looking outboard on port main U/C
Main U/C door details
U/C hinge casting
U/C pivot angle
Main leg details
Rake angle
Detail of U/C leg fitted with smaller wheel
Jack
Side stay
650mm x 250mm tyre
Nosewheel door details
Colour code
SG 70 Schwarzgrün 70 Varying shades of dark green
DG 81 Dunkelgrün 81
DG 82 Dunkelgrün 82
HB 65 Hellblau 65 Light blue
RLM.02 RLM Grau 02 Light slate grey
W Weiß White
B Schwarz Black
Y Yellow
LB Light brown
See Appendix One
Area over which pointed leading edge blends into round leading edge
Jacking point
Camera apertures on A-4 aircraft
Underneath view of A-Series aircraft
All undersurfaces HB 65
Leading edge sharply pointed in this area
U/C door bulges on B-Series aircraft
Underneath view of wing armament on B-Series aircraft
Spent shell case chute
Link chute
Incidence 2°
Incidence 1·5°
Incidence 1·5°
Incidence 3°
Underwing markings on production aircraft
Balence tab on ailerons,-production aircraft only
A.L.BENTLEY

seat, compressed air being used to propel the pilot clear of the cockpit. After these buttons had been depressed, the pilot then had to pull two large levers to jettison the canopy.

During May 1944 two further prototypes joined the test program. These were the Do 335 V7, W.Nr. 230007, CP+UG, which made its first flight on May 19 and the Do 335 V8, W.Nr. 230008, CP+UH, on May 31. The seventh prototype was later transferred to Junkers at Dessau where it was used as a test bed for the new 1,750 hp Jumo 213 engine. The V8 was probably the first aircraft to be fitted with Daimler-Benz DB 603 E-1 engines which were intended for the first production series. It also had slightly modified engine cowlings.

Successful testing of these aircraft led to the V9, W.Nr. 230009, CP+UI, which was to serve as the definitive prototype for the Do 335 A-1 series, by now known as the *Pfeil* (Arrow). It made its first flight on June 29, 1944, piloted by *Flugkapitän* Quenzler. Although similar to previous aircraft, the V9 had a redesigned undercarriage

Above: This port view of the Do 335 V1, again emphasis the large main-wheel covers and separate oil cooler intake below the forward engine's cowl. Both of these features were discarded with subsequent prototypes of the Arrow.

Left: Dornier mechanics perform checks with the front DB 603 A. Typical of most German fighters, the engine was easily accessible thanks to large cowl covers and engine support arms. Note the separate air intake for the oil cooler mounted on the lower cover. This arrangement was later dropped in favor of a cooler installed within the nacelle's forward ring collar.

Above and Below: Two additional views of the first prototype of the Do 335 Arrow. One can easily sense the large size of the Do 335 V1 standing atop its tricycle undercarriage. The first prototype was unarmed and, in addition to Hans Dieterle, was also flown by other Dornier test pilots including Werner Altrogge and Ivan Quenzler.

and an standard armament of two 20 mm MG 151 cannons with 200 rounds per gun and one 30 mm MK 103 with 70 rounds. It was the final prototype to serve as a model for the preproduction and production variant of the A-series. It was powered by two Daimler-Benz DB 603 A-2 twelve cylinder inverted "v" liquid-cooled, inline engines.

Soon after its first flight the aircraft was delivered to the *Luftwaffe* experimental station at Rechlin for performance tests. These were conducted by one of the station's most respected pilots, *Dipl.Ing.* Heinrich Beauvais. Beauvais possibly flew more different types of wartime German aircraft than any other pilot, logging time in such varied machines as the Ar 232 transport, the He 280 and Me 262 jets, the Me 163 rocket interceptor, the Fi 256 communications aircraft, the Ta 154 twin-engined fighter and the Fa 223 helicopter. During performance tests the Do 335 V9 attained a speed of 472 mph (760 km/h) at altitude. Beauvais well remembers flying a mock combat operation against a Fw 190 which was then the *Luftwaffe*'s foremost fighter. As soon as he pushed open the throt-

tles of the Do 335, it surged forward and left the Fw 190 far behind. Apart from its high speed and remarkable acceleration, the Do 335 possessed excellent handling characteristics, and was extremely maneuverable for its size.

Successful testing of the Do 335 V9 was followed by construction of a batch of ten A-0 preproduction aircraft (W.Nr. 240101 to 240110), a contract for which had been placed in December 1943. These aircraft were built at Dornier's airfield at Oberpfaffenhofen, west of Munich because of bomb damage caused to Dornier's Friedrichshafen factory. On April 28, 1944, some 750 American 8th Air Force B-17s struck Friedrichshafen and Oberpfaffenhofen, but because of stiff resistance aided by dense smoke screening, only partial damage was inflicted to assembly halls and workshops at Friedrichshafen. On July 20, 1944, heavy damage was sustained by assembly halls and workshops, but on August 3, 1944, bombing resulted in total destruction of Dornier's Friedrichshafen plant. In spite of this circumstance, continuation of work proceeded in the vicinity of Friedrichshafen

The first preproduction machine, the Do 335 A-01, W.Nr. 240101, VG+PG, made its first flight on September 30, 1944, and was generally similar to the production prototype (V9).

Apart from its unusual shape, the most striking feature of the fighter was its immense size - the average

Continued on p. 55

Above: The Do 335 V1 in flight. One great advantage of the aircraft's unique layout was that it could fly quite easily on one engine. In fact, tests were to prove that it was marginally faster with the forward propeller feathered than with the rear engine stopped. **Below:** A movie film still showing the Do 335 V1 about to touch down. **Opposite:** Port and starboard views of the new canopy fitted to the Do 335 V3. It differed from of the first prototype in two respects. First, to improve rearward visibility, two rear-view mirrors were mounted beneath plexiglas blisters, and secondly the whole canopy was designed to open by retracting extension arms which guided the canopy up and to the rear (see p. 54 top). All other Arrows were equipped with canopies hinged to open to starboard. **Next page:** Cockpit of the Do 335 V3.

Do 335 A-0, A-1

1. Cockpit canopy frame
2. Main blind flying panel
3. Main panel left section
4. Main panel right section
5. Left supplimental panel
6. Right supplimental panel
7. Operable panel
8. Equipment frame
9. Electrics switch panel
10. Pilot seat
11. Control column grip
12. Revi 16D gunsight
13. Oxygen flow guage
14. Oxygen pressure guage
15. Airspeed indicator
16. Pitot heating indicator
17. Artificial horizon
18. Variometer
19. Altimeter
20. Repeater compass
21. AFN 2 radio navigation
22. Propeller pitch indicators
23. Combined pressure-RPM indicators
24. Coolant temperature gauge
25. Oil temperature gauge
26. Fuel pressure guage
27. Oil pressure guage
28. Fuel transfer pump switch (aux. nose tank)
29. Fuel rate of use warning light
30. Fuel contents warning light
31. Fuel contents
32. Clock
33. Outside air temperature guage
34. Radio altimeter
35. UV light dimmer switch
36. Gyro control switch

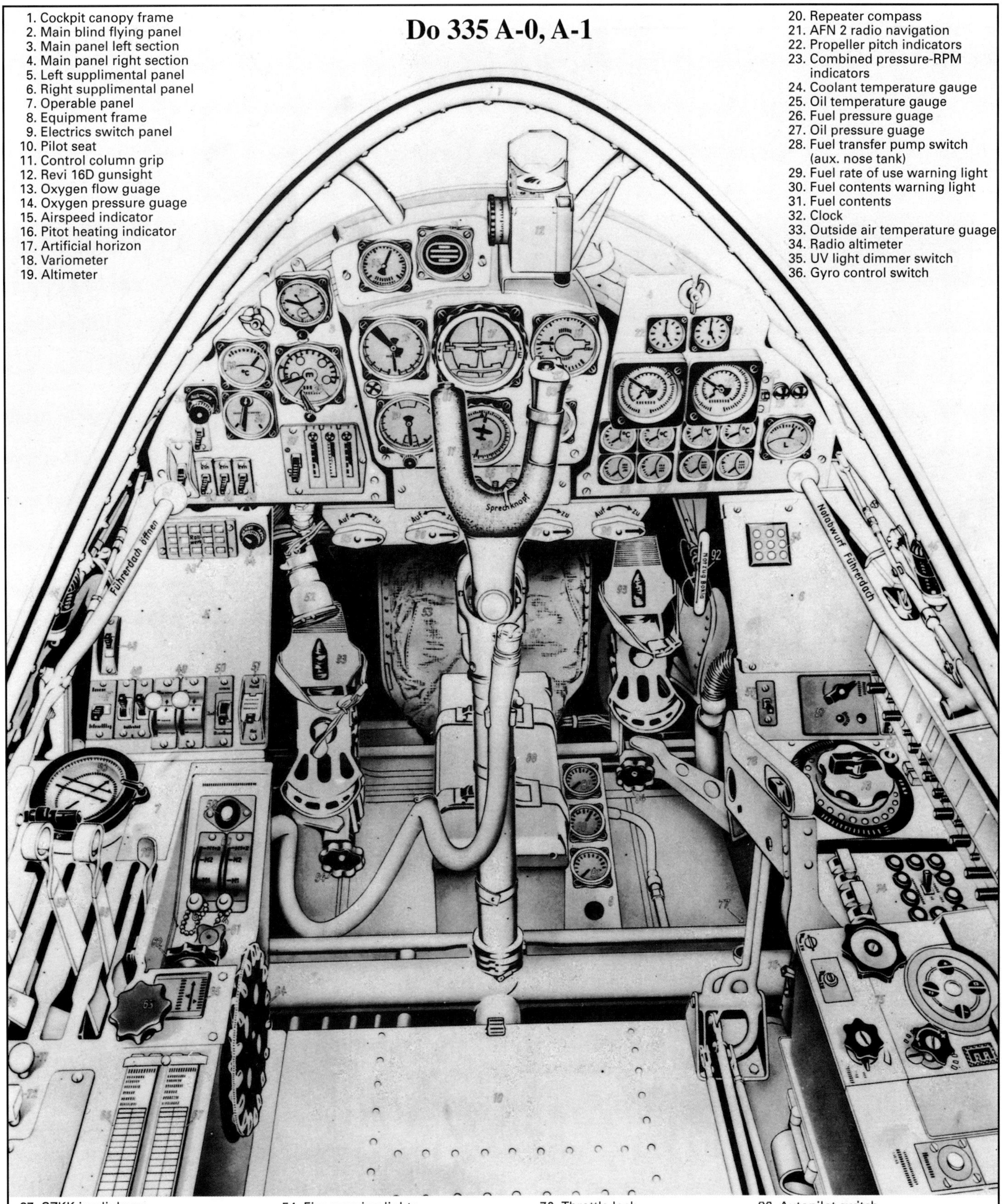

37. SZKK ing linkage
38. Pitot heating switch
39. Instrument panel lighting switch
40. Navigation lights switch
41. Landing lights switch
42. Auxiliary navigation lights switch
43. Five position undercarriage indicator
44. Compass lamp dimmer switch
45. UV lights
46. Explosive jettiston switch ventral fin
47. Stearing switch
48. Propeller selector switches
49. Propeller manuel control switches
50. Landing flaps switch
51. Undercarriage switch
52. Adjustable cabin spotlight
53. Engine cannon breech cover
54. Fire warning lights
55. Explosive detonator switch (abandon aircraft)
56. Course axial-switch
57. BG 25a control panel
58. Standby compass with lighting
59. Emergency switch for main electrics
60. Ignition switches
61. Oxygen flow valve
62. Aileron trim hand wheel
63. Rudder trim hand wheel
64. Elevator trim hand wheel
65. Trim indicator
66. Standby compass deviation table
67. Master compass deviation table
68. Fuel safety cock lever
69. Throttle levers
70. Throttle lock
71. Front engine fire extinguisher
72. Rear engine fire extinguisher
73. ZSK 246 fuse panel + selector switch
74. ASK 335 bomb release panel
75. FuG 16Z/Y control panel
76. Radio selector switch
77. FBG 2 location (if installed)
78. Ejection seat activitation unit
79. Canopy jettison lever
80. Canopy release lever
81. Bomb release button1
82. MK 103 firing button
83. MG 151 firing button on front
84. Autopilot course setting
85. Radio-telephone button
86. Autopilot switch
87. Oxygen connector point
88. Battery (24v)
89. Pressurized oil pressure guage
90. Emergency compressed air pressure guage
91. Ejection seat pressure guage
92. Bomb bay doors emergency lever
93. Rudder pedals
94. Rudder pedal adjustment wheel
95. Emergency undercarriage switch
96. Emergency landing flaps switch
97. Emergency stearing switch
98. Emergency bomb bay door switch

Opposite: Two views of the Do 335 V3 showing the main flap to the starboard wing, the unique aft-moving canopy and the ventral cooling intake for the aft engine. Proper cooling the rear engine was an unresolved challenge which plagued all Do 335s...and which was responsible for the tragic loss of several aircraft and their pilots. **Above and Below:** Two views of the Do 335 V3, W.Nr. 230003, CP+UC, the first reconnaissance machine of the Arrow, after it had been fitted with two large Rb 50/18 aerial reconnaissance cameras for service with the First Squadron of the Experimental Unit of the Air Force's High Command (*1./Versuchsverband OKL*). It had been planned to fly the Do 335 V3 over London, but it is unlikely such a flight was ever undertaken because of protracted serviceability problems with the aircraft.

Continued from p. 50

person being able to walk beneath it without even bowing his head. The fuselage was an all-metal monocoque structure with the forward DB 603 A-2 engine driving a huge 11 ft 5¾ in (3,5 m) diameter three-blade propeller with reversible pitch. The last feature could reduce the landing run by some 25 per cent. The main 325 US gal (1,230 ltr) fuel tank was positioned behind the cockpit, separated from it by an armored bulkhead, with the rear DB 603 QA-2 engine driving a pusher propeller via a hollow extension shaft. An internal weapons bay was provided beneath the center of the fuselage capable of carrying an 1,100 lb (500 kg) bomb or a jettisonable 132 US gal (500 ltr) auxiliary fuel tank.

The wings were built around a single box spar with all metal stressed skinning. Two 89 US gal (337 ltr) self-sealing tanks were mounted in the wing leading edges, on either side of the center section, and variable camber flaps were positioned inboard of the hydraulically powered ailerons. The cruciform tail was also built of metal with the exception of the leading edges of the fins which were wood. A sprung tail bumper was attached to the bottom of the lower fin which could be jettisoned in the event of a belly landing.

Initial series production was to commence in February 1944 at Luther *u.* Jordan, Brunswick. However, owing to continual development delays, none was completed by this firm. Following the completion of the ten Do 335 A-Os at Oberpfaffenhofen, work began on a batch of production Do 335 A-1 fighters. These differed in being powered by a pair of DB 603 E-1 engines rated at 1,800 hp for takeoff and 1,900 hp at 5,900 ft (1,800 m) with emergency power-boost. The guns were aimed with the aid of a Revi 16D reflector sight, and an FuG 16ZY transmitter, FuG 25a IFF and FuG 125 blind landing radio equipment were provided. As

Rüstsatz (auxiliary apparatus), two ETC 501 A-1 bomb racks could be positioned beneath the wings to carry either a 550 lb (250 kg) bomb or a 79 US gal (300 Ltr) drop tank.

The Do 335 A-2 was a proposed high-speed bomber version *(Kampfflugzeug)* powered by two DB 603 G engines and capable of carrying a 2,200 lb (1,000 kg) internal bombload. Due to changing war demands, it is doubtful if any aircraft of this series was completed.

It was intended to install the rather unusual combination of GM 1 and MW 50 powerboosting systems into the Do 335 A-3. This series was to have been a *Zerstörer* or heavy twin-engined day fighter. GM 1 (nitrous-oxide) was added to allow the aircraft to operate above the rated altitude of the engines while MW 50 (methanol-water), allowed extra power to be gained below the rated altitude of the engines. It is also doubtful if any examples of this version were completed before the wars end.

As early as the spring of 1944, the General of the Reconnaissance, *General-Major* Karl-Henning *von* Barsewisch, suggested using the Do 335 for long-range reconnaissance sorties over the British Isles, the VI to photograph the British fleet at Scapa

Above and **Below:** The Do 335 V3 with its operational code, T9+ZH, painted in black, as it was about to be handed over to 1./*Versuchsverband* OKL. The aircraft's permanent identification code (*Stammkennzeichen*), CP+UC, was removed from the exterior of the prototype after it was handed over to this special *Luftwaffe* unit, but not from it's official record card. Although not clearly shown in these views, the V3 continued to utilize round wheel wells without hinged doors in spite of the fact it was equipped with the new definitive landing gear covers.

Below and Right: The Do 335 was only the third piston-engined aircraft to have an ejection seat (the others being the Me 309 and He 219) as standard equipment. The system was operated by compressed air, but it is unknown if any Do 335 pilot ever had to use the seat in an emergency.

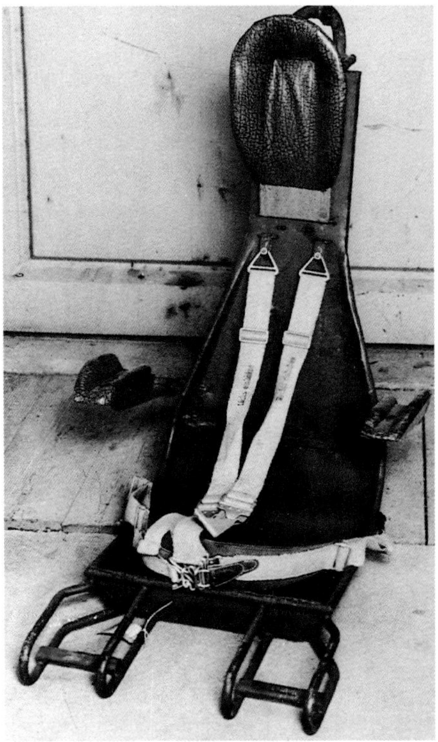

Below: An interesting series of photographs of the Do 335 V8 showing how the crew entry ladder was stowed and lowered. these photographs also give some idea of how far off the ground the aircraft sat. Most twin-engined German fighters of this period did not require boarding ladders. The first two letters of the air aircraft's primary identification code, CP+UH, are clearly visible. The Do 335 V8 was the eighth prototype and was equipped with DB 603 E engines and first flown on May 31, 1944 and was based at Mengen during October 1944 in order to participate in high altitude test flights. Its ultimate fate is unknown, but was at Rechlin during February 1945.

Above: The burnt out remains of the Do 335 V7, W.Nr. 230007, CP+UG, next to the tree line at Mengen during the summer of 1945. This photograph together with the close-up on page 175, are the only known surviving images of the seventh prototype. This aircraft was originally sent to Junkers at Dessau for test with the Jumo 213 installation, but was returned to Dornier in January 1945. Careful examination of the photograph suggests the forward engine to be the DB 603. **Left:** Close-up of the rear engine compartment for the newly completed Do 335 V8. The silver container on top of the exhaust stacks is one of two 3.8 gal (14.5 ltr) gycol coolant tanks for the rear engine. **Below:** The Do 335 V8, W.Nr. 230008, CP+UH, following a successful test flight. This prototype was the first Arrow fitted with the DB 603 E, which was to power the Do 335 A-1 series. The forward engine's supercharger scoop is slightly shorter in length than the standard Do 335 scoop.

Flow in the north Scottish island of Orkney and the V3 for a mission over London. Work had already begun on a reconnaissance version of the aircraft under the designation Do 335 A-4. This was to carry one or two Rb 50/18 cameras in the fuselage bay, with glazed apertures for the lenses in the bay doors.

A single camera was fitted experimentally to the Do 335 V3 and delivered to the First Squadron of the Experimental Unit of the *Luftwaffe*'s High Command (1./*Versuchsverband* OKL) in July 1944. Operationally coded T9+ZH, the airplane was piloted by *Leutnant* (Lt.) Wolfgang Ziese, but it is unknown if the proposed flights over Britain were attempted because of the aircraft's continued unserviceability. Ziese himself had a remarkable career. Earlier on in the war he had worked as a test pilot for the Siebel company at Halle, and following his testing of the Do 335, flew a number of reconnaissance operations with the remarkable Ar 234 jet. After the war he was taken to Russia to work on Soviet aviation development, and was engaged in Soviet testing of the German DFS 346 supersonic research aircraft at the time of his death in 1949.

As recounted earlier, the Do 335 V7 had been transfered to Junkers for trials with the Jumo 213. This promising engine had been promised during the autumn of 1943, but it was still under development during the first half of 1944. But, it was not until late 1944 that the engine had achieved a degree of reliability demanded by the *Luftwaffe*. Although supporting documentation remains elusive, it is nevertheless believed that the little known **Do 335 A-5** day fighter was to be powered by the Jumo 213. The Jumo 213 was also to power the **Do 335 A-7** high-speed bomber, the **Do 335 A-8** heavy day fighter, and the **Do 335 A-9** single-seat reconnaissance variant.

Above and Right: The newly completed Do 335 V9, W.Nr. 230009, CP+UI, represented the definitive prototype for the initial production model of the Arrow. It was first flown on June 29, 1944 by *Flugkapitän* Quenzler. It tested the engine-mounted MK 103 during July 1944 but crash landed on August 18, 1944. It was repaired and continued in it testing program. During the last days of the war, it was reportedly flown out of Rechlin by a pilot trying to reach Switzerland. However, due to inaccurate compass reading, the pilot bailed out over Allied-controlled territory and was taken prisoner. He was reported to have spent a long time incarcerated as a POW of the French.

Above and Below: The second preproduction Do 335 A-0, W.Nr. 240102, VG+PH, survived the war thanks to the efforts of Hans Lerche, a Rechlin test pilot who successfully flew this aircraft from Rechlin to the relative safety of Dornier's Oberpfaffenhofen facility at the end of April 1945. These photographs were taken after American troops occupied the airfield and show the aircraft collected among other Do 335s in a clearing outside one of the hangers (above) and being checked by Dornier mechanics (below) prior to being run-up. American intelligence officers were quite interested in the Arrow and were making plans to ship the two best examples back to the States for evaluation. **Opposite:** Two additional views of Do 335 A-02. The top photograph, taken at Oberpfaffenhofen, shows the crew entry ladder extended and additional Do 335 aircraft in the background. The lower image shows the aircraft in captivity with crudely applied American insignia. This aircraft was one of two brought to the States and assigned to the US Navy for testing.

102

Above: Do 335 A-02 after being stricken from the Navy's Tactical Test Division's roster and transferred to NAS Norfolk. It received the Navy's BuAer No. 121447, but it is unlikely the Navy ever flew the aircraft, in part because of serviceability problems. Instead, the Navy applied a special cocooning to the aircraft during the 1950s and parked the aircraft for outside long term storage. **Below:** A close-up of the nose spinner showing the aperture for the engine-mounted MK 103 cannon and the engine cooling radiator vanes enclosed within the cowling .

Above and Below: Photographed in April, 1971 at the National Air and Space Museum's Paul E. Garber Restoration Facility at Silver Hill, Maryland, the Do 335 A-02 awaits restoration minus its wings. In spite of outside storage for over a decade, it was in remarkably good condition, although a number of smaller parts were discovered missing.

Left: Close-up of the starboard side of the cockpit to Do 335 A-02 at Silver Hill, Maryland. Though the canopy was sealed, the small clear vision hatch is shown pushed open. Note the American-made forward hoisting bar attached to the cockpit.

Right: This October 1972 close-up view of the supercharger air intake for the rear engine shows the exhaust stacks and the American-made rear hoist bar which were used to lift the aircraft onto the British aircraft carrier, HMS Reaper (see p. 179).

Left: This detail view of the starboard side of the nose engine protective covering applied by the US Navy to protect the aircraft during its years of outside storage. Although very faded, the Dornier is still in its original wartime camouflage (see Appendix 1 p. 159).

Above: An interesting mystery! This set of Do 335 wings, photographed at Silver Hill in 1971, are from the US Army Air Corps' aircraft, Do 335 A-1 and not the Navy's A-02. The Air Corps' Foreign Equipment number FE-1012, painted in white, was still clearly visible on the top surface of the wing. This begs the question of what happened to the original Do 335 A-02 wings kept in storage by the US Navy? However, since the two sets of wings were interchangeable, final assembly after restoration was not a problem. **Below:** Dornier personnel work to complete restoration at Oberpfaffenhofen. Shown here is the exposed forward DB 603 A-2.

Above and Below: Taken during autumn 1975 at Dornier's Oberpfaffenhofen factory, these two views of Do 335 A-02 clearly show the restoration project moving forward. The forward engine is in position and the cowl radiator support collar has been attached.

Top: Close-up view of the side to the forward DB 603 A-2 showing the alloy engine bearer arm and ancillary equipment. **Above:** The original spinner to the front engine, shown left, has been cleaned while the original rear spinner was lost over the years. A new fiberglass replica is shown to the right. **Above Right:** A close-up of the wing leading edge stall strip. This device acts as a stall originator which improves lateral control thereby allowing the wing tips to stall last. **Right:** A detail shot of the port wheel well cover door. This design was adopted after the original circular one-piece wheel cover proved impractical.

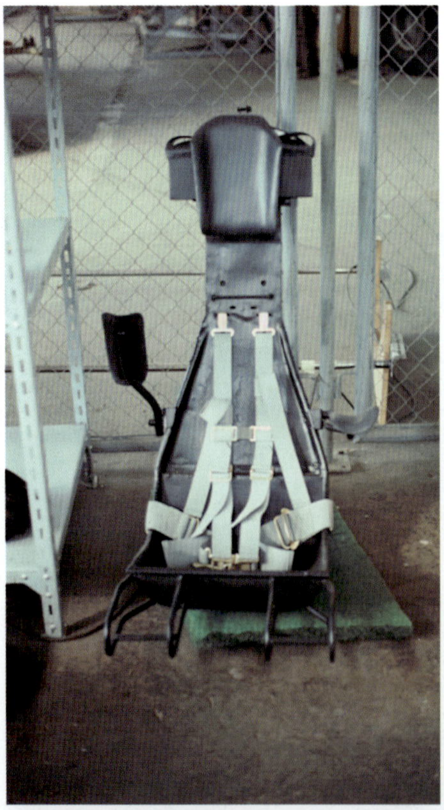

Above left to Right: The pilot's seat complete with arm rests, the main gear cover, and the empty rear engine bay during restoration. **Left:** Close-up of the rear propeller shaft.
Below Left: The Revi C/12 D reflector gun sight planned for installation. The correct gun sight for the Do 335 A-0 was the Revi 16 D. **Below:** This view of the top port side to the DB 603 A-2 shows the cast allow engine bearer arm, port engine coolant tank and new exhaust stacks.

Above: December 1975. Thirty-one years and three months after being built, the newly restored Do 335 A-02 serves as an impressive backdrop to the Dornier personnel who assisted in the restoration process of this unique aircraft. **Below:** Photographed in the spring of 1976 outside one of the hangers at Oberpfaffenhofen, the Do 335 A-02 awaits completion of the addition to the Deutsches Museum in nearby Munich. Although the aircraft appears to carry cowl weapons, these are in fact simulators as it is against German law for actual weapons to be installed. Note too, that the two clear vision hatches to the canopy plexiglas were not reproduced when new glass was fitted.

Above: The cockpit of the Do 335 A-02 showing some variation in instruments from what was originally specified (see p. 53). Unlike many German fighters of the period, the Dornier cockpit was spacious and well laid out. Like most German fighters, the flight instruments were mounted on a suspended panel attached to the center of the main panel. Engine instruments were positioned to the right. Most of the interior was painted in Color 66 Black-Gray while Color 02 RLM Gray was applied to lower sections of the cockpit.

Lower photograph: A glimpse inside the cockpit of the Do 335 V8. Note the addition of a FK 38 magnetic compass, type Fl23233, mounted in place of the gun sight. Faulty compass readings were a common complaint of Do 335 pilots.
Opposite: Two views of the restored Arrow with the lower photograph taken in 1987 while the Dornier was still on public display at the Deutsches Museum.

102
VO PH

VG

Above: This photograph of Do 335 A-03, W.Nr. 240003, VG+PI, taken at Oberpfaffenhofen after American occupation of the field, shows other airframes in the background. This particular aircraft was located at Rechlin late in the war, and was to be flown out by Hans Lerche, but due to a tire puncture, it could not on that occasion. Obviously, another pilot was able to get the aircraft repaired and flown out prior to the field falling to the advancing Russians.

Below: Another preproduction Arrow found after the war. This is Do 335 A-05, W.Nr. 240005, VG+PL, found abandoned at Oberpfaffenhofen with substantial bullet damage to the rear fuselage.

Above and Below: Two additional views of Do 335 A-05 captured by American troops at Oberpfaffenhofen. The lower photograph shows Col. Harold E. Watson standing on the wing next to the cockpit with an unidentified German officer looking on. In a letter to Hitler's adjutant, Nickolaus von Below, General Milch said that he saw the Do 335 as "the piston-engined, high-speed bomber and day fighter of the future". There is little doubt that he was right, but Allied bombing slowed production to the point that the aircraft was too late to see operational service.

This page and Opposite: Dornier factory photographs of complete production aircraft are very rare with the exception of these views of Do 335 A-07, W.Nr. 240107, VG+PN. Completed during September 1944, this seventh preproduction Arrow was extensively photographed prior to participating in its test program. Because of the threat of Allied aircraft over flying Oberpfaffenhofen, this series of photographs were apparently purposely taken on an overcast wet day. The ultimate fate of this aircraft is unknown.

107

107

Above: Hans Lerche's Do 335 A-02 running up its engines at Oberpfaffenhofen.
Opposite: A recent view of the final approach to the main runway at Rechlin. Some of the old *Erprobungsstelle* buildings are still standing.

My last fight with the Do 335

It was mid-April 1945 at the *Luftwaffe* Test Center at Rechlin in Mecklenburg. Fewer and fewer German aircraft were to be seen in the skies, and it was obvious that the war was nearing its end. However, in spite of fuel shortages and other limitations, I still had to complete a series of urgent test flights with three captured Allied fighters, a British Hawker Tempest, a Soviet Lavochkin La-5FN, and a Yakovlev Yak-3.

We also had orders to ferry, if possible, available German test aircraft from Rechlin back to their manufacturers, and this, together with the speed of the Do 335, spurred me to ferry one of the two Do 335s still at Rechlin to Dornier's facility at Oberpfaffenhofen near Munich. I also had another, and a more personal, reason for wanting to make this flight; my future wife lived in the area.

The necessary preparations were soon completed, but, as I was taxiing to the take off point, one of the tires had a puncture, and I had to abandon my first attempt. The puncture was probably caused by one of the innumerable steel bomb splinters lying over the runway. As it was impossible to repair the tire at that time I had to leave Do 335 A-03, VG+PI, to her fate[1] and prepare the last remaining Do 335, which was A-02, VG+PH, for the ferry flight.

Because of the numerous air raids I was unable to take off until the evening of April 20, 1945. The night before I had heard on the BBC that the Soviet encirclement of Berlin from the east and north was progressing rapidly, and I prepared my flight plan accordingly. I intended to bypass Berlin by flying south west of the city, and keep as low as possible to avoid enemy fighters and anti aircraft guns. I was of course well aware that navigation under these conditions would not be easy with such a fast aircraft as the Do 335 which clocked around 342 mph (550 km/h), throttled back. There were railroads and *autobahns*, however, which would help me in my flight preparations. All this was vital because my aircraft did not carry ammunition and, in any case, I had no experience in aerial gunnery. Moreover, I was not familiar with the radio and navigation systems of the Do 335. Up to that time, I had only made blind-approach flights with the help of a radio operator, but this time I was flying a single-seater. It was also questionable if the ground organization was still intact and if, by using the radio, one would not simply attract the attention of prowling enemy fighters. In short, I was going to fly low and fast and orientate myself as in the old days. I stowed my few personal belongings in the bomb-bay and was ready to go.

The take off went well, and in short sequence I had completed all the necessary operations: retract the gear, throttle back the engines, set the prop pitch, stow the flaps, and trim for level flight. Both engines were running smoothly, and all the instruments were reading the correct values. I was on my way! The first lakes and woods around Rechlin, well known to me from countless previous flights (including soaring) offered reliable orientation points. As it turned out, this was more accurate than the compass reading which, to my surprise, indicated a different direction than the one I was actually flying. The reason for this deviation became clear to me only later on. The master compass in an aircraft is usually situated in the rear of the fuselage, that is, as far as possible from the engine(s), which affect the compass's normal functioning. But in the Do 335, with its tandem-engine layout, it was not possible to place the compass in the fuselage. Instead, the master compass had to be mounted in the port wing where, unfortunately for the pilot, it had a life of its own, being influenced by rapid acceleration which defeated its own purpose. This willful behavior of the master compass, as I

heard much later, caused another Do 335 to land in enemy controlled territory resulting in the long incarceration in a POW camp for its pilot.[2]

I made quick progress. Soon I saw the Nauen radio towers appearing to port; I was on course. Berlin was also easily distinguishable. Only then did I become aware of approaching darkness. I would have had more daylight if the take off from Rechlin had not been delayed.

Since my Do 335 was not fully tanked up, to be on the safe side (and to test the installation) I switched on the fuel- transfer system which was supposed to pump fuel from the wing tanks into the main fuselage tank behind me. The combined 3,600 horses of both engines drank at least 237 gal. (900 liters) of fuel an hour! After a short while, however, I realized the pumps were not working. This and the rapidly approaching dusk made it clear that it would be impossible to reach Lager-Lechfeld, south of Augsburg, in one hop. The K.d.E. (Commander of Test Establishment) was there at the time, and I had to deliver some important documents to him. On the spur of the moment, I decided to fly in the direction of Prague where I was familiar with the large Rusin (Rusyne) airfield, having made a series of instructional flights there (with captured B-17s for the *Luftwaffe* fighter groups based in the area).

The district of Beelitz-Heilstätten, south west of Berlin, whisked by underneath me, and already I was flying along the southern *autobahn.* On no account could I afford to miss the turn to Dresden - and there it was. Still flying low, I suddenly spotted some figures scattering in all directions as my Do 335 thundered over them at some 490 ft/sec (150 m/s). They were easily recognizable as Russians with their vehicles. At this speed and so close to the ground, an aircraft is no easy target, even for light antiaircraft guns, but I asked myself what was the point of having a fast aircraft if not for this, as I pushed the throttle forward even more. Now I had a bit more time. The *autobahn* was clearly visible in spite of fast approaching night.

Despite the encroaching darkness, I decided not to switch on my position lights. Why invite unnecessary attention? Shortly afterward I rushed past Dresden, left the *autobahn*, and very soon the lights of Prague appeared before me. I quickly found the airfield, which was already lit for night operations. Out with the undercarriage, and down she goes! But, I had spoken too soon! The wheels would not budge. Thank God there was an emergency lowering system! It should really be second nature to a pilot to know the service instructions of his aircraft by heart. Junkers Ju 88 pilots could operate all controls and switches blindfolded, the first group, to my knowledge to do so. Of course it is more difficult if one is flying a different, and often completely unknown, aircraft daily, as I did while testing captured enemy aircraft. I imposed this precaution on myself after circling an airfield thirteen times on my first flight with the American Airacobra, trying desperately to find out how to operate the emergency undercarriage release system on this nosewheel fighter. Aircraft with such undercarriages are particularly tricky in this respect, especially as regards the nosewheel itself. If the main gear is locked down, but the nosewheel leg is not, the consequences can be more unpleasant than with a normal belly landing. A forced landing with the Do 335 had its own tricky side; the ventral fin would have tilted the machine forward and made it plow up the field with the front engine.

At a touch down speed of approximately 124 mph (200 km/h), my chances for survival would have been poor, as the ventral fin of the Do 335 could be blown off by explosive charges in an emergency landing. Nevertheless, I was glad that I did not have to try out these refinements, including the ejector seat of my Do 335, because in the meantime I had felt around the cockpit and had found the handle for the pneumatic emergency undercarriage lowering system. The typical slight thumps caused by the locking down of the gear in flight as well as the three small green lights on the instrument panel indicated that all was clear for a normal landing on the long, well-lit runway. It was

already 20:20 hours (8:00 pm), and quite dark.

After a short rest, I went to refuel, as I wanted to take off again first thing the next morning. However, despite my urgent flight orders, I was told that the coveted high-octane fuel was simply not available[3]. To make a long story short, after a bit of palaver and a few packets of scarce cigarettes had changed hands the precious fuel began to flow into the tanks of my Do 335. Soon they were full to the brim, as I had no intention of relying once more on the electrically operated fuel-transfer system! The only thing which worried me was the reluctant undercarriage, but finally I managed to interest a mechanic from the hangar workshop in my problem. To this day I am deeply grateful for his kind help.

After a quick meal, we met again in the hangar, jacked up the Do 335 and retracted the undercarriage. An easily rectified slight mechanical defect had been responsible for the problem. Of course, it was also possible that the aircraft had simply not been properly serviced during these last weeks of the war. In any case, my Do 335 was soon ready for flight.

Unfortunately, the weather people did not hold out much hope for my takeoff the next morning, and so I went to bed. True enough, early the next morning it was IFR (instrument flight rules) conditions. Low clouds and pouring rain made any kind of flying impossible. Even the sparrows had to walk, as airmen used to say! I had to stay put. After all, it was necessary to find my way through a valley in the Bavarian forest! Trouble was also brewing in Prague; our troops were pulling out throughout the city. I had to leave as soon as I could. The next day was just as bad. Even though the forecast for the following day was for more of the same, I decided to take the risk and resume my flight. According to the meteorologists, the weather was supposed to be improving over southern Germany.

I arose at 04:00 hours in order to make use of first light. It was still raining, but the clouds were finally lifting. I will never forget the date; it was April 23, 1945. All preparations went according to plan and take off was no problem. I flew a little higher at first to get my bearings in this strange area as I still could not rely upon the compass. Who would be after my neck at this unearthly hour in this soaking gray weather?

I put my trust in fate and my own intuition and actually found a valley to fly along in the Bavarian forests - to this day I don't know which one - and began to think I already had the worst part of the journey behind me. Even the weather began to improve.

Suddenly, tracers whipped past the Do 335 from behind. I still have no idea if this welcome came from the ground or some enemy fighter, but it made me instinctively take violent evasive action and ram the throttles forward while plunging to almost tree top level. When I recovered from the shock, I slowed down a little and began to check the instruments for any tell tale signs of damage, especially any increase in temperature from the rear engine. If the oil or cooling system had been hit, the engine would have sized in about thirty seconds. With both engines intact I had nothing to fear as no enemy fighter could overtake me. In retrospect, the fiery greeting had probably come from some American ground troops who had already advanced past Nürnberg. In the meantime I set my course due south, crossed the Danube, and, helped by the appearance of the Alps panorama in the gradually improving visibility, I was able to get my bearings even before reaching Munich. I flew past the Pasing railway station at telegraph-pole height and turned westward. High above me I noticed the first contrails of my "comrades from the other side." I had to keep an eye on them just in case!

The railroad has always been an ideal navigational help to pilots, and if I followed the old airman's rule of "left wheel on the right-hand track" I only had to determine that the points were set correctly beyond the Pasing rail station. I avoided Fürstenfeldbruck airfield as I didn't want to run into enemy fighters, and our own light flak could have also taken a shot at me. It was now quite easy to find Lager-Lechfeld airfield. After a tight circuit around the field, the gear came down on the first try, and I was back on the ground once more. I taxied to the flight-control building where they told me that there was yet another air-raid alarm on, and I had practically no hope of seeing my Do 335 in one piece again afterward. It was too late to try and reach another airfield. We could already hear and see the approaching bombers and fighter-bombers. There was no time to spare! I took cover in a ditch while all around me bombs and shells wreaked havoc. In all, sixteen well-camouflaged aircraft were destroyed there that day, and the nearby Schwabstadel ammunition depot literally went up in the air before our eyes, together with a small wooded area around it. But, unbelievable as it may sound, my Do 335 out there on display remained untouched! The enemy pilots had probably thought it was an airfield decoy as it looked unusual enough.

I completed my mission as well as I

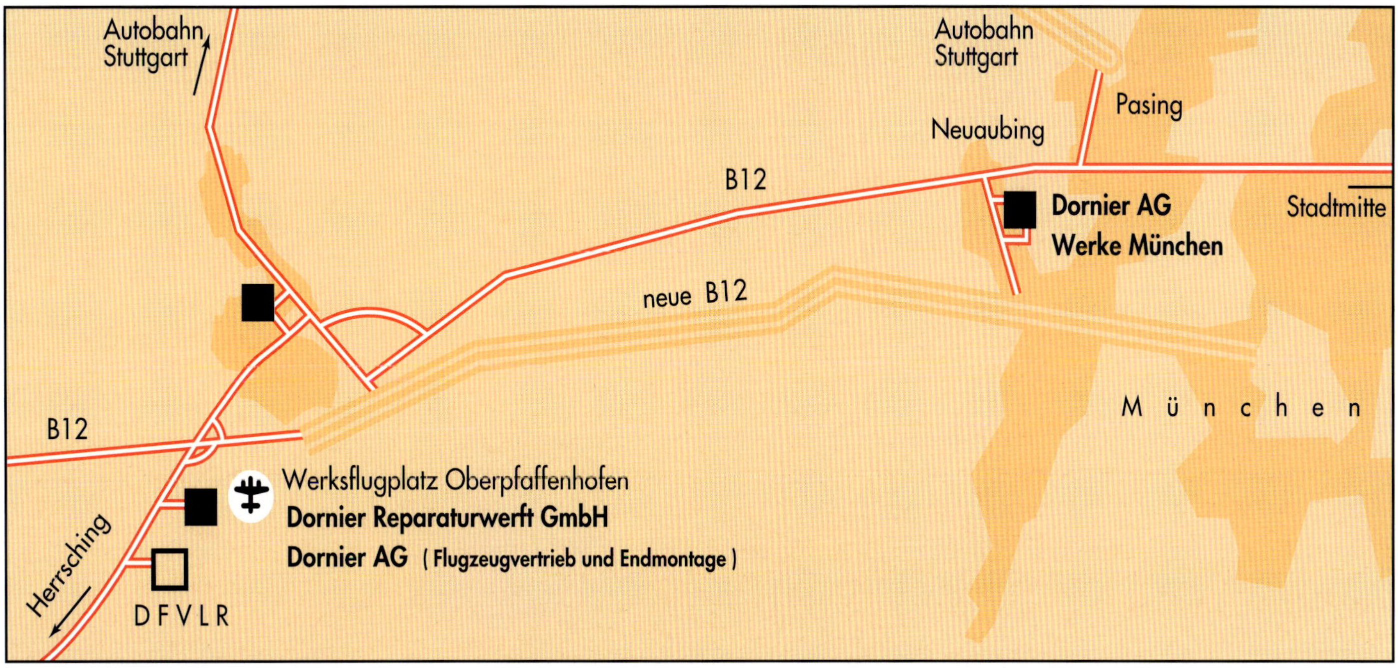

Opposite Left: Thirty-year old *Fl. Hauptingenieur* Hans-Werner Lerche in 1944. **Below:** A current view of the Dornier airfield at Oberpfaffenhofen. Although there are many new buildings, several of the old wartime structures are still standing.

could under the circumstances. After the air raids had abated, and with new flight orders directing me south, I climbed back into my Dornier that evening. I was now on the last lap of my journey to Oberpfaffenhofen, the Dornier works airfield, in my unscratched Do 335. And this time I decided to leave the gear locked down. One never knows!

The take off, which proved to be my last of the war, went well and a few minutes later I landed my valuable aircraft intact at Oberpfaffenhofen and parked it nicely in front of the main building, to the utter surprise of the Dornier staff who could hardly believe their eyes.

Dipl. Ing. Hans-Werner Lerche

1 This aircraft was later flown from Rechlin by another pilot to Oberpfaffenhofen.

2 This incident may have involved the Do 335 V9 and its last flight which ended in France.

3 In fact, the Do 335 did not require C3 fuel (96-100 octane), but instead flew normally with B4 (87 octane) fuel.

DORNIER Do 335 A-0
W.Nr. 240102, VG+PG
December 1975 - Oberpfaffenhofen, Bavaria

Do 335 A-0, A-1

1. VDM metal propeller 3.5 m Ø
2. Oil cooler radiator
3. Coolant radiator
4. Hydraulic coolant flaps
5. Hydraulic coolant flaps adjusting equipment
6. DB 603 A-2 (or E)
7. Engine bearer arm
8. Coolant tank 3.8 gal (14.5 ltr)
9. Forward firewall, fuselage frame 1
10. MG 151 cannon brackets
11. Nosewheel 685 x 250
12. Nosewheel damper
13. Nosewheel oleo leg
14. Nosewheel retraction strut
15. Hydraulic service cylinder
16. Landing gear door
17. Directional stear
18. Rudder pedal
19. Elevator linkage
20. Double hand grip on control column
21. 12 GL 3 battery
22. Pressurized air for emergency operations
23. Backside of the instrument panel
24. Electrics panel
25. FuG 16Z radio
26. Operations panel
27. Trim handwheel
28. Pilot's ejection seat
29. Pilkot's back armor
30. Fuselage frame 2
31. Fuel filter canuister for the forward engine
32. Pressurized air containers for emergency operations
33. Pressurized air containers for the ejection seat
34. Oil tank for the forward engine 11.9 gal (45 ltr)
35. Oil tank filler point
36. Fuselage frame 6
37. Main fuel tank 325 gal (1230 ltr)
38. Fuel filler point
39. Fuel distribution head
40. Fuel tank support braces
41. Rear firewall at fuselage frame 11
42. Fuselage bay
43. Hydraulic control for high speed and slow flight
44. Ventral intake for rear engine
45. Coolant outlet flap
46. Fire extinguisher 1.3 gal (5 ltr)
47. Fuselage frame 18
48. Hollow propeller extension shaft
49. Rear propeller lubricant feed lines
50. Camber adjustment for elevator and rudder trim

51. Elevator control lever
52. Elevator
53. Outer elevator trim tab
54. Elevator tim tab
55. Horizontal stabilizer
56. Rudder control lever
57. Dorsal fin
58. Rear propeller pitch control
59. VDM metal propeller 3.3 m Ø
60. Fuselage frame 24
61. Jettisonable ventral fin
62. Ventral rudder
63. Ventral rudder trim tab
64. Tail skid shock absorber
65. Tail skid
66. Landing flap
67. Hydraulic piston for flaps
68. Flap control linkage
69. Aileron trim tab linkage
70. Aileron
71. Aileron trim tab
72. Aileron connecting linkage
73. Wing rib 26
74. Wing tip section
75. Navigation light
76. Pitot tube
77. Master compass
78. Box spar
79. Wing rib 14
80. WheeljackWing spar protecting edge
81. Wing leading edge section
82. Landing light 130 E 2
83. Mainwheel 1015 x 380
84. Landing gear cover
85. Hydraulic retraction piston
86. Auxiliary retraction jack and guide
87. Guide cable of the auxilary retraction jack
88. Main gear wheel well
89. Wing fuel tank 99 gal (375 ltr)
90. Wing tank fuel vent line
91. Pressurized oil container
92. Oxygen bottles
93. Engine primer fuel tank 1.6 gal (6 ltr)

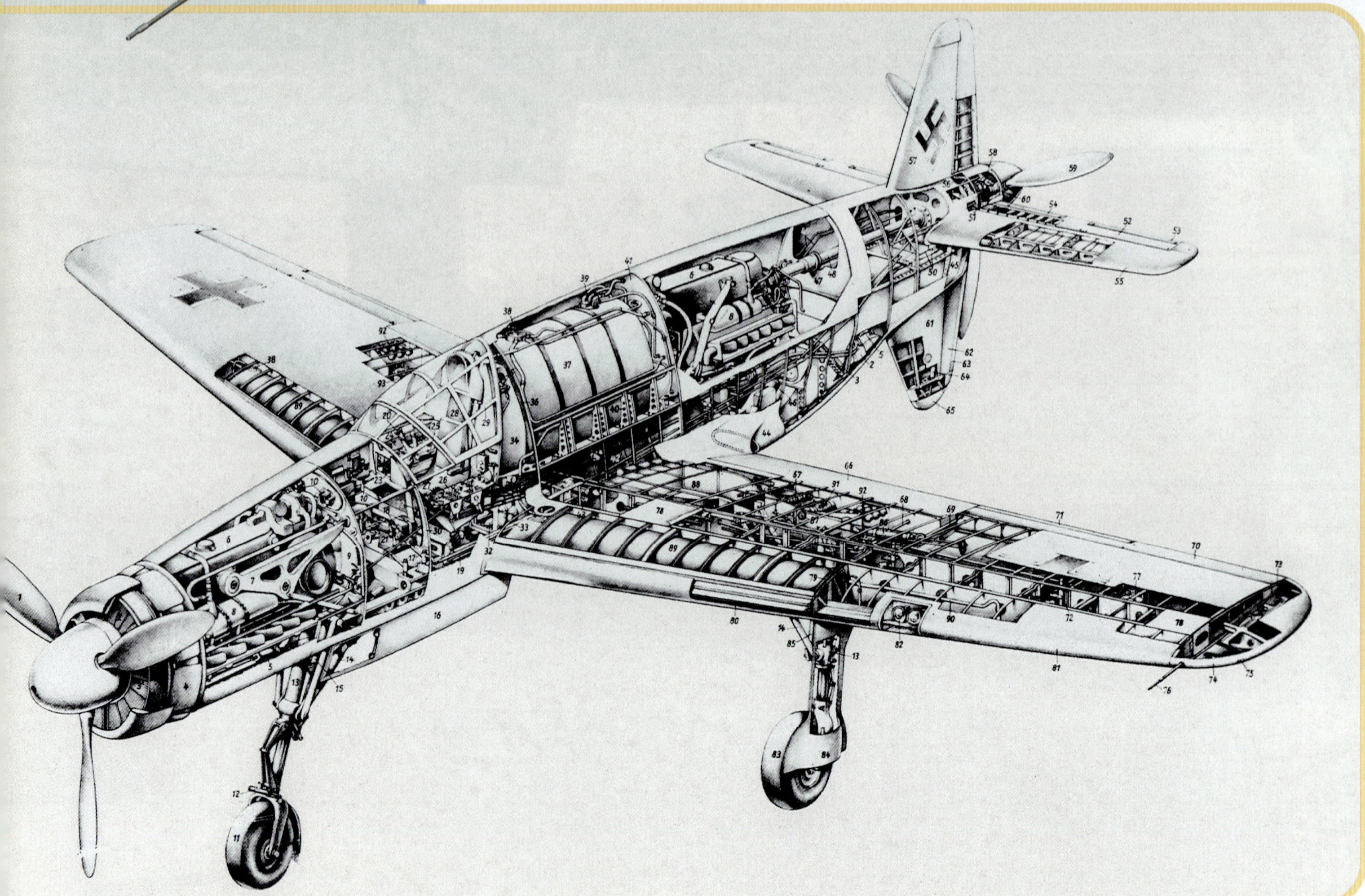

Above: *Dipl. Ing.* Hans-Werner Lerche stands proudly beside the aircraft he successfully flew to the relative safety of the Dornier factory at Oberpfaffenhofen on April 23, 1945 two weeks before the end of the war in Europe. This photograph, taken in 1983 shortly before his death, dramatically illustrates the size of the Do 335. Born during 1914 in Posen, Germany, Hans Lerche learned to fly in 1931 and ten years later was posted to the *Luftwaffe* Flight Test Center at Rechlin as a test pilot. While at Rechlin, he flew a wide range of German and captured Allied aircraft including the single-engined Bf 109, P-51 B Mustang, Yak-3 and twin-engined Me 262, B-26 Marauder and the Ar 232A. He also flew three-engined aircraft such as the Ju 352 and Italian SM.79. *Dipl. Ing.* Lerche also test flew large aircraft such as the 4-engined Ju 290, the B-17G and the huge 6-engined Ju 390 and Me 323. In 1976 he was made an Honorary Fellow of the Society of Experimental Test Pilots.

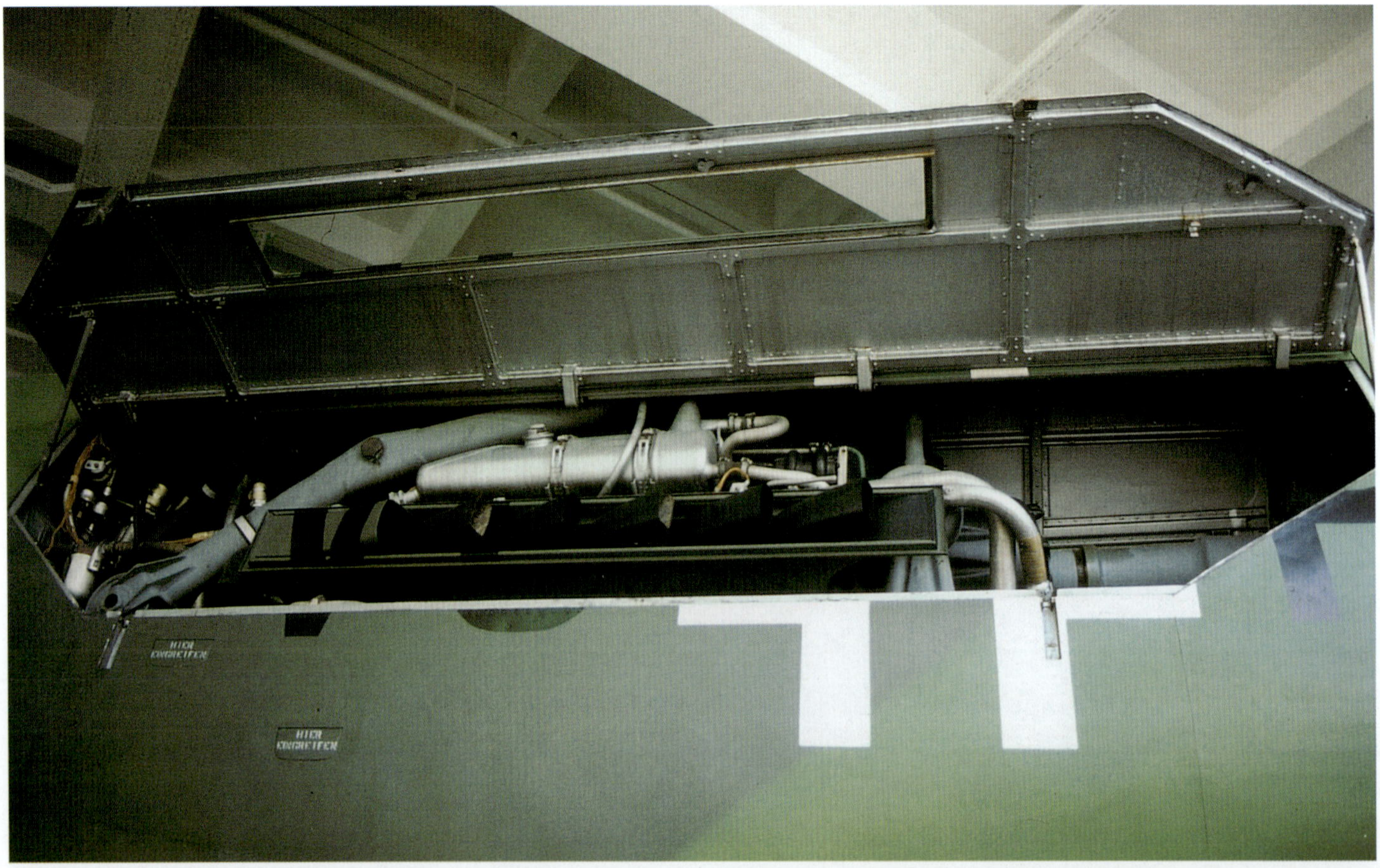

Above and Below: Two views of the rear engine area of Do 335 A-02 taken while the aircraft was on exhibit at the Deutsches Museum in Munich, and during restoration in 1975. Cooling difficulties associated with the rear engine were never completely solved. This was the Achilles Heel of the aircraft and was responsible for a number of engine failures, fires and at least one fatality. The engines were reliable and powerful, yet the rear engine cooling system was prone to fail due to blockages and other problems. Pilots were warned to constantly monitor engine instruments for any sign of overheating or fire. However, when the system was functioning normally, as designed, the aircraft was a pleasure to fly.

Above and Below: A close-up of the rear port engine area and an overall view of the port side to Do 335 A-02 taken during the summer of 1983 at Oberpfaffenhofen. The top photograph clearly shows the aircraft's *Stammkennzeichen* (primary identification code), VG+PH, which was assigned to this aircraft at the time of manufacture, and which stayed with the aircraft throughout its career. However, if this particular Dornier had been assigned to an operational *Luftwaffe* unit, this four-letter code would have been removed from the exterior of the aircraft, but would have been retained by the aircraft's identity card located in the cockpit. Note the Dornier 31 in the background of the lower photograph.

A-96

This page and Opposite: Three color views of Do 335 A-02 taken after restoration and while on exhibit in Munich. The black and white view shows the starboard 11.8 gal (45 ltr) oil tank plus the three pressurized tanks for GM 1 powerboosting containing nitrous-oxide. Note the mud guard for the nose wheel. This feature was eliminated in the Do 335 B-series due to a slightly larger tire and stowage considerations.

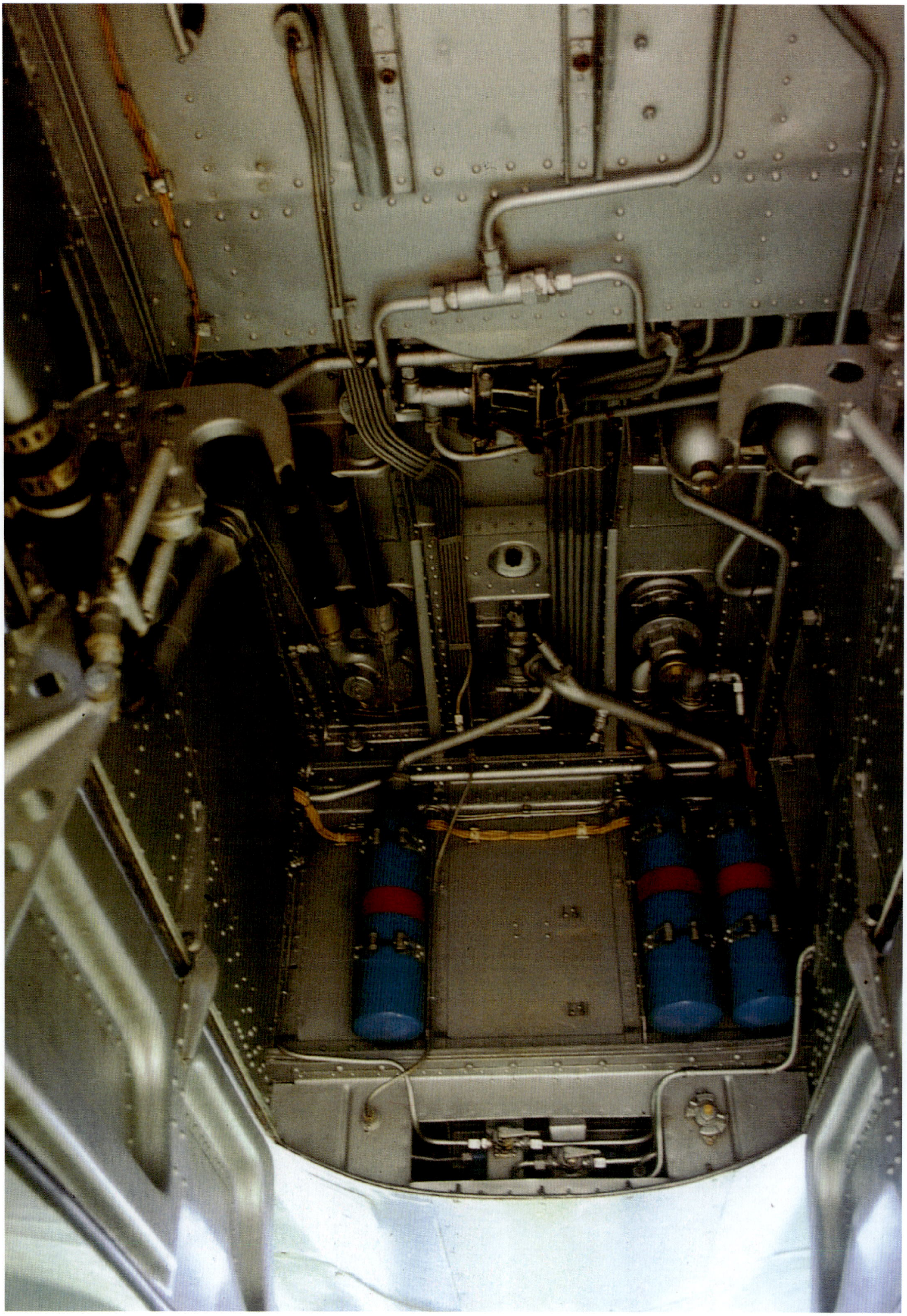

Above: Do 335 A-02 after restoration. **Opposite:** Close-up of the nose gear bay, looking forward, for Do 335 A-02 showing the three blue and red compressed air bottles. **Below:** Close-up of the bomb detonator switch box, SZK 246, found on the right side console. **Below Right:** The small oxygen instrument panel from a Do 335 B-series usually installed to the left of the gun sight (see pages 92 and 93). **Bottom Right:** Close-up of the adjustable right rudder pedal holder and the brake valve which was installed between the holder and the tip of the pedal (see page 93).

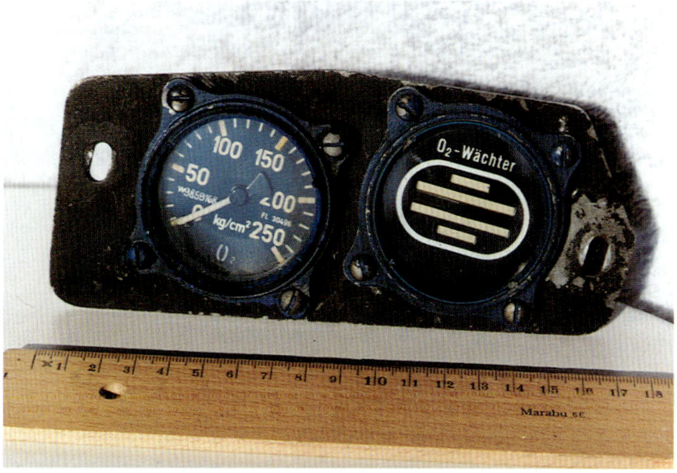

Above: A beautifully restored main instrument panel for the Do 335 showing the engine and flight instruments correctly positioned. The trapezoidal shaped panel carrying the flight instruments was independently sprung to minimize interference from engine vibration. The four red controls at the base of the main panel are emergency switches for the (l to r) undercarriage, flaps, steering and fuselage bay doors. **Below:** A close-up of the standby compass which was installed in the left console. **Right Opposite:** Contemporary factory view of the cockpit of a Do 335 A-0. All instruments were within easy reach and well positioned. Note that only the gyro control switch (far left) is missing in this view.

GM1-Anlage
36

Above and Below: Two views of Do 335 A-1, W.Nr. 24016?, taken at Neubiberg after having been flown out of Oberpfaffenhofen by the Americans prior to the aircraft being handed over to the British as part of the reciprocal agreements between the Allies. Unfortunately, this particular aircraft did not reach England.

Above and Below: Two additional views of the Do 335 intended for the British. In these views, the temporary, crudely applied, American national aircraft insignia, has been removed from the fuselage in anticipation of the application of RAF insignia. This aircraft crash-landed at Merville, France, in December 1945, when the nose gear failed to extend.

Above: One of the aircraft found at Oberpfaffenhofen was this Do 335 A-1, which in this view, lacks its rear engine and has sustained damaged to its ventral rudder. It is believed this aircraft was the Do 335 M1 as indicated by the number atop the dorsal tailplane. The number 2 represents the last digit in the serial number, 240162. **Below:** Taken in June 1945 at Dornier's Friedrichshafen facility by an American serviceman, this photograph shows the results of deliberately destroying a Do 335 prior to capture. It appears that an explosive device was detonated in the rear engine bay accompanied by a fire which ate through a large portion of the airframe. The exact model of Arrow is difficult to determine, but careful examination of the original photographs shows a B-series canopy resting upside-down near the wing root.

Right: A close-up of the rear engine area of Do 335 A-1, W.Nr. 240113, RP+UC, found by American forces at Bindbach near Bayreuth. This aircraft was severely damaged when the night fighter ace, twenty-three year-old *Major* Wolfgang Schnaufer, misjudged his approach on landing.

Below: A port side view of the Do 335 flown by *Major* Schnaufer showing severe damage to rear fuselage. It appears as though the *Major* bent the rear fuselage while landing nose high causing the ensuing severe damage to the ventral rudder and fin, and buckling of the fuselage at the tailplane.

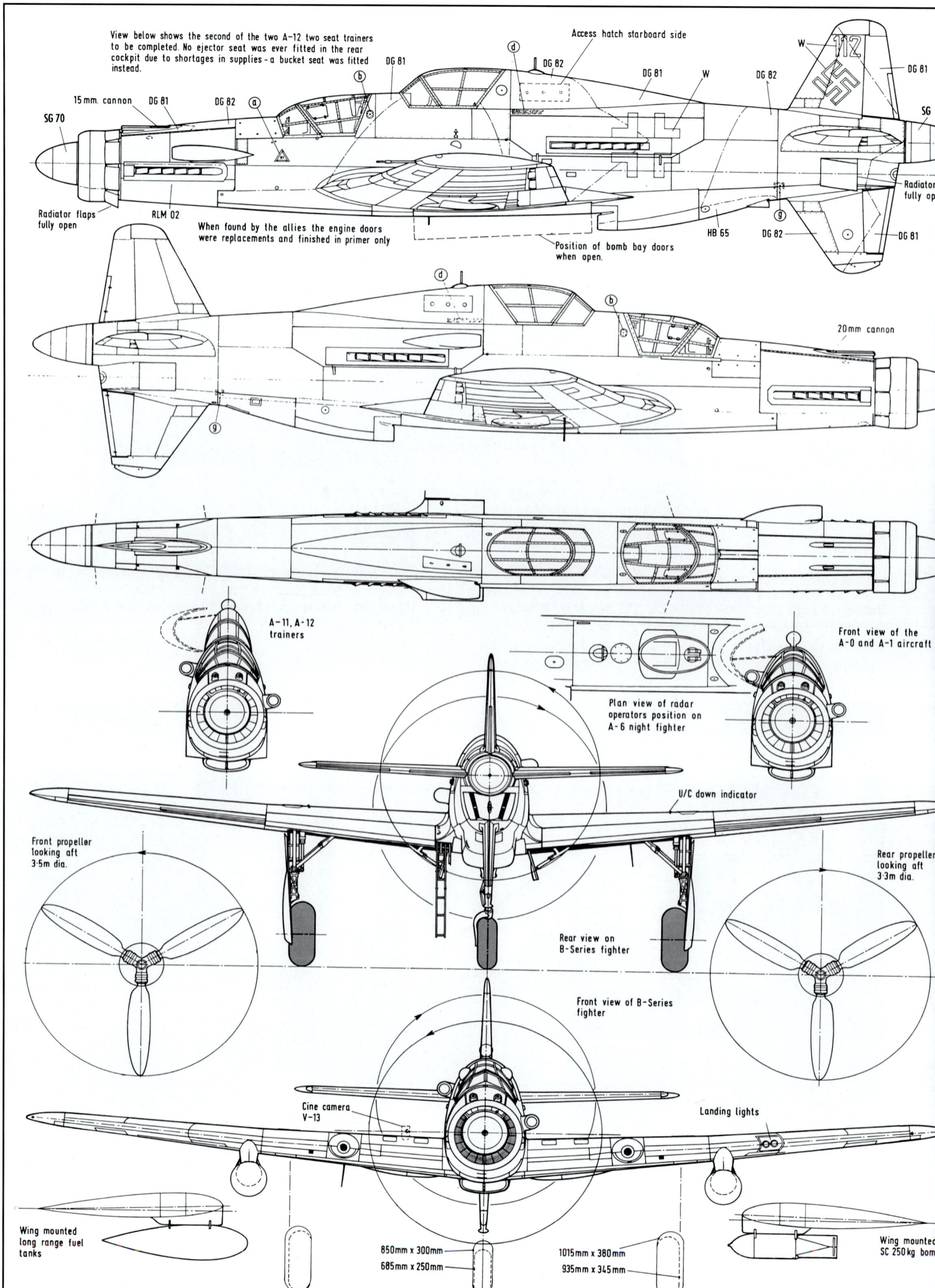
View below shows the second of the two A-12 two seat trainers to be completed. No ejector seat was ever fitted in the rear cockpit due to shortages in supplies - a bucket seat was fitted instead.
Access hatch starboard side
15 mm. cannon
DG 81
DG 82
SG 70
SG
W
HB 65
RLM 02
Radiator flaps fully open
When found by the allies the engine doors were replacements and finished in primer only
Position of bomb bay doors when open.
20mm cannon
A-11, A-12 trainers
Front view of the A-0 and A-1 aircraft
Plan view of radar operators position on A-6 night fighter
U/C down indicator
Front propeller looking aft 3·5m dia.
Rear propeller looking aft 3·3m dia.
Rear view on B-Series fighter
Front view of B-Series fighter
Cine camera V-13
Landing lights
Wing mounted long range fuel tanks
850mm x 300mm
685mm x 250mm
1015mm x 380mm
935mm x 345mm

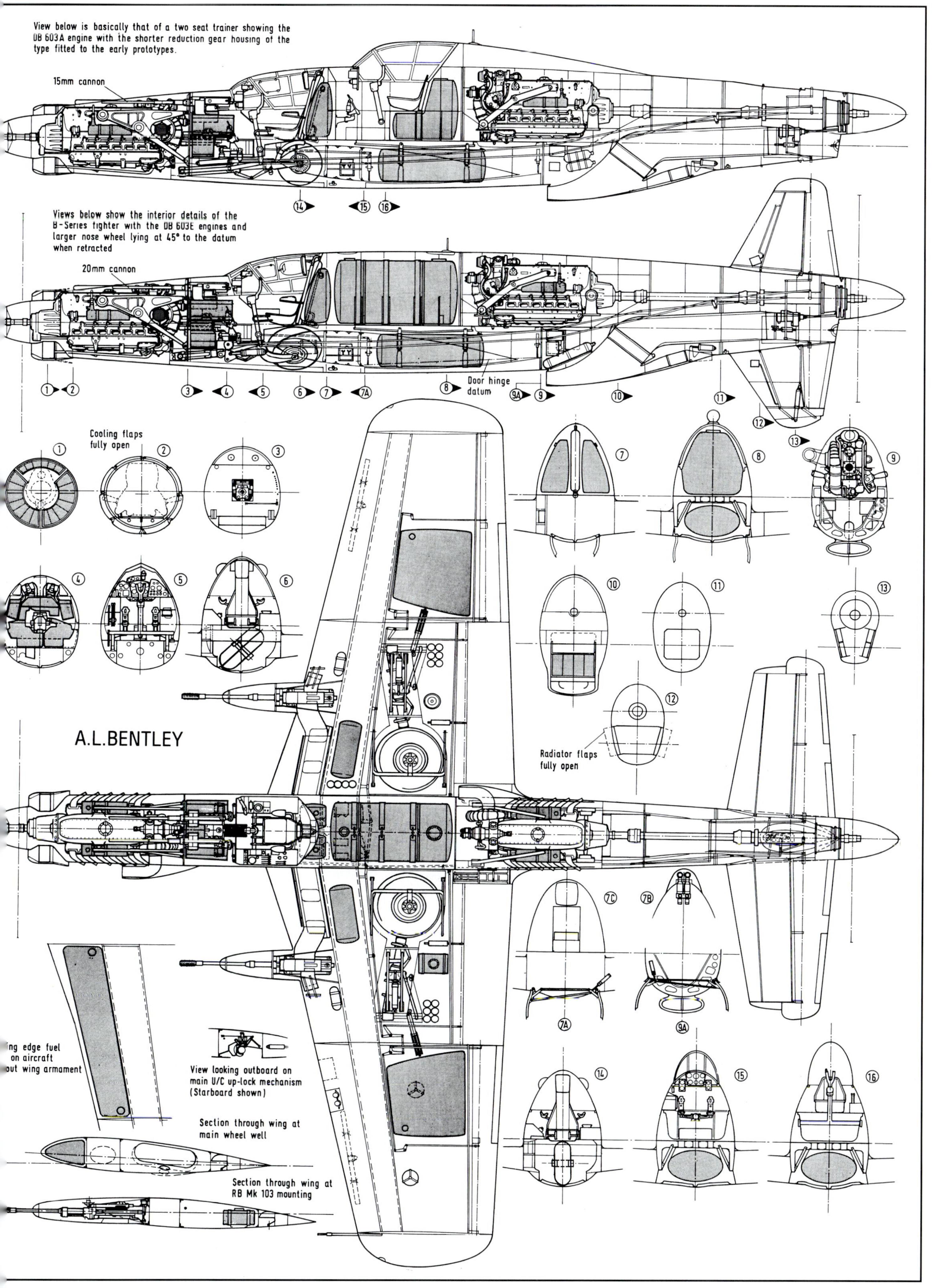

View below is basically that of a two seat trainer showing the DB 603A engine with the shorter reduction gear housing of the type fitted to the early prototypes.
15mm cannon
Views below show the interior details of the B-Series fighter with the DB 603E engines and larger nose wheel lying at 45° to the datum when retracted
20mm cannon
Door hinge datum
Cooling flaps fully open
Radiator flaps fully open
A.L.BENTLEY
View looking outboard on main U/C up-lock mechanism (Starboard shown)
Section through wing at main wheel well
Section through wing at RB Mk 103 mounting

Above: Do 335 A-1, W.Nr. 24016?, being serviced by American mechanics. **Left:** The unrestored fuselage bay, looking forward, to Do 335 A-02. **Below:** An Rb 50/30 reconnaissance camera mounted in the fuselage bay.

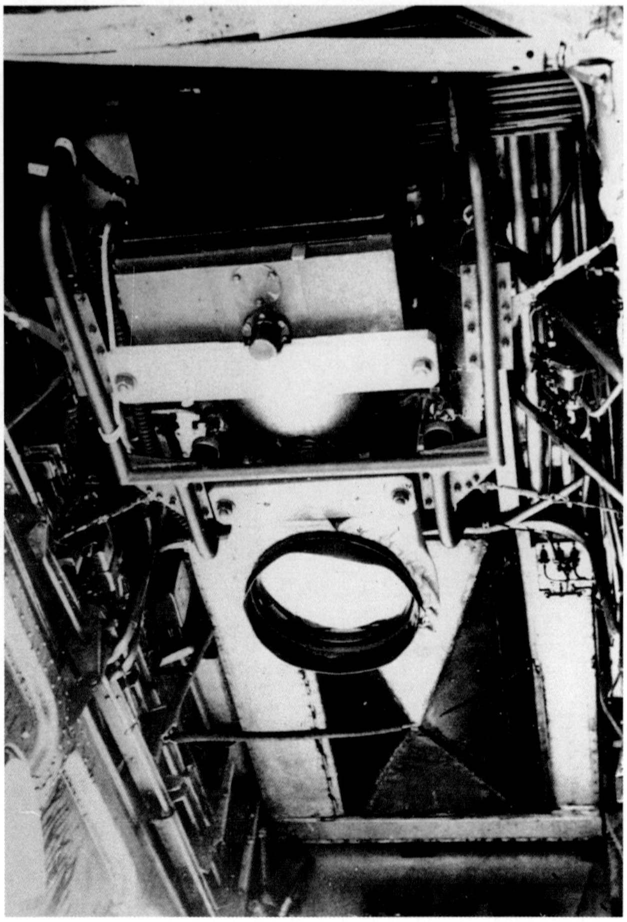

Above: To fulfill the bomber requirement of the original specification, Dornier created full-scale simulation models. The photograph, shown above left, illustrates how a 2,205 lb (1,000 kg) SC 1000 bomb would fit within the fuselage bay. The photograph shown above right, shows how a 1,102 lb (500 kg) SC 500 bomb would be loaded into the fuselage bay. See page 183 for further details.

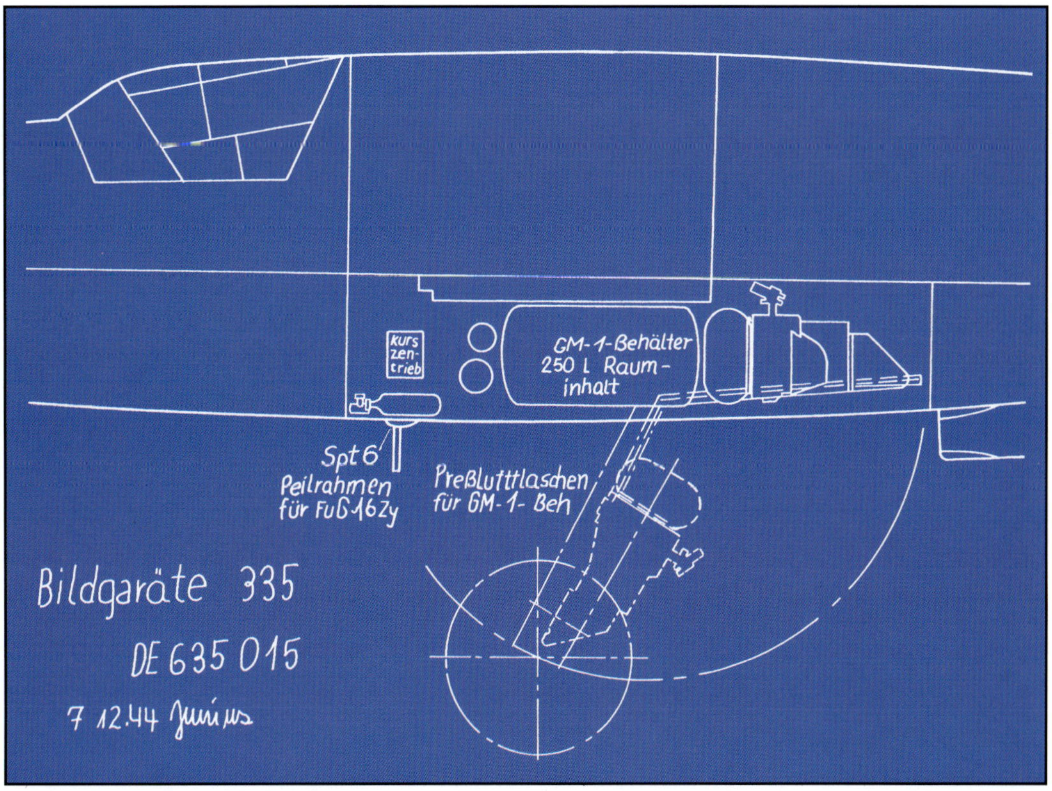

Right: In addition to bombs, the fuselage bay was designed in such a way, that it could accommodate other equipment such as one or two photographic reconnaissance cameras plus a supplemental fuel tank. In this Junkers sketch, a 66 gal (250 ltr) GM 1 fuel tank is shown just ahead of an Rb 50/30 reconnaissance camera. GM 1 was nitrous-oxide, a power-boosting fuel contained under pressure for improving engine performance above the rated altitude.

THE ARROW AT NIGHT

During the fall of 1944 proposals were put forward for adapting the Do 335 for the nightfighting role under the designation **Do 335 A-6**. This was basically similar to the A-1, but with a second seat behind the pilot for a radar operator. The latter was to be provided with a flush-fitting canopy and a specially designed Heinkel ejector seat. The installation of a second seat resulted in the main fuselage fuel tank being reduced in capacity to 158 US gal (600 Ltr), the deficiency being made up by two 79 US gal (300 ltr) drop tanks under the wings. Two small MW 50 tanks were also installed in the wings to provide water-methanol injection for the DB 603 E engines. The use of MW 50 increased engine power to 2,000 hp for short periods.

In addition to the standard radio equipment, the A-6 was to carry Telefunken FuG 220 *Lichtenstein SN-2* air-borne interception radar (later to be replaced by the lighter Siemens FuG 218 *Neptun V* set which operated on higher frequencies). Also fitted was Telefunken FuG 350 Naxos Z "passive" radar which worked on the emissions of the British H2S set, and a Siemens FuG 101 radio altimeter. The installation of radar necessitated the attachment of four "toasting fork" antennae in the wings, the two for the lateral beams on the port side, the two for the vertical on the starboard. The standard armament of one MK 103 and two MG 151 cannons was retained, and a 1,100 lb bomb could be mounted in the weapons bay in place of the 132 US gal (500 ltr) auxiliary fuel tank. It was estimated that the second seat, radar equipment and flame damping exhausts would reduce the A-6's maximum speed by some 43 mph (70 km/h).

Above: An artist's impression of the two-seat Do 335 M10, which was the first prototype for the night fighter version.

The prototype night fighter was the Do

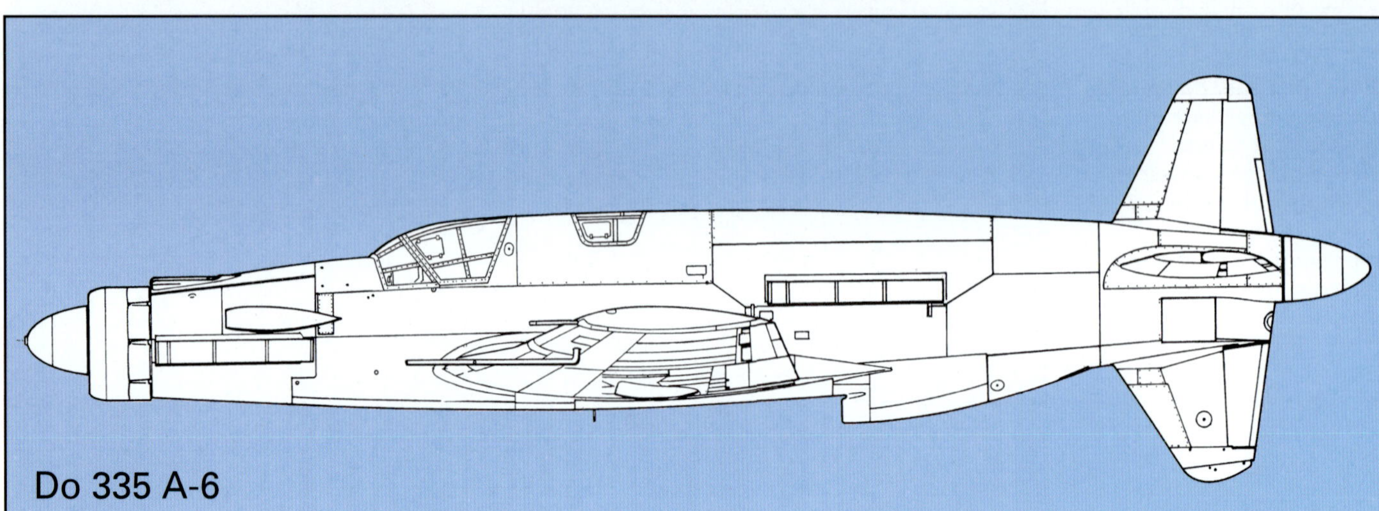

335 M10, W.Nr. 230010, CP+UK, which made its first flight from Diepensee on January 24, 1945. It had a second seat positioned behind the first with a flush-fitting multi-piece canopy with clear vision panels installed as in the pilot's canopy. The second night fighter prototype, intended for delivery early in February 1945, was the Do 335 M17. It was to serve as prototype for the **Do 335 B-6** night fighter and was to be fitted with FuG 218 radar but the war ended before it was completed. However, after being captured intact by the French at Mengen and, working with former Dornier employees, it was finally completed two years after the war as recounted in Appendix 3. A further B-series night fighter prototype was proposed, the Do 335 M21 but this aircraft was never completed. After delivery these development machines were to be passed to the radar test center at Werneuchen for evaluation.

Apart from the various types of radar, other systems were to be developed for the Do 335 night fighter. These included de-icing equipment (which was tested on the Do 335 A-05), the EZ-42 gyroscopic gunsight (to be installed in the Do 335 M13) and the Messerschmitt P 8 high speed reversible-pitch propeller (to be tested in the Do 335 A-08). The latter feature installed in place of the standard VDM forward propeller, was found to reduce the landing run by some 650 feet (200 m) at maximum landing weight.

At a conference of the Special Commission for the Development of Night and Bad Weather Fighters held in Berlin on January 24, 1945, Dornier promised that he could deliver the first of a batch of fifty Do 335 A-6s by March 1945, these to be subcontracted by Heinkel North at Oranienburg. All fifty airplanes were to be equipped with FuG 220 D *Lichtenstein* SN-2 radar sets. Doubts were expressed, however, about the effectiveness of the Dornier 335 as a night fighter. The head of the Commission, *Professor* Kurt Tank of Focke-Wulf considered that "it will only be adequate until around mid-1945; after that only the Me 262 and Ar 234 jets will be suitable until the development of a new three-seater." After some discussion, it was agreed to further examine the Do 335 night fighter in parallel with a mixed power derivative, and abandon them both at the outset if they proved too costly.

As part of the testing of the Do 335, Germany's leading night fighter ace *Major (Maj.)* Wolfgang Schnaufer, was given the opportunity to fly one of the early production Do 335 A-1s, (W.Nr. 240113) According to Schnaufer's radio operator, *Leutnant (Lt.)* Fritz Rumplehardt, the young ace crashed the aircraft at Gutersloh which did not exactly endear him to the Dornier flight test staff! However, he did put forward a suggestion that the aircraft be fitted with the *schräge Musik* (jazz music) upward firing gun installation for night fighter operations.

It is quite likely that the Do 335 M10 was later delivered to I./NJG 3 under *Hauptmann (Hptm.)* Werner Baake for operational testing. This group also flew the Focke-Wulf Ta 154 A-4 in the night fighting role. A special operational unit was in fact set up to fly the Do 335 night fighter as early as September 1944.

Designated V./NJG 2, the group was formed from III./KG 2, but never received the *Pfeil*. Its last ground attack operation was in fact flown with a Junkers Ju 88 G-6 on the night of April 27/28, 1945.

NIGHT FIGHTER CAMOUFLAGE

Our illustration at the top of page 102 depicts the Do 335 M10 in a possible, but unverified paint scheme. Since no photographs of this prototype appear to have survived, aviation artist Sonny Schug has suggested an attractive scheme based upon an earlier February 1943 Dornier night fighters scheme for the Do 217 N-1. This camouflage scheme called for the top surfaces of the aircraft to be painted in colors 74 Gray-Green and 75 Gray-Violet while the fuselage sides, including the vertical tailplane, were mottled in the same two colors over base color 76 Light Blue, or alternatively a base of color 02 RLM Gray. All undersurfaces were a continuation of the fuselage base color; either color 76 or 02. Spinners and metal propeller blades were each in the usual color 70 Black-Green. Our photograph below of Do 217 N-2, PE+AW, illustrates a simplification to night fighter camouflage. This newly completed aircraft featured an overall application of color 76 Light Blue with an interlocking pattern of color 75 Gray-Violet sprayed over top surfaces. Note the fuselage national aircraft insignia has been created by simply spraying a simplified white cross over a solid application of color 75 Gray-Violet.

THE *AMEISENBÄR*

During early 1944, development of a dual control trainer of the Do 335 was begun. It was anticipated that even experienced pilots would require a certain amount of familarization before transitioning to the new aircraft. Resultingly, two two-seat prototypes, the Do 335 M11, W.Nr. 230011, CP+UL, and the Do 335 M12, W.Nr. 230012, RP+UO,were produced which quickly earned the affectionate nickname *Ameisenbär* (Ant Bear - Anteater) because of its characteristic humped fuselage. Dornier engineers created the second, raised

Above and Below: The Do 335 M11, W.Nr. 230011, CP+UL, was the first prototype for the Do 335 A-11 trainer. It was the first Arrow to test the explosive jettison system of the rear propeller and was damaged during a landing accident at Dornier's Mengen airfield.

cockpit by redesigning and reducing the main fuselage fuel tank's capacity. The instructor enjoyed a much elevated view from his cockpit which was equipped with a dual set of controls, but lacked the otherwise standard ejection seat. The Do 335 M11 made its first flight on October 11, 1944, with *Flugg-kapitän* Appel at the controls. The Do 335 M12, which was completed in September 1944, was essentially similar powered by two DB 603 A-2 engines. Both prototypes were forerunners for the planned Do 335 A-11 series. The Do 335 M11 was severely damaged due to undercarriage failure while landing at Dornier's Mengen facility. It was subsequently used to test the rear propeller jettison system. The Do 335 M12 was completed with the Messerschmitt designed Me P 8 reversible pitch propeller which had been installed to investigate reducing landing roll distance.

To shorten delivery time for the new trainers, eight production Do 335 A-1s (240111, 240112, 240114, 240119, 240120, 240121, 240122 and 240123) were selected for modification to become Do 335 A-12 trainer series which, like the A-1 series, were powered by two DB 603 E-1s. Of these, only half were actually completed at Oberpfaffenhofen before the end of the war. The proposed Do 335 A-10 trainer series was to have been similar but powered by Jumo 213s. Although not completed, a two-seat trainer was also earmarked for the B-series as the Do 335 B-5.

Finally, it has been alleged by several postwar authors that the two-seat trainer was adapted to night fighter duties, but this assumption is incorrect. The *Ameisenbär* was strictly a two-seat trainer.

Above: Because of its distinctive profile, the two-seat trainer was affectionately known as the *Ameisenbär* (Ant Bear, or Anteater). Shown here is a Giant Anteater (Myrmecophaga Jubata) and resident of the San Diego Zoo. **Right:** The remains of the second two-seat trainer, the Do 335 M12, W.Nr. 230012, RP+UO, which had been purposely destroyed at Dornier's Friedrichshafen facility prior to the arrival of American troops. This aircraft had been fitted with a Me P 8 reversible-pitch propeller.

Left: Nose gear failures were not uncommon as shown in this photograph of Do 335 A-12, W.Nr. 240111, RP+UA. This aircraft was originally built as an A-1 series, but was modified for the training role.

Right opposite and Below: Two views of Do 335 A-12, W.Nr. 240112, RP+UB, as it was captured at Oberpfaffenhofen at the end of the war. The first batch of these two-seat trainers were essentially identical.

Left: In this photograph of "112" the aircraft is still in its original German insignia, and was one of the more popular examples of the Do 335 with American troops.

Do 335 A-11, A-12

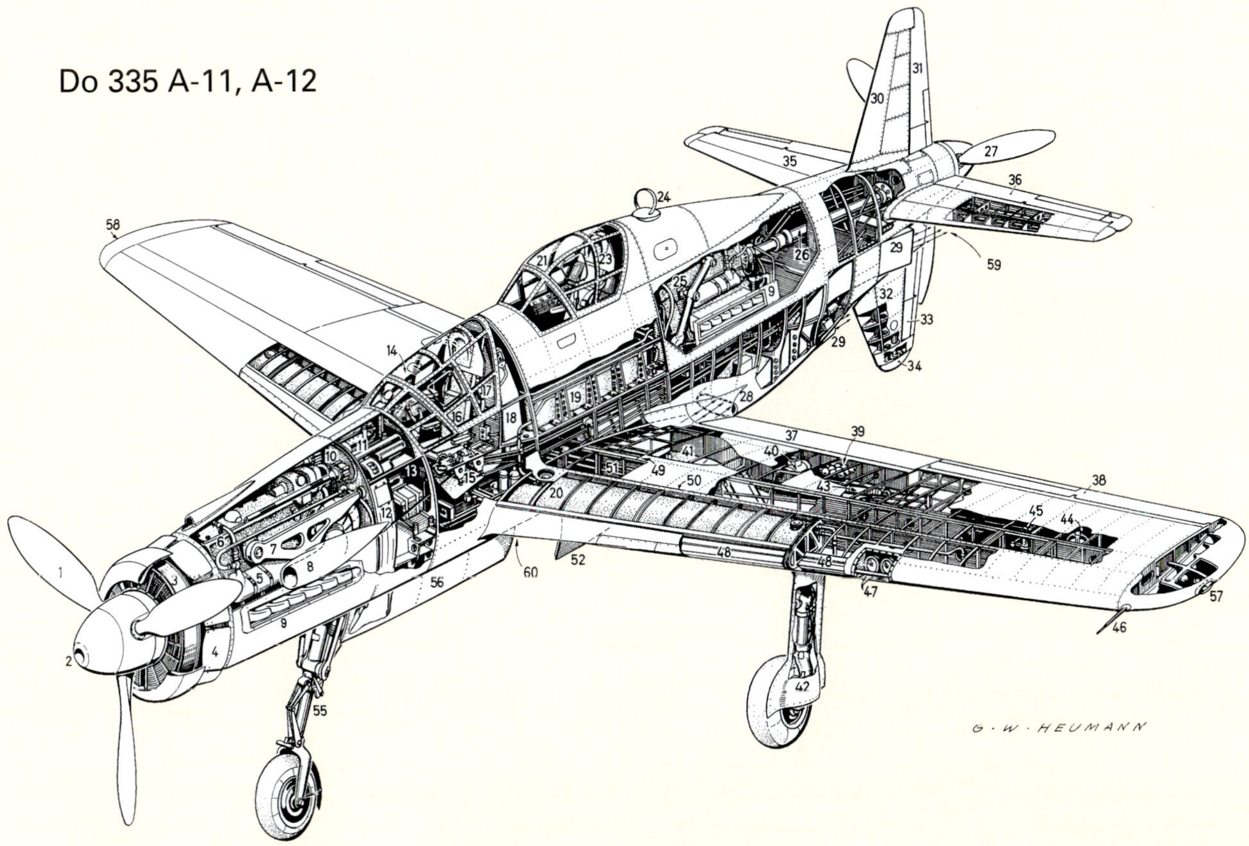

1. VDM Propeller
2. Front Spinner
3. Forward radiator
4. Radiator flaps
5. Port coolant tank
6. DB 601 E-1 engine
7. Engine bearer arm
8. Supercharger intake
9. not used
10. Forward firewall
11. Twin MG 151/20 cannon
12. Ammo tank for MG 151/20
13. MK 103 cannon
14. Jettisonable canopy
15. Engine control rods
16. Ejection seat
17. Rear armor plate
18. Port lubricant container
19. Main fuel tank
20. Wing fuel tank
21. Jettisonable canopy
22. not used
23. Ejection seat
24. FuG 16Z d/f loop
25. DB 603 E-1 engine
26. Hollow extension shaft
27. Jettisonable VD Propeller
28. Rear engine radiator intake
29. Radiator exit flap
30. Jettisonable dorsal fin
31. Jettisonable dorsal rudder
32. Jettisonable ventral fin
33. Jettisonable ventral rudder
34. Tail skid with shock absorber
35. Horizontal tailplane
36. Elevator
37. Port variable chamber flap
38. Port aileron
39. Compressed air tanks, port only
40. Armored hydraulic fluid tank
41. Port mainwheel well
42. Port undercarriage leg
43. Undercarriage operating jack
44. Master compass
45. Aileron control rods
46. Pitot tube
47. Landing lights
48. Balloon cable cutter
49. Main wing box spar
50. Forward wing spar
51. Aileron/flap contol rods
52. Fuselage bay doors
53. not used
54. not used
55. Oleo leg for nose wheel
56. Door for nose gear
57. Red port navigation light
58. Green starboard navigation light
59. White rear navigation light
60. Sharp wing root airflow disrupter

Left: All of the photographs on this page show "112" the second production two-seat trainer to be completed. **Below:** Preparatory to its flight from Oberpfaffenhofen to Neubiberg, where it was to be formally handed over to the British, it was hastily repainted with American insignia.

Left: Some idea of the size of this example of the *Ameisenbär* can be gained in this view of American troops standing by the large Dornier.

Above: After arrival in England, "112" was assigned Air Ministry number AM223 and repainted with RAF insignia prior to going on display at Farnborough. It crashed on January 18, 1946, killing Group Captain Hards. Cause of the crash was blamed on a rear engine fire which burned through vital control cables. **Right:** Do 335 A-12, W.Nr. 240114, RP+UD, was also captured at Oberpfaffenhofen but was not airworthy. **Below:** Do 335 A-12, W.Nr. 240119, RP+UI, was one of the last trainers completed before the occupation. Most of the aircraft is unpainted.

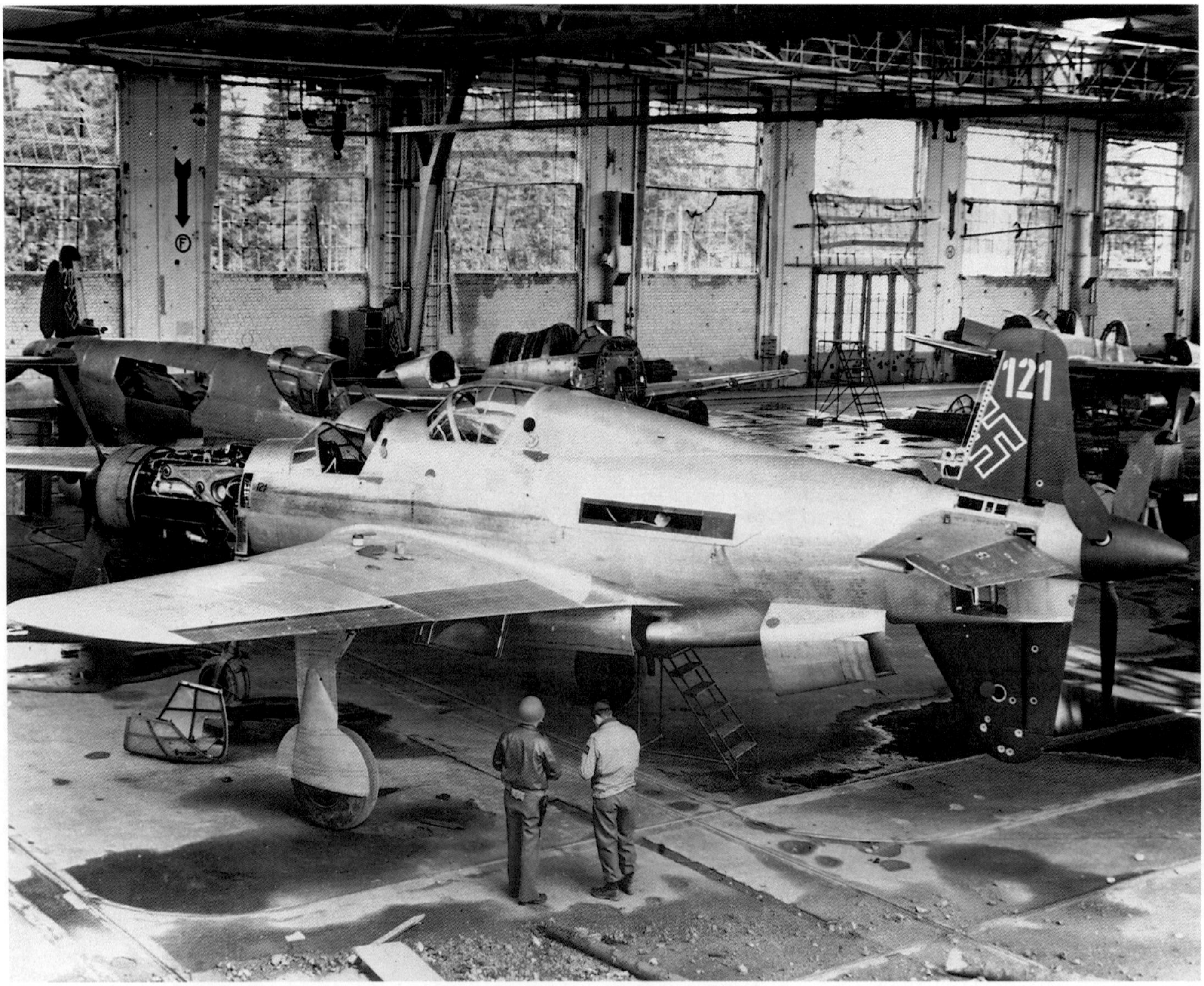

Above: A view inside the final assembly hall at Oberpfaffenhofen shows American officers examining Do 335 A-12, W.Nr. 240121, RP+UL, which was almost finished when American troops arrived. In the background are two incomplete B-series prototypes, thought to be the M20 (left) and the M18 (middle).

Below: The incomplete Do 335 A-12, W.Nr. 240122, RP+UM, sits in the grass at Oberpfaffenhofen. Though not damaged when captured, its back was broken by troops incorrectly pulling the aircraft.

Above: American servicemen pose with "114" at Oberpfaffenhofen. **Right:** A view inside the instructors cockpit of the two-seat trainer. Visibility was excellent, but instrumentation sparse in contrast to the main cockpit. Unlike the main, or students cockpit, the instructor's area was not fitted with an ejection seat. **Below:** Another view of "114" showing both canopies in the open position.

Above and Left: Two additional views of "114" at Oberpfaffenhofen. These unusual German aircraft became ideal backdrops for servicemen with extra film and a working camera. **Below:** This photograph shows three of the two-seat trainers pulled into the open at Oberpfaffenhofen including "119" in the foreground, the incomplete remains of Do 335 A-12, W.Nr. 240123, just behind, and "114" in the background.

Right: This detail view accurately depicts the shape and placement of the main fuselage fuel tank, which was redesigned for the trainer version, and which differs from the provisional view shown on page 99. **Below:** Two final photographs of "112" at Oberpfaffenhofen. Aside from the four complete Do 335s and assorted spare parts requisitioned by the Americans and British at Oberpfaffenhofen, no other complete aircraft were saved from demolition and destruction.

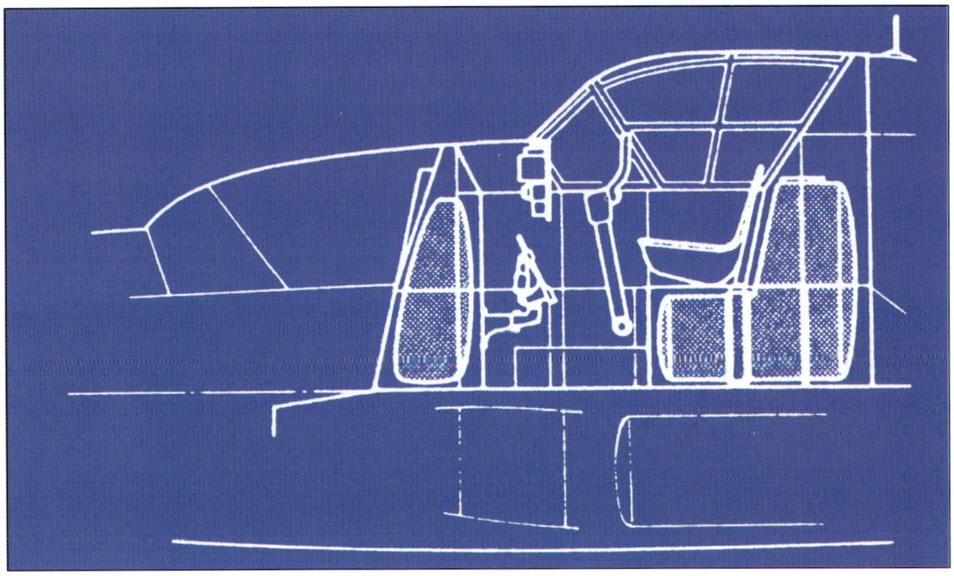

Chapter III

THE B-SERIES

By J. Richard Smith & Thomas H. Hitchcock

Opposite Left: Noted aviation artist, John Amendola's superb impression of the Do 335 M14 accurately conveys the essence of this aircraft as it overflys the majestic landscape. The M14 was the second development aircraft of the Do 335 B-2 series which was completed during November 1944.

During the summer of 1944 work began on the improved B-series for which eight different versions were planned, each powered by either the DB 603 E or LA engines. The first of these, the **Do 335 B-1** single-seat day fighter, was generally similar to the A-1 series, but incorporated an armored windshield replacing the non-armored windscreen of the A-series, a larger nose wheel and certain internal equipment changes. However, this model was armed with the same three cannon employed by the A-series; namely 1 x MK 103 plus 2 x MG 151/20. Two prototypes were allocated to the Do 335 B-1, the Do 335 M15 and M16, but these were still under construction at the end of the war.

However, higher priority was attached to the **Do 335 B-2** *Zerstörer* for which the Do 335 M13, W.Nr. 230013, RP+UP, and Do 335 M14, W.Nr. 230014, RP+UQ, were the two designated development prototypes. This heavily armed version was characterized by two wing-mounted 30 mm MK 103 cannon contained in special fairings each with 70 rounds in addition to the normal engine-mounted MK 103. To make way for this ammunition, the two 82 US Gal (310 Ltr) wing tanks were removed and replaced by two smaller containers of 58 US Gal (220 Ltr) capacity in the outer panels. The B- series also standardized on larger tires which, when retracted into the confined space, required the nose wheel to rotate through 45 degrees for stowage. The Do 335 M13 was first flown on October 31, 1944, powered by two DB 603 E-1 engines with the rear unit being identified as the DB 603 QE-1. The M14 was completed late in 1944 and was captured by French troops at Mengen airfield and subsequently tested over a period of three years after the war. Series production was issued to Heinkel at Oranienburg in May-June 1944 but because of numerous problems, none were delivered until February 1945. It is unclear if any Heinkel-produced B-2s were actually begun before the end of hostilities in Europe.

The **Do 335 B-3** *Zerstörer* was similar to the B-2 but was to be equipped with the more powerful DB 603 LA engine as soon as this new powerplant became available. In a letter to Daimler-Benz from the Chief of Powerplant Development dated May 5, 1944, *Dipl. Ing.* Schilo reaffirmed the urgent need for two flight-cleared DB 603 L engines for the Do 335, which were scheduled for delivery in June 1944. To expedite delivery, the planned configuration of the engines with heat exchangers were to be deferred and instead outfitted with the charge-air cooling scheme of direct water-menthanol (MW) injection. However, Daimler-Benz was unable to deliver the DB 603 L until the autumn of 1944. The Do 335 M18, M19 and M20 were assigned to B-3 development trials but none of these three prototypes were completed by May 1945.

The *Zerstörer* class of aircraft were heavily armed twin-engined day fighters which were basically utilized to attack Allied bombers. With their heavy caliber weapons they were capable of bringing down heavy four-engined bombers with but a few well-placed hits. The Do 335-2 and B-3 *Zerstörers* would have been formidable gun platforms with up to three 30 mm cannon produced by Rheinmetall-Borsig augmented by two faster firing 20 mm Mauser MG 151/20 cannon above the cowl. As potent as this weaponry array was, it was planned to upgrade the engine-mounted cannon from the 30 mm MK 103 to the newer Rheinmetall 55 mm MK 112 as soon as the latter weapon became available. This aircraft cannon was essentially a scaled up version of the firm's MK 108. By the end of the war only ten prototypes of this remarkable weapon were manufactured but none had been installed in the Do 335. With a weight of 600 lb (272 kg) and a rate of fire of 300 rounds a minute, it would

have been a devastating aircraft cannon.

The **Do 335 B-4** reconnaissance version was based upon Dornier project P 237/3 and was similar to the A-4 apart from the new high aspect ratio wing developed by Heinkel coupled with the 2,000 hp DB 603 LA engines with two-stage supercharges. The new wing, first tested on the Do 335 V4, had a wing span of 60 ft 4½ in (18.4 m) and an area of 463 sq ft (43 m^2). Athough high speed reconnaissance aircraft were highly valued by the declining *Luftwaffe*, development of this series appears to have been given relatively low priority as no prototype was assigned to the B-4 program.

The two-seat **Do 335 B-5** trainer was also to be fitted with the new Heinkel wing but was otherwise quite similar to the Do 335 A-12. Apparently no examples of this series were built.

The two-seat **Do 335 B-6** night fighter was based on the Do 335 A-6 apart from being structurally strengthened, and featuring a new bubble canopy over the radar operators position. The variant also was to be built by Heinkel at Oranienburg, fifty aircraft being ordered. The first of these was due for delivery in April 1945, but it is very doubtful any were completed . Early B-6s would have had FuG 220 radar, this being replaced by FuG 218 from the thirty-first production machine.

A more advanced night fighter version having 2,000 hp DB 603 LA engines and an enlarged laminar flow wing with an area of 441 sq ft (41 m^2) was also planned under the designation **Do 335 B-7** for which the Do 335 M22 was to have been the development prototype. Again, no examples of this model were completed prior to the end of the war in Europe.

The final B-series variant, which was to go into series production in September 1945, was the two-seat **Do 335 B-8** night fighter, for which the Dso 335 M23 was the designated development prototype. A high-altitude night fighter with the 463 sq ft Heinkel wing and the usual heavy armament of 1 x MK 103 plus 2 x MG 151/20 cannon.

Continued on p. 135

Above: Inside the main assembly hall at Oberpfaffenhofen shortly after capture by American forces, are many B-series aircraft under construction. In the foreground to the left, is the incomplete airframe of the Do 335 M18, which was a development aircraft for the B-3 series. The aircraft to the right is the Do 335 M20, which was also a B-3 development aircraft. The unusual tail numbers identify the last two digits of the aircraft's serial number combined with larger digits denoting the *Muster* (Model) number. The Do 335 B-3 series was to have been heavily armed day fighters of the *Zerstörer* class.

Above and Below: Two views of the Do 335 M13, W.Nr. 230013, RP+UP, photographed at *Löwenthal* (German code name was Luchsberg) on March 15, 1945. This aircraft was the first development aircraft for the Do 335 B-2 series of heavily armed day fighters of the *Zerstörcr* class and was completed on October 31, 1944. Unfortunately, it was among the aircraft blown-up at Friedrichshafen prior to the arrival of American troops. The B-2 and B-3 series of *Zerstörer* aircraft were heavily armed with three 30 mm MK 103 cannons plus two 20 mm MG 151/20 cannons.

Above: In this close-up of the Do 335 M13, the small movie camera temporarily mounted on top of the wing, and visible just behind the wing cannon, was used for evaluating the effectiveness of the aircraft's devastating firepower.
Below: This large hanger sustained bomb damage, to the roof and doors. In addition, at least five Do 335 B-series fuselages and components located within the hanger were also damaged. One of these fuselages is shown here partially covered by camouflage netting.

Above: Another view the damaged hanger at Oberpfaffenhofen showing another incomplete and damaged Do 335 B-series fuselage found by American troops when they captured the facility late in April 1945. Production of the Do 335 had been shifted from Friedrichshafen to Oberpfaffenhofen during the summer of 1944 following several heavy American bombing raids. Earlier in 1944, the firm of Luther *und* Jordan had been contracted to build the Do 335, but by the autumn of 1944, this firm was already over committed with the license manufacture of other aircraft such as the Bf 110 G-4 night fighter. The Heinkel firm, located at Oranienburg, was also expected to begin series production of the Dornier Arrow in May or June 1944. Reportedly, the first Do 335 was completed there in February 1945, but no further details are known.

Below: A phantom illustration of a B-series *Zerstörer* aircraft showing the wing, vertical tailplane and fuselage ribbing location.

1. VDM metal propeller
2. Oil coolant radiator
3. Engine coolant radiator
4. Jack for radiator flaps
5. DB 603 E
6. Supercharger for DB 603
7. Engine bearer arm
8. Engine coolant container
9. Armored windscreen
10. Hinged canopy
11. Clear vision windows
12. Rear view mirrors
13. Canopy lock
14. Canopy stay line
15. Instrument panel
16. Side console radio equipment
17. Side console for engine + prop
18. Control column
19. Rudder pedals
20. Rudder pedals parallelogram linkage
21. Identification flare pistol
22. Ejector seat activating control
23. Pilot's ejector seat
24. Ejection seat compressed air tanks
25. Oil tanks for front and rear engines
26. Main fuselage fuel filler point
27. Main fuel tank
28. Wing fuel tanks when armament displaced leading edge fuel tanks
29. Auxiliary fuselage bay tank
30. DB 603 E
31. Rear engine bearer arm
32. Engine coolant tank
33. Auxiliary MW 50 fuel tank
34. Hollow rear prop extension shaft
35. Rear propeller gear box
36. VDM metal propeller
37. Rear engine coolant radiator
38. Rear engine oil cooler
39. Actuator for oil cooler flap
40. Coolant air outlet flap for rear radiator
41. Actuator for rear engine radiator flap
42. Rudder and elevator control rods
43. Flying control mechanisms in fuselage
44. Aileron control linkage in wings
45. Throttle control rods

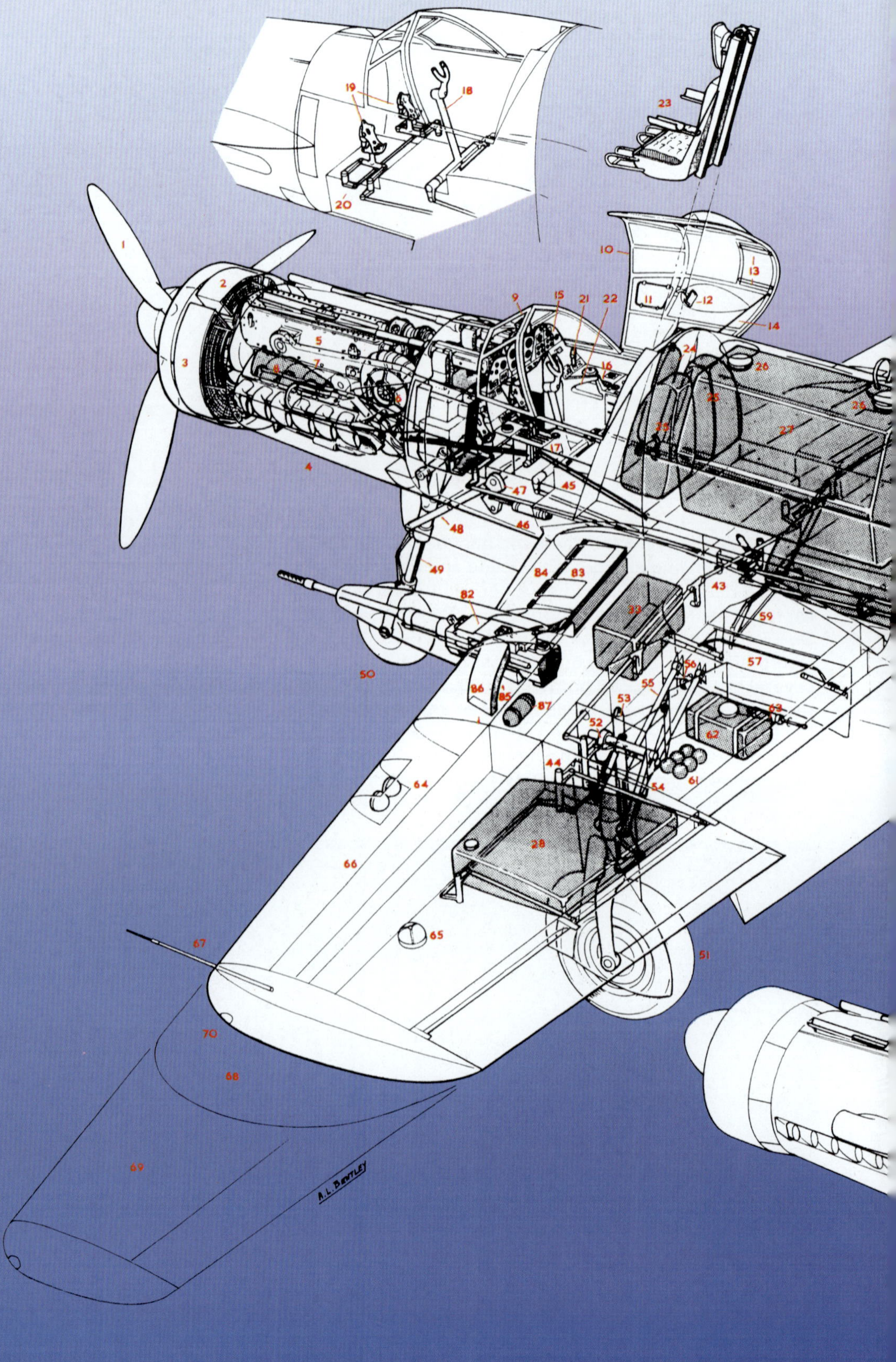

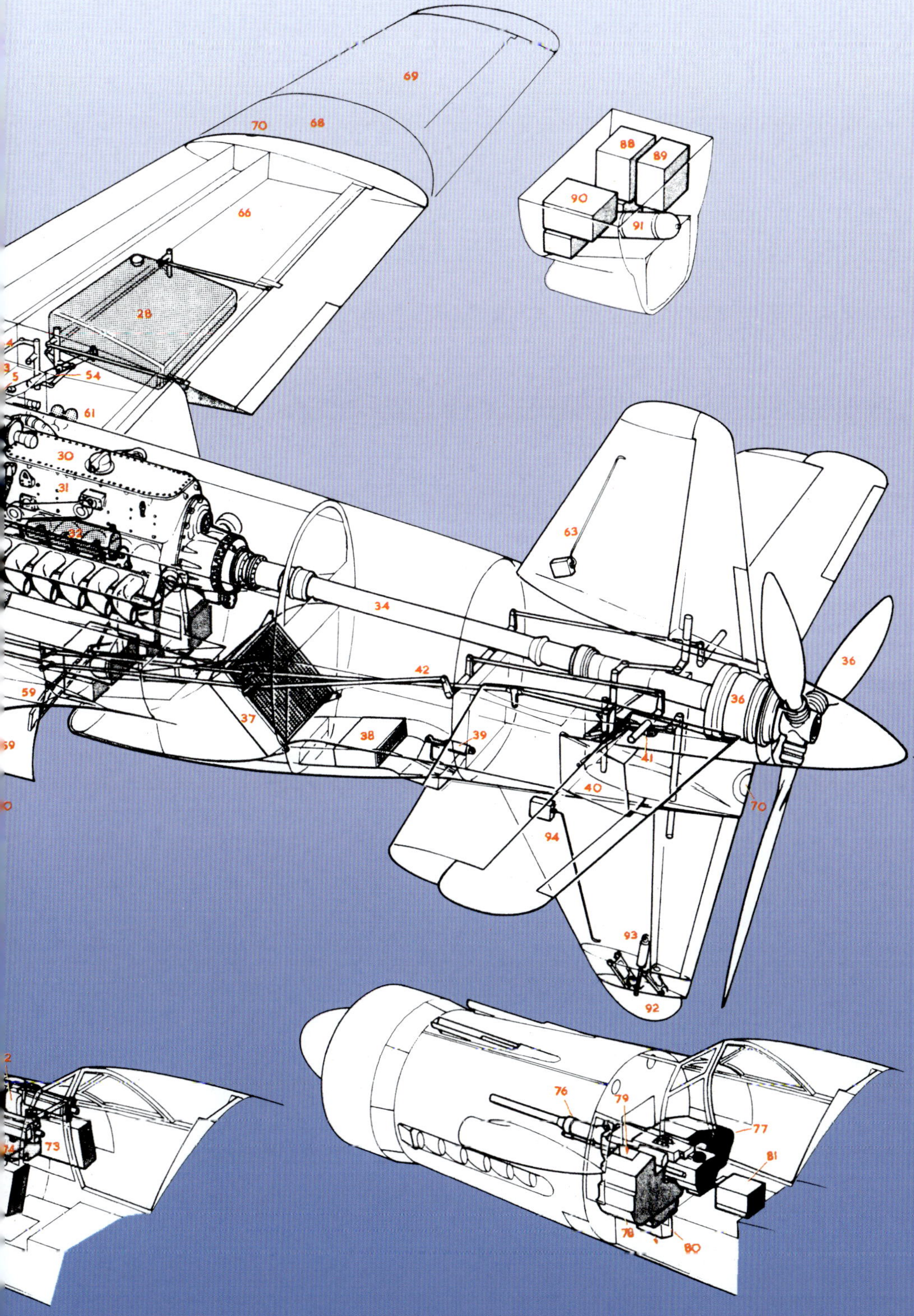

Do 335 B-Series

46. Nose wheel actuating jack
47. Gear type operating mechanism
48. Nosewheel side stay
49. Nosewheel leg
50. Nosewheel
51. Main wheel
52. Main wheel leg
53. Main actuating jack for main wheel
54. Auxiliary actuating jack for main wheel
55. Main wheel side stay
56. Main wheel up-lock
57. Main wheel door
58. Fuselage bay doors
59. Bomb bay door mechanism
60. Folding boarding ladder
61. Oxygen tanks
62. Hydraulic reservoir
63. Jack for landing flaps
64. Landing lights
65. Master compass
66. Main wing box spar
67. Pitot tube
68. Extended wing tips
69. Heinkel-designed outer wing panels
70. Navigation lights
71. Two MG 151/20 cannon
72. Ammunition feed chutes
73. Ammunition boxes with 200 rpg
74. Spent shell collection boxes
75. Chute to drop spent shells
76. MK 103 engine cannon
77. Ammunition box - 70 rounds
78. Collector box for spent shells
79. Shell opening
80. Chute for unloading spent shells
81. Battery
82. Wing-mounted MK 103
83. Ammunition container
84. Armor for ammunition container
85. Spent shell chute
86. Chute for spent links
87. Compressed air tank for cocking guns
88. FuG 125
89. FuG 25a
90. FuG 15
91. Fire extinguisher
92. Tail skid
93. Tail skid shock absorber
94. Radio antennas

Above: The Do 335 M14, W.Nr. 230014, RP+UQ, was captured intact by American and French troops at Dornier's Mengen facility, near Sigmaringen in Württemberg, approximately 50 miles (80 km) north of Lake Constance. This aircraft was the second development machine for the B-2 series of heavily armed day fighters known as *Zerstörers.* By agreement, the M14 was given over to the French **Below:** French and German personnel at Mengen prepare the M14 for its road journey Lyon-Bron airfield.

Above and Below: The Do 335 M14 was to be thoroughly reconditioned before French testing could begin. In these photographs, taken while the spring of 1945 while the aircraft was still at Mengen (German code name was Mangold), show the Dornier still in its original markings and being serviced. Its rear engine had been removed for overhaul and work was being carried out on the front engine as well as the wing-mounted cannon.

Above and Below: Two additional views of the Do 335 M14 at Dornier's Mengen facility. The two French officers are Paul Badré (seated in the cockpit) and Robert Pascal (standing on the wing). The French were thorough in their assessment of the Dornier's overall condition, and they were particularly concerned about the reliability of certain components made during the last year of the war. They received cooperation from former Dornier personnel, but experienced problems with the availability of replacement parts.

Above: On August 8, 1945, Col. Badré carried out a routine test flight in the restored and repainted M14. On his landing approach the Dornier began violently vibrating and smoke filled the cockpit. Badré shut down both engines and dead-sticked the aircraft heavily onto the airfield bursting the right tire. With no hydraulics and no brakes, the M14 left the runway and slammed into a parked B-26. **Right:** The M14 undergoing repairs in the spring of 1946 at the SNCASO near Paris. Locating replacement parts and overhauling existing hardware presented a constant challenge. **Below:** This view of the M14, taken in September 1945 at the SNCASO plant at Surennes, show the aircraft being repaired to resume flight testing. The final flight of the M14 occurred in June 1948.

This page: Two overall views and one close-up of the Do 335 M14 after restoration and repainting entirely in French camouflage color Khaki Green (approximate Munsell match: 10Y, 4/1). Note the armor plate attached to the canopy sides and center panel above the pilot's headrest. The circular impression in the lower right corner of the photograph to the left is merely a French identification stamp made directly onto the photograph. It was not part of the aircraft.

Above and Right: A good rear view of the M14 plus a close-up of the open canopy showing the two large French instruments installed on the instrument panel in the space normally occupied by the gun sight. Note the French aviation triangle denoting the filler point for engine lubricant.

Dornier Do 335 M14

Above: Apart from the first prototype, in flight photographs of the Do 335 are quite rare. This official French image of the M14 climbing is therefore historically significant.
Below **Left**: A close-up of the M14's nose gear showing the larger 840 x 300 tire common to all B-series aircraft. Compare this with the nose gear and wheel of A-series shown on page 174. Because of the larger wheel of the B-series, a complicated retraction movement was required to completely stow the wheel within its compartment.

Below Right: A close-up view of the boarding ladder located within the aft section of the port wing root. Because of the height of the wing from the ground, such a folding ladder was essential for access to the cockpit.

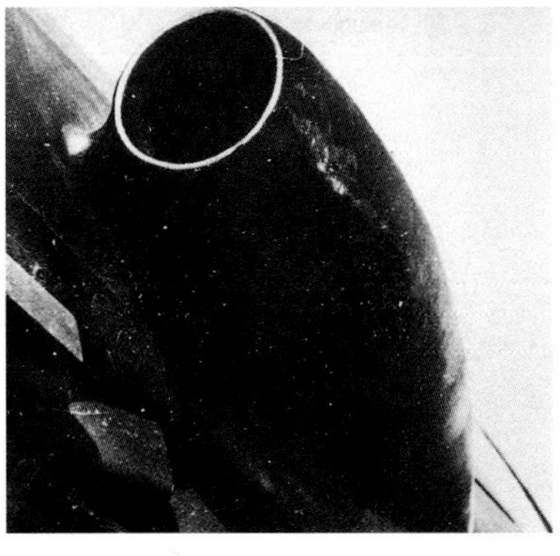

Above: *Capitaine* Reni Receveau in the cockpit of the M14 at Bretigny in 1947. **Right:** Close-up of the adjustable ventral outlet from the rear engine oil cooler. **Left:** Close-up of the forward supercharger air intake to the M14. The air intake for the rear engine was similar.

Right: Close-up of the port main landing gear leg showing the bulged cover, the main retraction jack and the side stay. Main wheels were 1015 x 380, Torque links were also fitted but these are obscured by the gear cover.

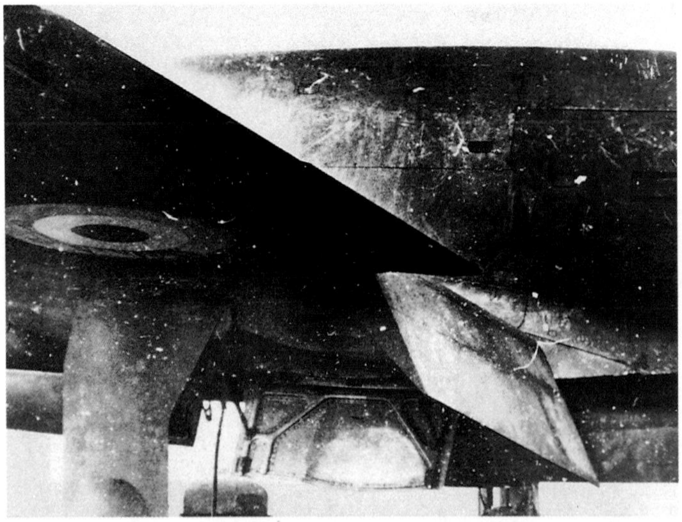

Top Left: A view of the port landing flap on the Do 335 M14. The flaps were a camber changing type with the hydraulic actuating jack located within the wing. **Above:** Detail view of the M14's ventral tail skid. This hard surface skid was internally attached to two compression arms and a heavy-duty shock absorber. **Left:** An overall view of the M14's tailplane. It is interesting to note that two French insignia were applied to both the dorsal and ventral fins. **Below:** This March 1949 photograph of the derelict M14 was probably the last snapshot taken before this historically significant aircraft was scrapped. During its postwar career with the French, it had accumulated a total fight time of 11 hours and 25 minutes. **Opposite Right:** The cockpit of the Do 335 M13. Compare this with the similar cockpit for the A-series cockpit shown on pages 53, 92 and 93. Typical of German fighters of the late war period, the flight instruments are grouped on a single independently sprung panel, whereas the engine instruments are grouped separately on adjacent panels. Note the canopy jettisoning levers on either side of the cockpit. It is rumored that activation of these could cause the pilot serious discomfort if he failed to quickly release the levers prior to being jettisoned from the aircraft.

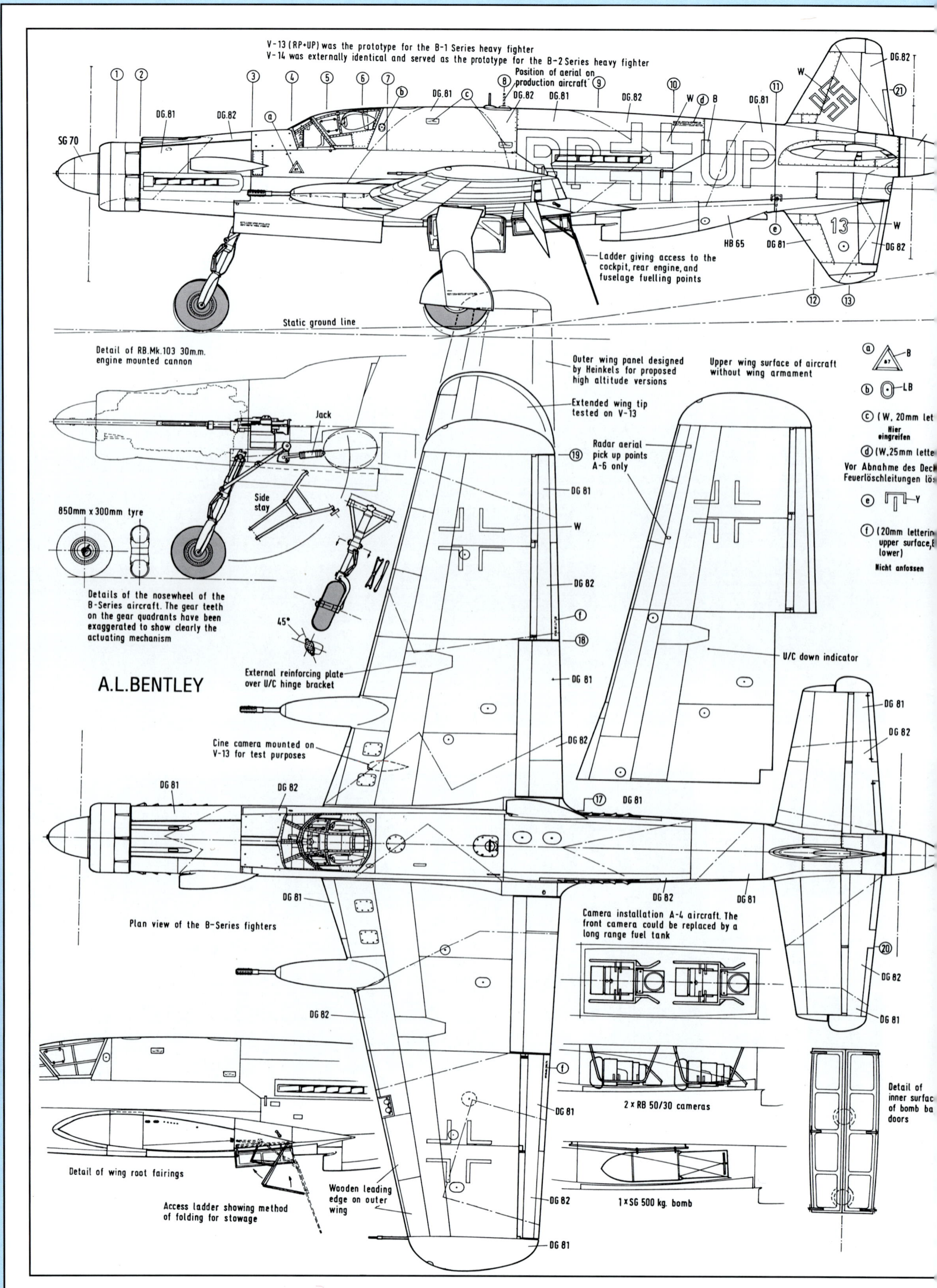
V-13 (RP+UP) was the prototype for the B-1 Series heavy fighter
V-14 was externally identical and served as the prototype for the B-2 Series heavy fighter
Position of aerial on production aircraft
SG 70
DG.81
DG.82
HB 65
Ladder giving access to the cockpit, rear engine, and fuselage fuelling points
Static ground line
Detail of RB.Mk.103 30m.m. engine mounted cannon
Jack
Side stay
850mm x 300mm tyre
Details of the nosewheel of the B-Series aircraft. The gear teeth on the gear quadrants have been exaggerated to show clearly the actuating mechanism
45°
External reinforcing plate over U/C hinge bracket
A.L.BENTLEY
Outer wing panel designed by Heinkels for proposed high altitude versions
Extended wing tip tested on V-13
Radar aerial pick up points A-6 only
Upper wing surface of aircraft without wing armament
U/C down indicator
Cine camera mounted on V-13 for test purposes
Plan view of the B-Series fighters
Camera installation A-4 aircraft. The front camera could be replaced by a long range fuel tank
2 x RB 50/30 cameras
1 x SG 500 kg. bomb
Detail of wing root fairings
Access ladder showing method of folding for stowage
Wooden leading edge on outer wing
Detail of inner surfac of bomb ba doors
(W, 20mm let
Hier eingreifen
(W,25mm lette
Vor Abnahme des Deck
Feuerlöschleitungen lös
(20mm letterin upper surface, lower)
Nicht anfassen
LB
W
B
Y

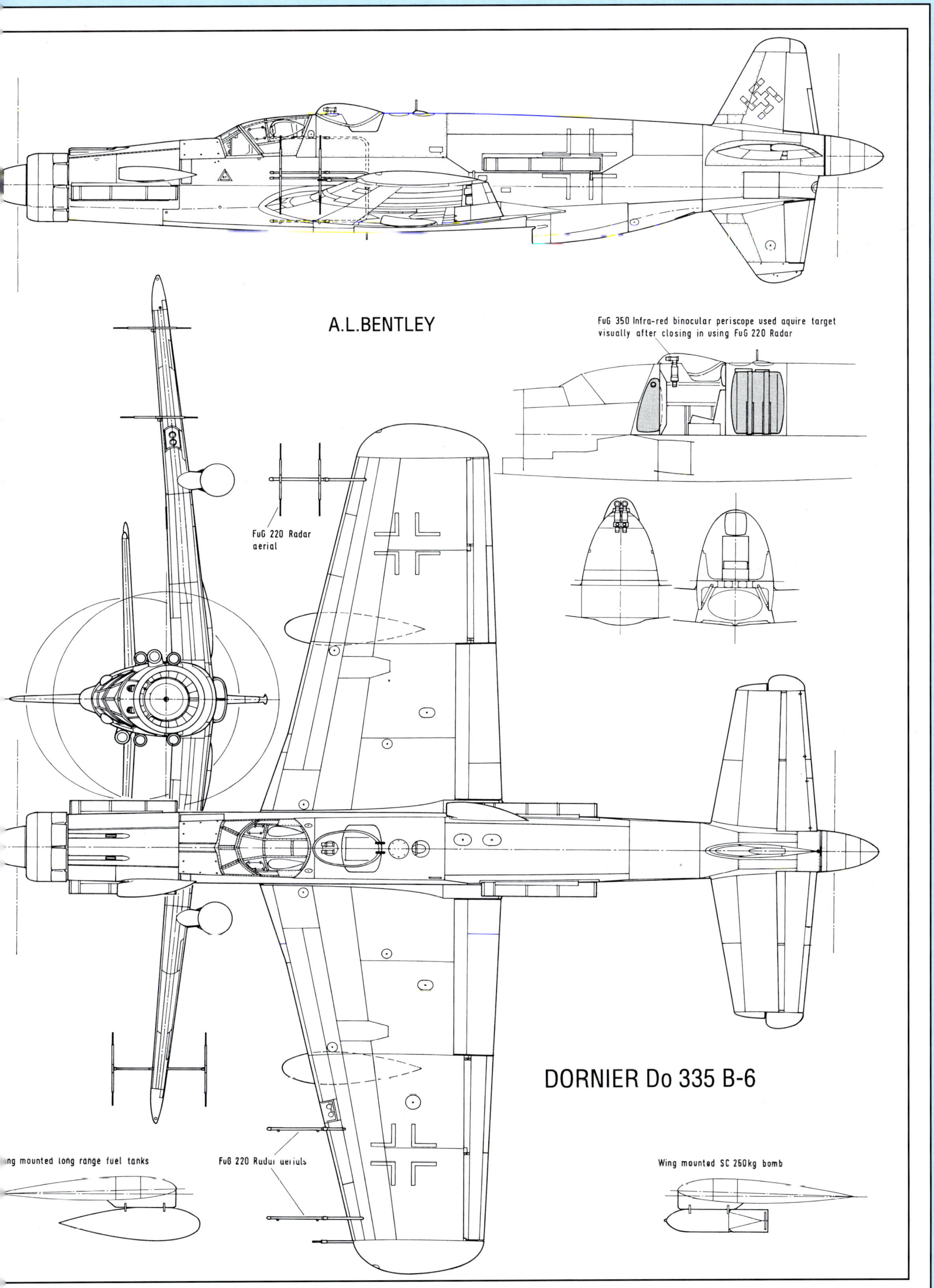
A.L.BENTLEY
FuG 350 Infra-red binocular periscope used aquire target visually after closing in using FuG 220 Radar
FuG 220 Radar aerial
DORNIER Do 335 B-6
ng mounted long range fuel tanks
FuG 220 Radar aerials
Wing mounted SC 250kg bomb

Left: A view of the DB 603 L. This 12-cylinder, inverted "v", liquid-cooled engine was fitted with a two-stage supercharger with aftercooler and developed 2,100 hp for take-off and war emergency power at 2,700 rpm. When paired with MW 50 powerboosting system, the designation was amended to DB 603 LA. It had an overall length of 8.9 feet (2,740 mm) and weighed 2,145 lb (975 kg). This long-awaited powerplant was to power the Do 335 B-3 *Zerstörer,* the B-4 reconnaissance variant, and the B-7 and B-8 high altitude night fighters.

Right: A perspective illustration of the Rheinmetall-Borsig MK 112. This 55 mm automatic aircraft cannon was essentially an enlarged version of the company's 30 mm MK 108 but apart from test prototypes, it failed to enter production before the end of the war. The weapon had a length of 80 inches (2,032 mm) and weighed 605 lb (274 kg). It had a rate of fire of 300 rpm with a muzzle velocity of 1,950 feet (594 m) per second. Ammunition was belt fed along the top side. The weapon fired a shell weighing 3.3 lb (1.5 kg) with an overall length of 8.8 inches (225 mm). This aircraft cannon was to have been installed within the Do 335 as an engine-mounted cannon replacing the MK 103, but by the end of the war, only ten examples had been manufactured and none were made available to Dornier.

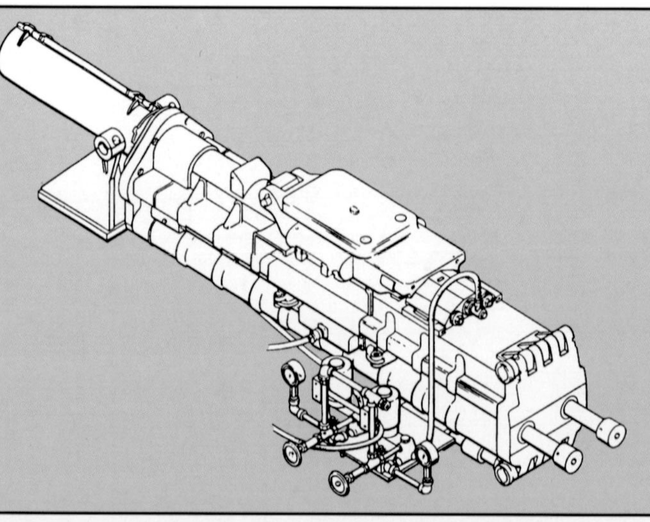

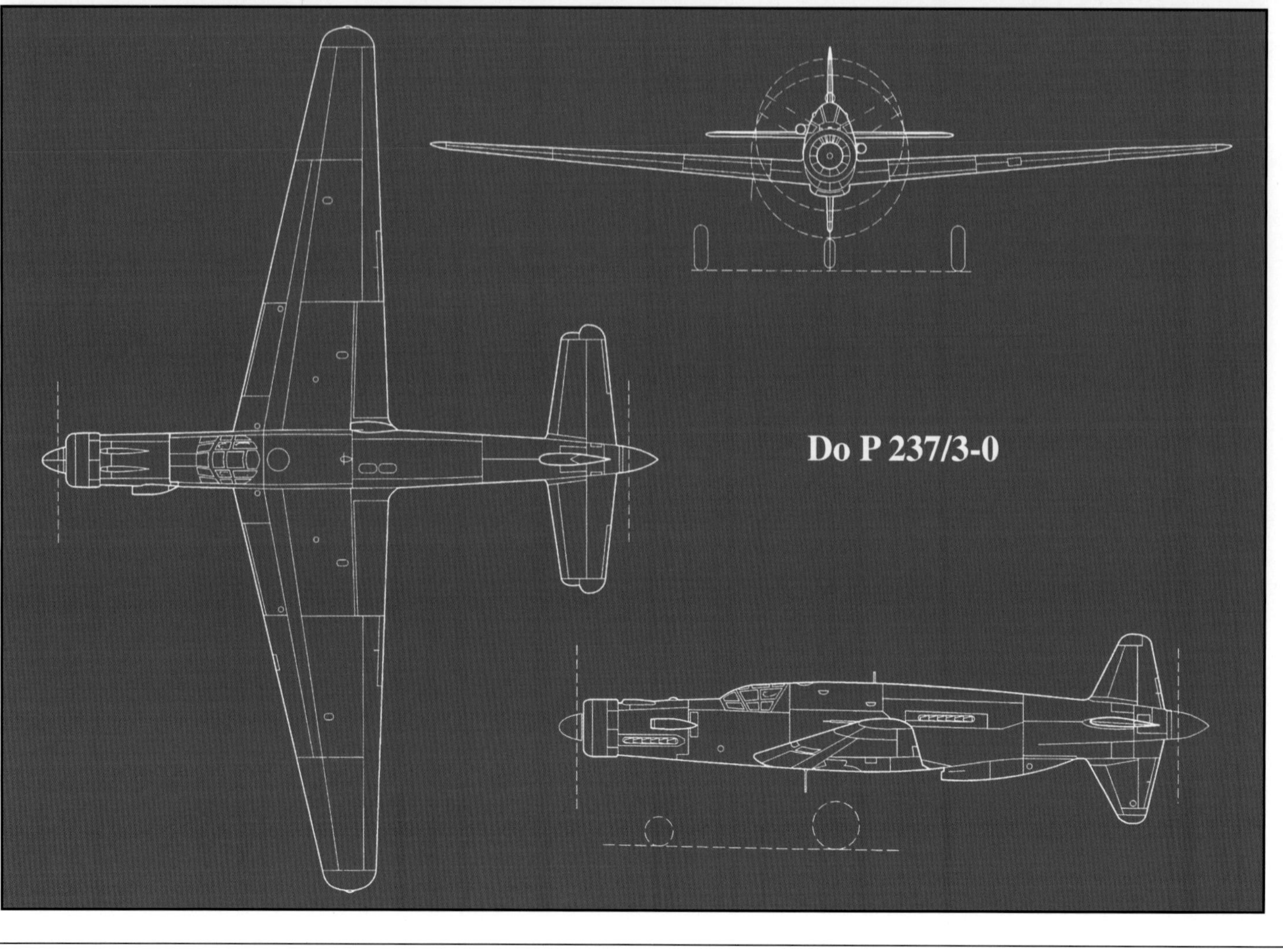

Above: An artist impression of the Do 335 B-4. This single-seat reconnaissance aircraft would have been equipped with the new long-span wing developed by Heinkel and powered by the DB 603 LA engines. However, no examples were completed prior to May 1945.

Continued from p. 116

On September 4, 1944, an experimental unit had been set up at Rechlin to introduce the Do 335 to operational service. Designated *Erprobungs- kommando* 335, the unit had the dual tasks of developing the *Pfeil* as an anti-Mosquito night fighter and developing fighter bomber and reconnaissance tactics. Its commander was *Hptm.* Alvon Meyer. It suffered its first casualty on December 24 when Do 335 A-0, W.Nr. 240108, piloted by *Fw.* Alfred Wollank crashed at Donefeld during a transfer flight from Oberpfaffenhofen to Rechlin. Although details are unknown, it is possible this Do 335 fell victim to an Allied fighter. *Fw.* Wollank was killed in the crash.

The testing of the Do 335 led to an aircraft recognition memorandum being issued to German flak units on October 26, 1944.- "The following information is given to prevent the new fighter airplane *Pfeil* (Do 335) being fired on by our own guns. The aircraft has tandem twin engines, with the second propeller behind the tail unit. The latter is in the form of a cross." Despite all this there are only isolated reports of the Do 335 having been met by Allied aircraft. In mid April 1945, Tempests of No 3 Squadron RAF chased a *Pfeil* over the River Elbe, but it easily outpaced them and made off. In another case a Do 335 was seen by Mustangs of the 325th Fighter Group, US 15th Air Force over southern Germany but the Do 335 again made off at high speed. Two other pilots from *Erprobungs-kommando* 335 were however lost, *Ogef.* Konrad Schäfer in March 1945 and *Ogef.* Gustav Tesche in April of the same year.

The precise number of Do 335 Arrows produced is unknown, but approximately 52 were actually completed. Of this quantity, 15 were prototypes, 10 preproduction aircraft and approximately 27 production examples were completed with another 12 development machines in various stages of assembly. These are summarized in Appendix 2 (p. 166) and 3 (p. 172).

Above and Left: The two-seat night fighter prototype, the Do 335 M17, W.Nr. 240313, photographed at Bretigny during 1947. This aircraft was a development aircraft for the Do 335 B-6 series and was captured in an incomplete state by French troops when Dornier's Mengen airfield was occupied in late April 1945. It was finally completed by French and German personnel. It was first flown by *Capitaine* Receveau, shown in the cockpit in the photograph to the left, on April 2, 1947.

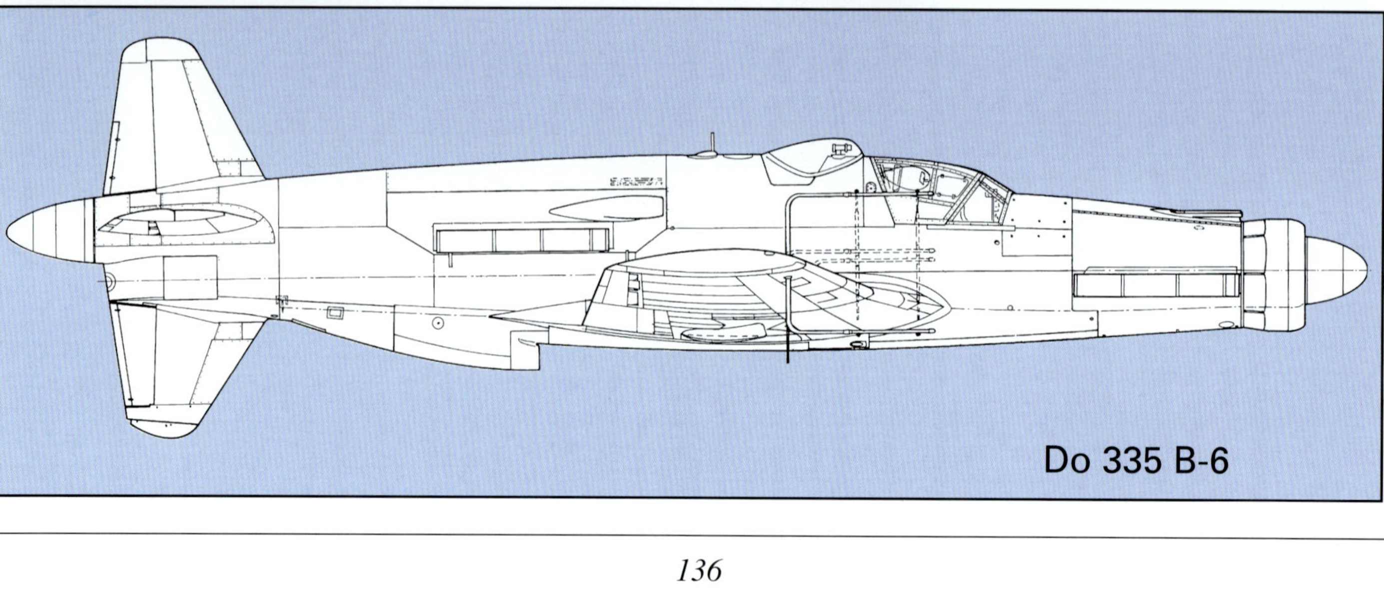

Do 335 B-6

Above: The Do 335 M17 being taxied at the *Centre d' Essais en Vol* (CEV) during 1947. Like the M14, the aircraft was painted overall in French color Khaki Green. **Left:** A companion photograph to the one shown opposite, this view shows *Capitaine* Receveau climbing a wooden ladder to board the M17 for its maiden flight from Mengen. Note the two cowl gun barrel troughs designed to brace the 20 mm MG 151/20 cannons.

Below: A group portrait of the French and German teams celebrating the successful first flight of the M17. Working under primitivc conditions without adequate spare parts, it is little wonder than it took this team just over two years to finish building the M17.

Above and Left: On November 27, 1948, the starboard landing gear leg accidentally retracted during taxiing tests causing damage to the rear propeller, ventral fin and rear fuselage. It was decided not to repair the Do 335 M17.
Below: On December 15, 1948, the M17 was dragged to a remote area of the airfield and subjected to ejection seat and rear propeller ejection tests. In March 1949 it was scrapped along with the M14.

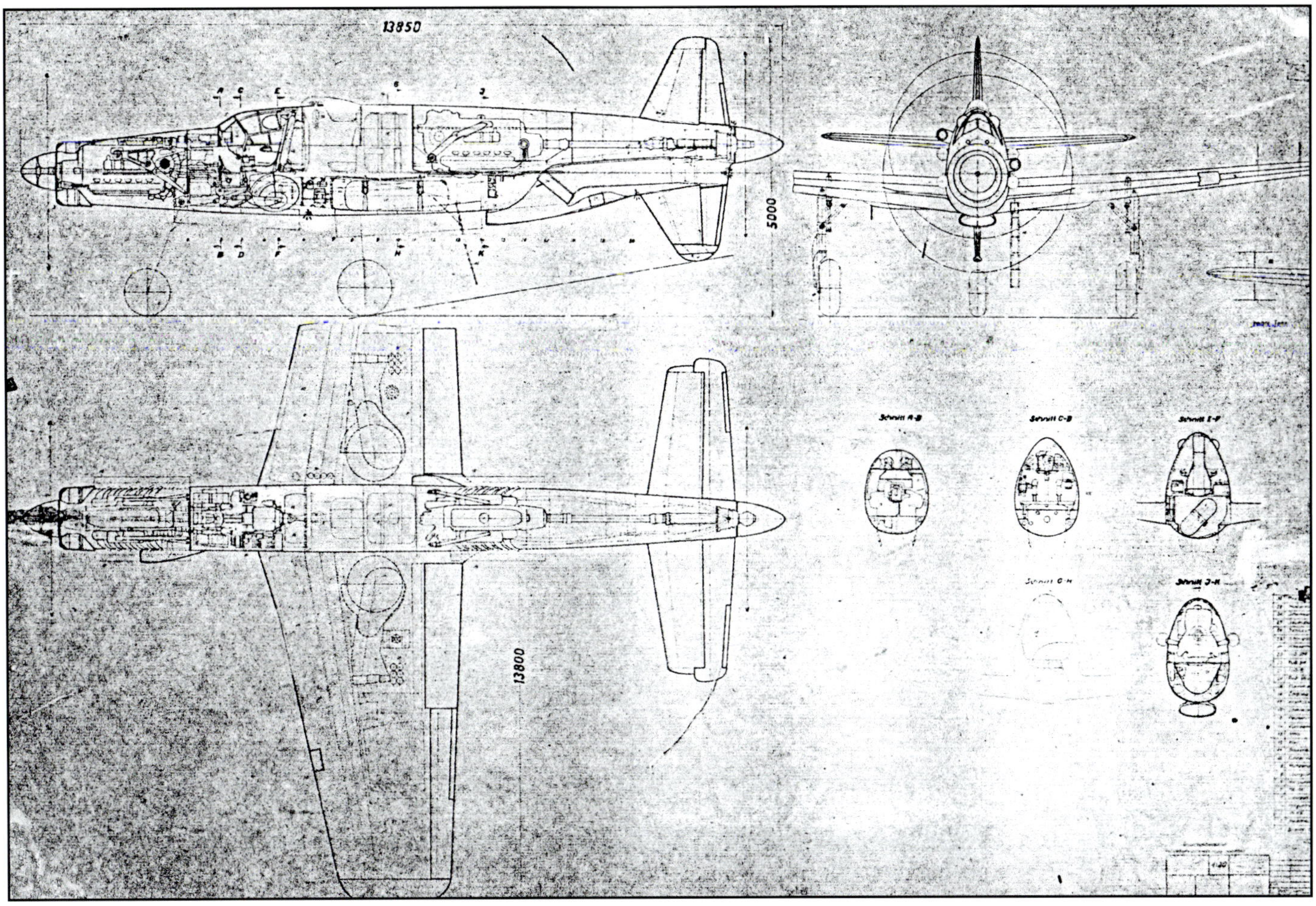

Below: An artist impression of the definitive two-seat night fighter version of the Arrow, the Do 335 B-8 is shown complete with its wing-mounted radar, flame dampers and enlarged wing. The development aircraft for this series was to have been the Do 335 M23. The B-8 was scheduled for production during September 1945, powered by a pair of the long-awaited DB 603 LA. **Above:** A drawing of the Do 335 B-6.

Above: This official US Army Air Corps photograph taken above Dornier's shattered Oberpfaffenhofen facility just after the war, shows a number of incomplete Do 335s which had been collected into one group on the airfield. In addition there are a number of incomplete Do 335 fuselages within the large hanger at the top left portion (see pages 118 and 119) as well as the debris pile in front of the hanger to the right. One incomplete fuselage is also visible amongst the nine airframes clustered above the bomb crater. Five German civilians are shown walking across the field, while American personnel relax around a water test pool near the top hanger. The nine incomplete airframes include, clockwise from left to right, the M19 allocated as a B-3 series development aircraft with the vertical tailplane number of 15/19, the M21 with both propellers installed and carrying the tailplane number 17/21, the M18 with a tailplane number 14/18 and intended as a development aircraft for the B-3 series. Near the center of the top row, facing the camera, is another unidentified B-series airframe while to the right of this is an unidentified A-series airframe, without its tailplane. In the upper right corner, there appears to be a rather complete B-1 series aircraft. Just above the bomb crater are two incomplete two-seat trainer conversions. To the right of the crater is the incomplete remains of W.Nr. 240123 which was the last of the A-series two-seat conversions. Off the right wing of "123" is "121" which was W.Nr. 240121 (see p 110) another two-seat trainer conversion. The last airframe, shown above and to the left of the crater, is that of the M11 with a tailplane number of 18/11. It is believed that this aircraft was to have been a development aircraft for the B-5 series of two-seat trainers, and that it was also undoubtedly a replacement for the previously damaged first M11 (W.Nr. 230011, see p 104).

Right: An interesting view, which was included within a British technical description of the Do 335, of one of the incomplete B-series fuselages acquired at Oberpfaffenhofen from the Americans. In addition to incomplete fuselages, a number of additional components were also brought to England after the war for study and evaluation. **Below:** The clean lines of the twin-engined Arrow are especially evident in this frontal view of the Do 335 M13. Sitting high off the ground on its tricycle undercarriage, it was a radical departure from most other twin-engined German fighters.

Right: Close-up of the rear fuselage of the aircraft shown at the top of this page, which was also part of a British intelligence report prepared during July 1946.

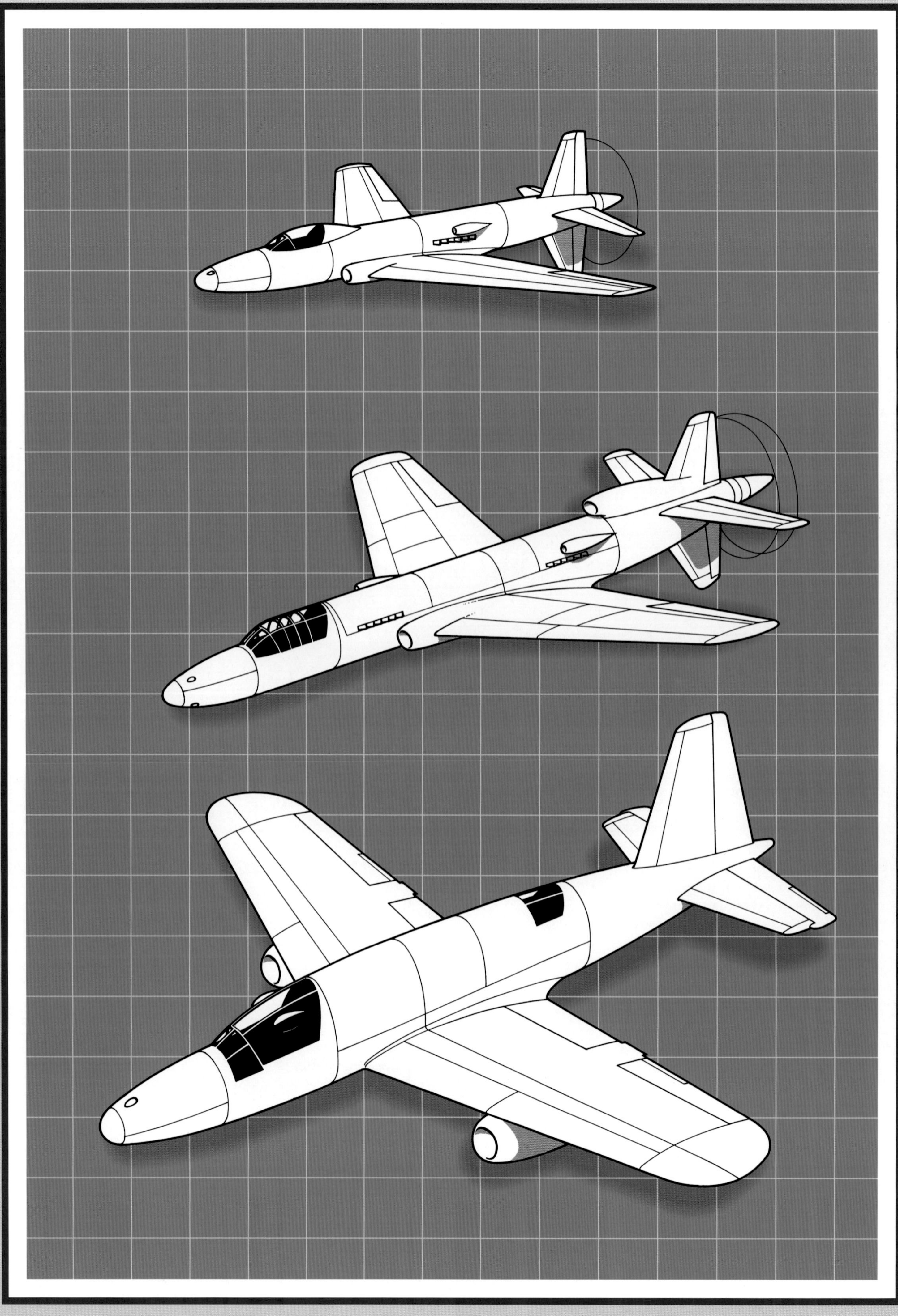

Chapter IV

ARROW PREDICTORS, THE PROJECTS

By Thomas H. Hitchcock

Opposite: Three interesting Dornier projects which are described in Chapter IV. These include the Do P 247/6 of 1942 (top), the Do P 252/3 of 1943 (middle) and the Do P 256/1 of 1944 (bottom).

This chapter describes projected developments of the basic Do 335 design, none of which were completed before the end of the war in Europe.

The foregoing chapters have conclusively proved that *Prof.* Dornier and his able staff of designers, engineers, draftsmen, metalworkers, assemblers, and certainly his test pilots were extremely creative, talented, and dedicated. Yet, in spite of these admirable qualities, much depended upon resources outside the control of the Dornier firm. Existing and new powerplants, propellers, weapons, instrumentation, and electronic equipment were each extremely important in the overall big picture. Moreover, the availability of aviation fuels, lubricants, tires, plastics, aviation glass, and landing-gear assemblies further ensured the success or failure of the manufacturing process. In addition, the complex network of suppliers had to be interconnected with adequate means of supply both on the ground and in the air. During wartime conditions, the whole process is speeded up. Things that normally took years to develop were rushed forward at breakneck speed; often at the expense of quality and/or durability.

Insofar as the Do 335 was concerned, the entire development history of this warplane was directly influenced by the above-mentioned factors and conditions. It is difficult to extract one area from another as being more important, but certainly aircraft engines must be placed high on the list. Throughout this book the authors have mentioned various engines in the context of pairing the right aircraft with the right engine. *Prof.* Dornier and his design staff were kept apprised of the latest advances in aircraft internal combustion engines coming principally from Daimler-Benz and the Junkers Motor Works. Although the Daimler-Benz DB 603 was the principal engine of choice for the Do 335, others were being evaluated for possible inclusion within the program. As recounted in Chapter 2, the Junkers Jumo 213 was a serious contender, but because of this engine's protracted development, it was not ready when expected. Promised by autumn of 1943, it was still in development in the spring of 1944. Up to this time only 130 examples of this 1,776 hp engine had been produced, and these were spread throughout the industry dependent upon this new powerplant. The primary complaint about the Jumo 213 was its unreliability. Finally, late in 1944, the administration of the Junkers *Motorenwerke*, who were determined to make this engine reliable, as demanded by the *Luftwaffe,* locked their best engineers in the factory for four weeks, forbidding them to see their families until the problems were identified and corrected. By the end of 1944, production had risen to a total of 551 units with far fewer complaints about reliability.

Another engine which appeared to offer great potential for the Do 335 was the Junkers Jumo 222. This powerplant, designed in 1939, was a twenty-four cylinder, liquid-cooled, multi-bank radial, with a displacement of 46.5 liters. The cylinders were arranged in six banks of four, disposed radially about the crankcase. Junkers calculated that the Jumo 222 A/B was capable of delivering 2,500 hp at 2,900 rpm at sea level. The fist series of this new engine did not deliver the required power, and a second series was instituted which increased the displacement to 51 liters by boring out the cylinders from 135 mm to 140 mm. Still referred to as the Jumo 222 A/B, the second series per-

formed closer to its rated power. By April 1944, 167 examples had been manufactured by Junkers at Dessau (MSD), but unfortunately the engine was still not reliable enough for service use.

Meanwhile, *Prof.* Dornier and his staff had evolved a modified version of the Do 335, which was to be powered by the Jumo 222 based upon *projekt* study P 238. Designated **Do 435**, the new series was similar to the Do 335, but incorporated a new pressurized cockpit and a long-span wing with wooden outer panels. Published sources have identified proposed aircraft series A,B,C and D for the Do 435, but it is unclear if these were finalized.[4] A January 1946 Allied intelligence summary (A.I.2(g) Report No. 2383) reported that the Do 435 was intended as a night- fighter with a wider cockpit seating the two-man crew side-by-side, a pressurized cabin, radar equipment, and the aforementioned larger wings. It further stated that the flying weight was nearly 26,000 lb (11,794 kg). This all-up weight contrasts to 22,266 lb (10,100 kg) for the two-seat Do 335 A-6 night-fighter. The fuselage was slightly increased in width allowing the two-man crew to be located under the main canopy. But, a more accurate description would be a staggered arrangement with the radar operator seated slightly aft and to the right of the pilot (see P 238/1 opposite).

4 Do 435 A-1 = Bomber
2 x DB 603LA, short wing.
Do 435 A-2 = Bomber,
2 x DB 603LA, long wing.
Do 435 B-1 = Zerstörer,
2 x Jumo 222, short wing.
Do 435 B-2 = Zerstörer,
2 x Jumo 222, long wing.
Do 435 C-1 = Night fighter,
2 x Jumo 222, short wing.
Do 435 C-2 = Night fighter,
2 x Jumo 222, long wing.
Do 435 D-1 = Night fighter,
2 x DB 603 LA, short wing.
Do 435 D-2 = Night fighter,
2 x DB 603 LA, long wing.

Above: An artist impression of the Do 435 two-seat night fighter powered by two Jumo 222 engines and with extended wing tips.
Left: The 24-cylinder Jumo 222 offered great potential, but was never fully developed.

Right: This strange aircraft, purportedly based on the Do 335, has been labeled as the Do 435. However, exhaustive research has failed to locate evidence to support this assumption, leaving the authors to conclude this "stretch 335" to be a work of fiction.

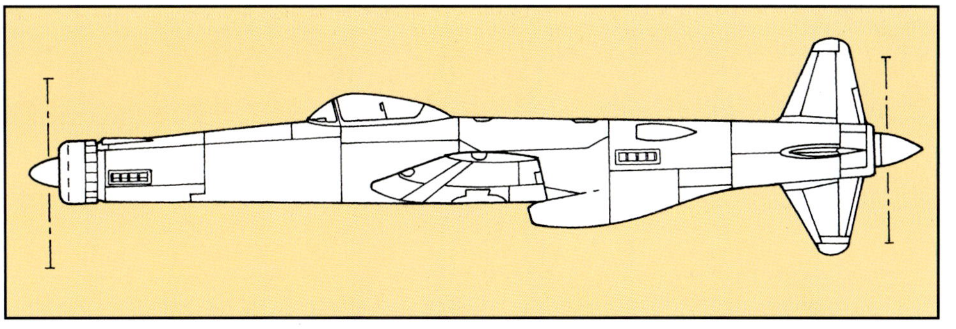

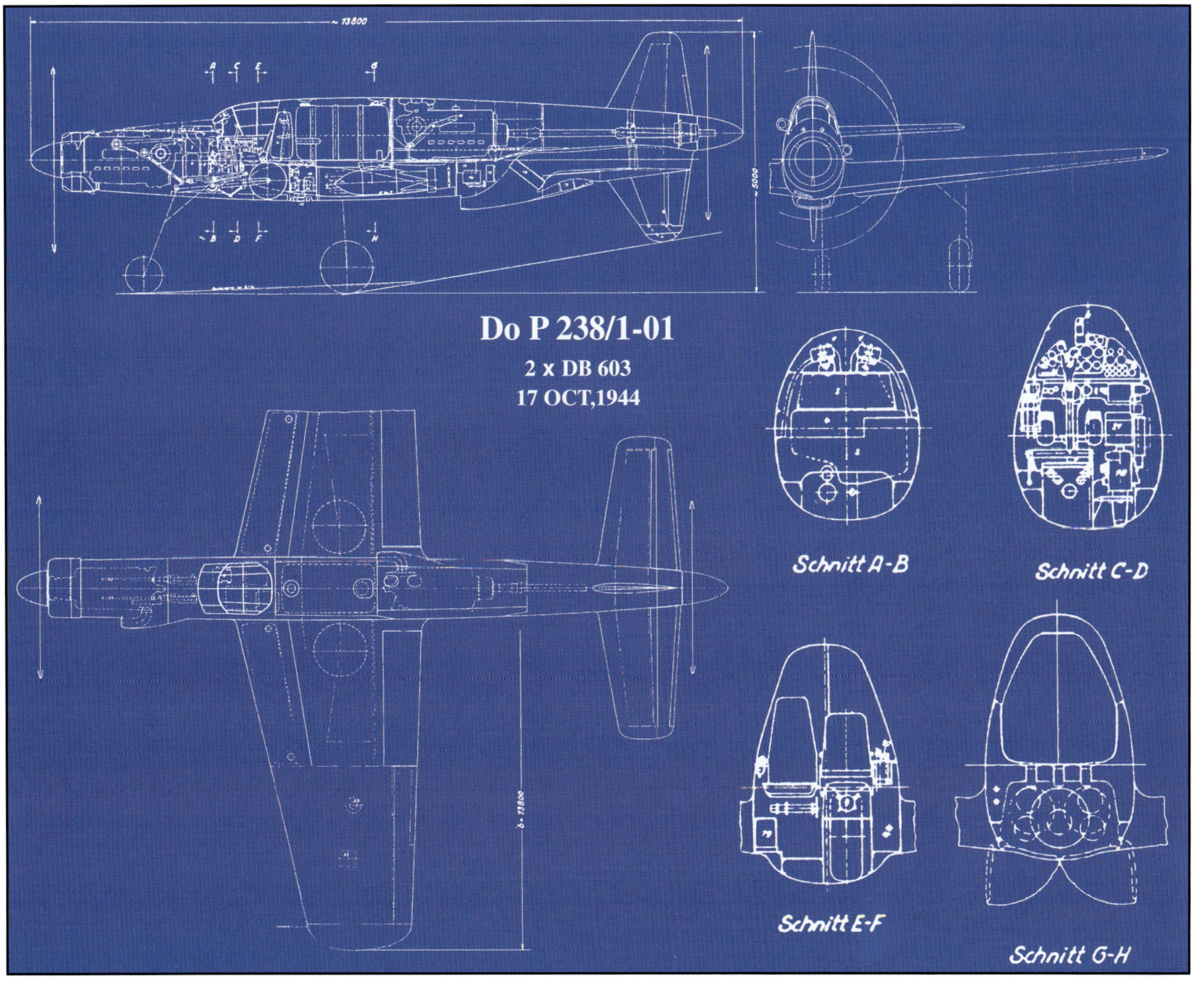

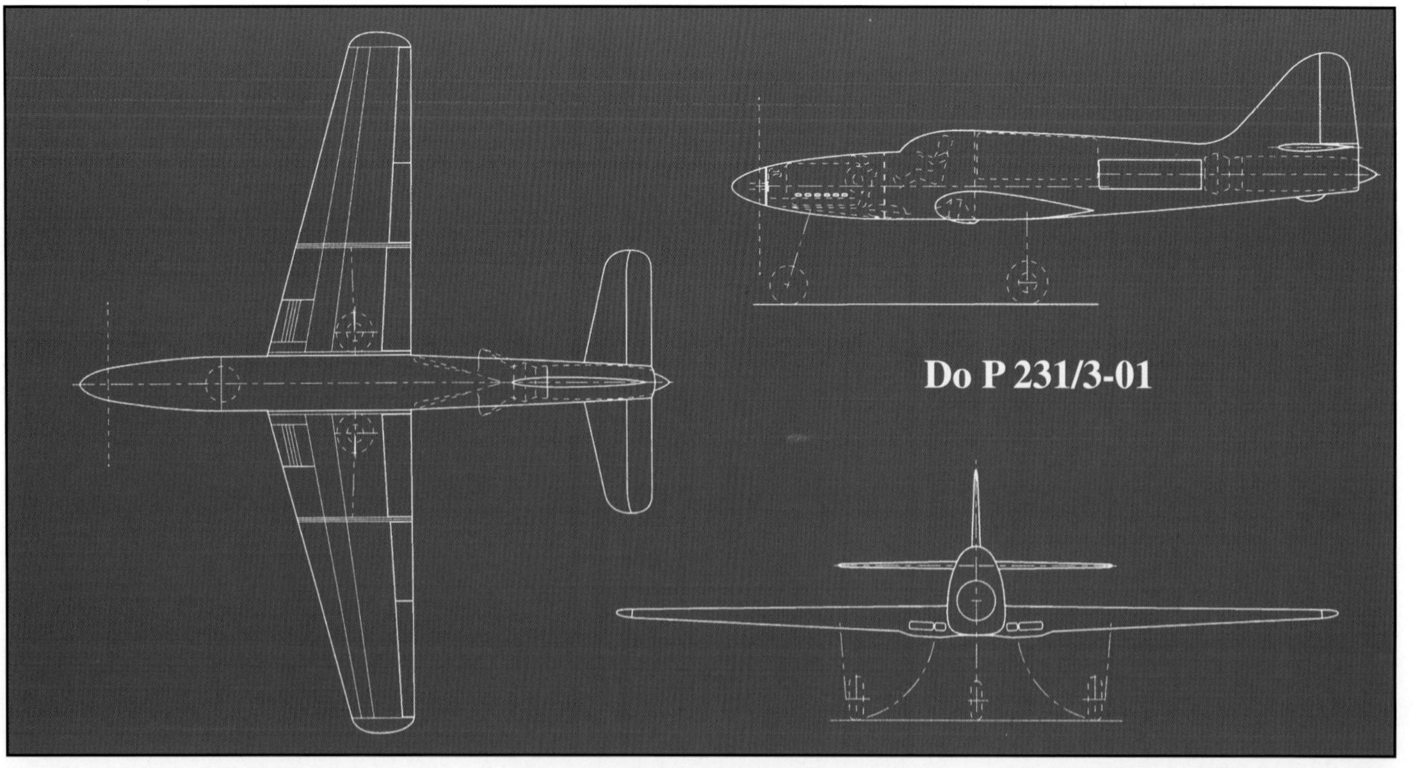

Development of the Do 435 proceeded slowly throughout 1944 . An interesting adjunct to the Do 435 was provided by Allied Interpretation Report No. L. 298: "An aircraft resembling the Do 435, but with an increased wing span of approximately 58 ft. was photographed at the Dornier factory at Lowenthal during April 1945, and it seems very likely that this aircraft was the Do 435 described in A.I.2(g) Report No. 2317. So far as can be seen the redesigned wing, which is slightly more tapered as well as greater span than that of the Do 335, is the only modification, although the fuselage may possibly have been widened. This probable Do 435 remained in a netting-covered shelter during most of April, but may have been destroyed - as were other aircraft at Lowenthal - prior to the Allied capture of the factory". Previously, in December 1944, during a conference chaired by Kurt Tank, who had been appointed technical overseer of night-fighter production, the Do 435 program was reaffirmed, thus lending credence to existance of at least one Do 435 prototype.

By the end of 1942, the German experiments with turbojets were showing positive results. The firms of Junkers and Heinkel-Hirth were each deeply committed to the development of the turbojet as a prime powerplant for aircraft. Concurrently, Dornier evolved a series of mixed power *projekt* studies in which a turbojet was positioned as the aft engine. The earliest study, P 231/3, was somewhat sketchy, but it called for a DB 603 to be installed in the nose and an unidentified turbojet in the rear. Project P 232/2 of May 1943, was more specific. It called for a high-speed bomber, similar to the Do 335, powered by a DB 603 G driving a Me P 8 prop in the nose,

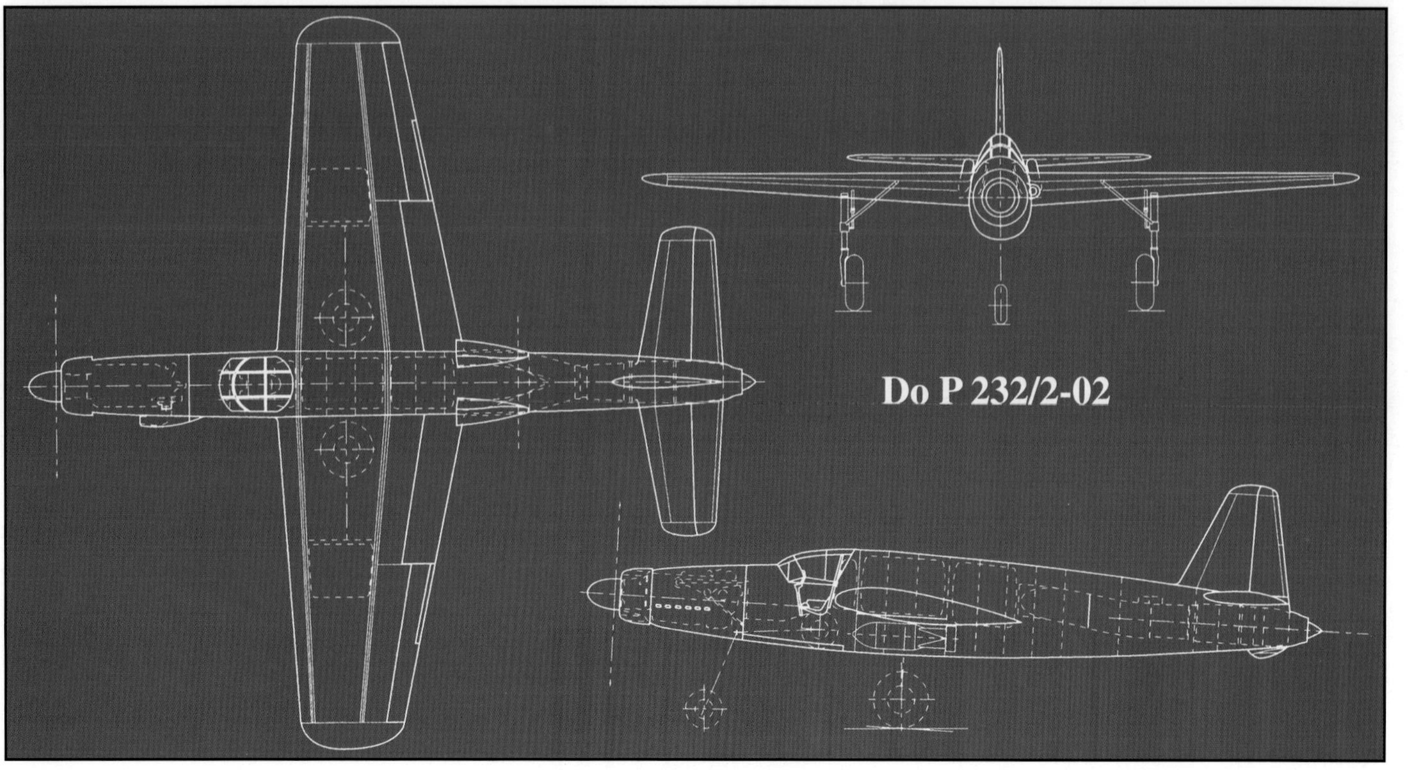

Above: An artist impression of the He 535 A, single-seat heavy day fighter of mixed propulsion.

and a Junkers Jumo 004 turbojet in the tail. The aircraft was to use the tricycle undercarriage, but the nose was to sit higher than the tail. Air intakes for the jet engine were positioned on either side of the rear fuselage. Project P 232/3, of the same period, was similar but elevated the tail level with the nose centerline. The wing and horizontal tailplane both resembled the standard Do 335 arrangement while the twin air intakes were eliminated for a single dorsal intake mounted midway atop the fuselage. At this stage, Dornier did not consider that the combined mixed- power arrangement be used throughout the flight range. Instead, the rear-mounted jet would only be used at takeoff and during the attack, when high speed was essential. In all other flight regimes, the aircraft would fly on the front engine only.

During mid 1944, Dornier decided to proceed with the mixed-power concept adapted to the night-fighter role, even though the early jet engines were anything but fuel efficient. The RLM correspondingly decided to transfer development to the firm of Ernst Heinkel AG at Oranienburg because of that firm's experience with jet engines, and

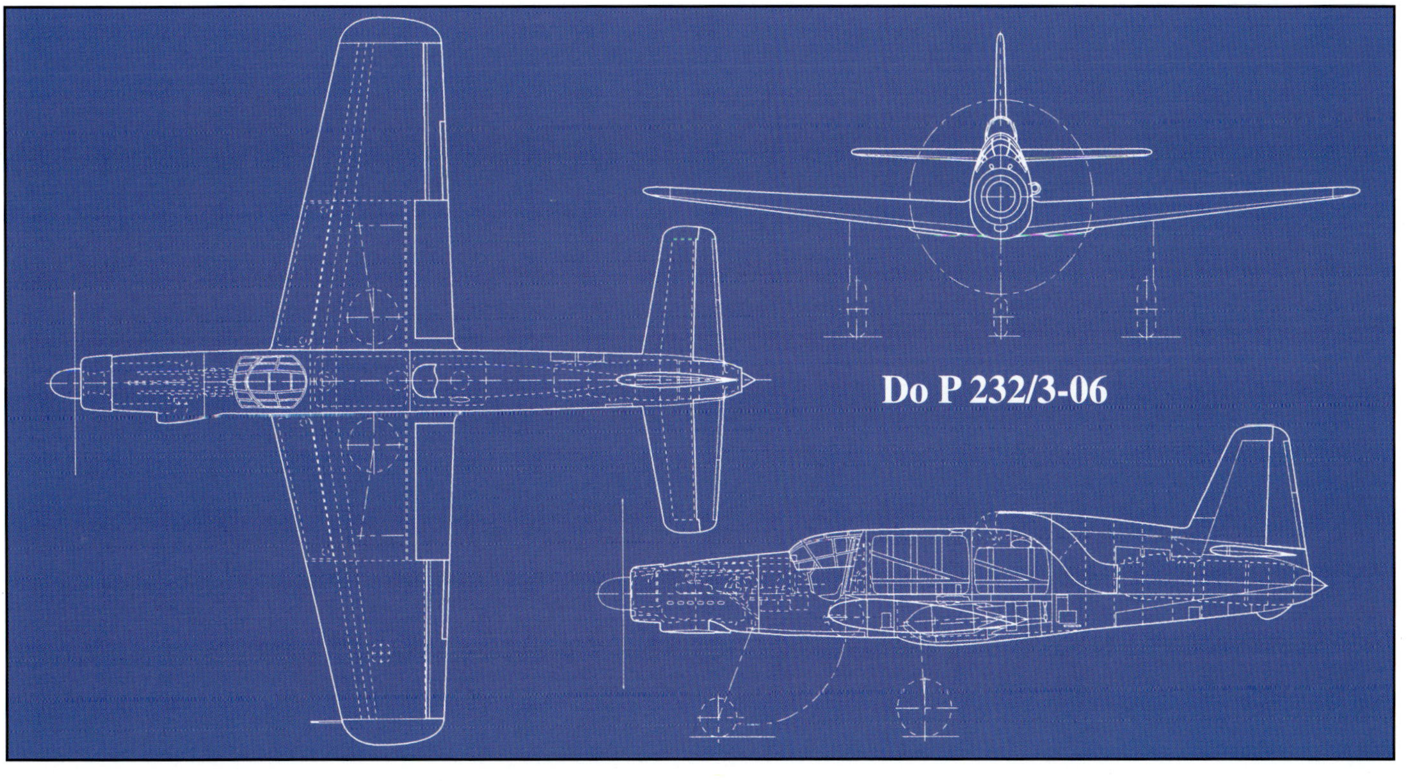

because of their greater manufacturing capacity.

Designated Heinkel **He 535**, the new night-fighter was based upon the Do P 254. Two variants were planned, the He 535 A, based upon the Do P 254/1-02, and featuring a standard Do 335 fuselage and wing modified to accept a Heinkel-Hirth HeS 001A turbojet in the rear fuselage. The radar operator was located between the wing and the jet engine. Two obliquely aimed, fixed 30 mm MK 108 cannons were mounted ahead of the radar operator. The second version, the He 535 B, patterned after the Do P 254/1-03, was similar but had extended tips to the wing and a blister canopy over the radar operator which also enclosed the FuG 350's rotating scanner. Both versions were to use the DB 603 LA as the nose engine (with the Jumo 213 J as an alternate) and were

Above: **An artist impression of the He 535 B, two-seat night fighter of mixed propulsion.**

equipped with FuG 218 radar.

By January 1945, it had become clear to Heinkel that the HeS 011 turbojet would not be ready for service use for many months. The engine was still in the prototype stage because severe problems

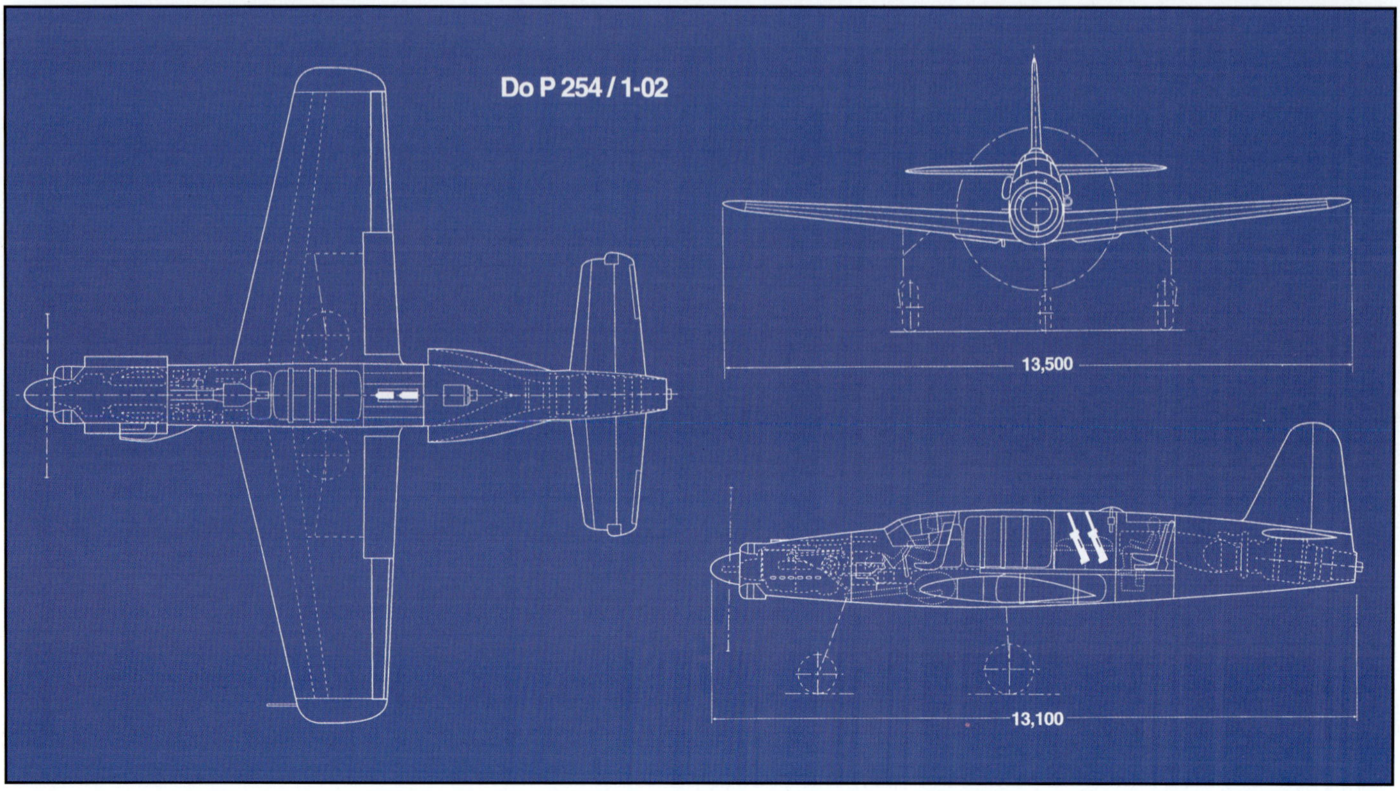

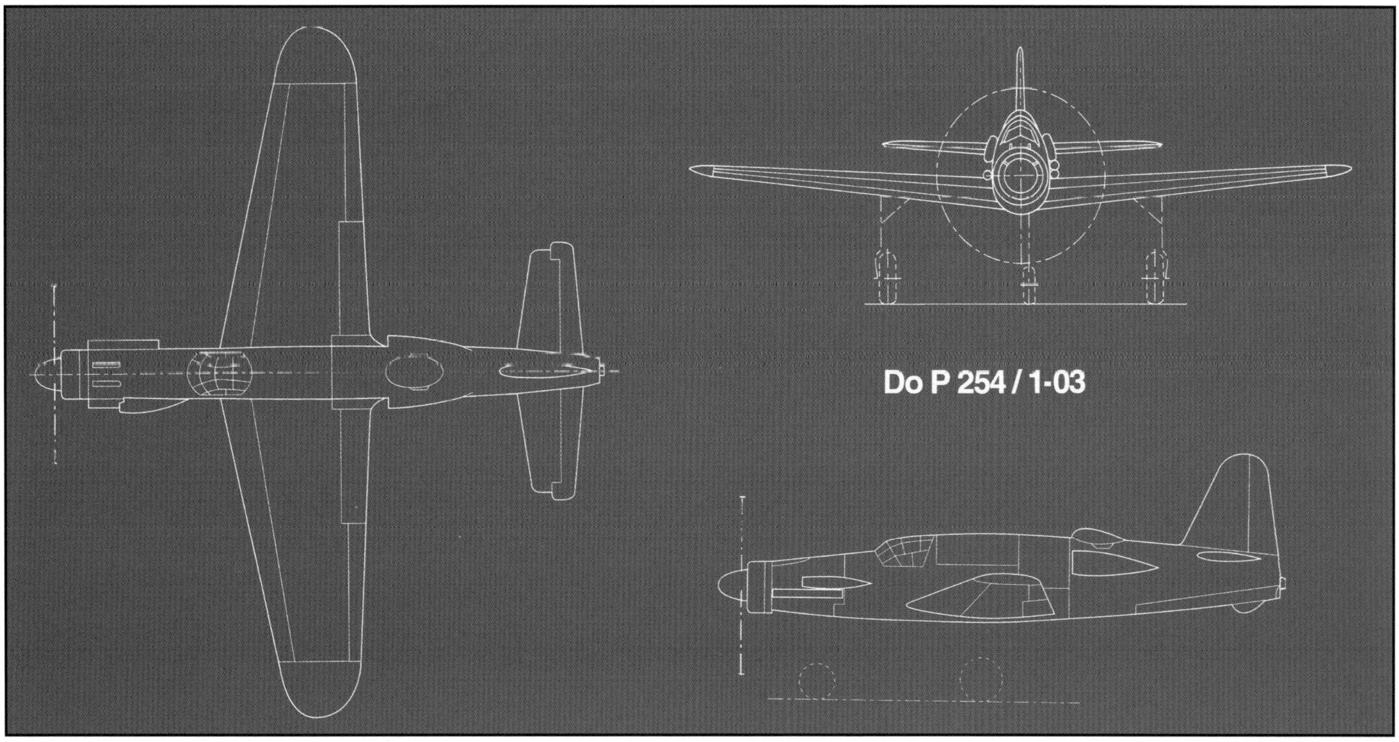

were encountered with the engine's unusual use of both axial and diagonal flow compressors. A total of 184 hours of bench running had been achieved, but the anticipated output of 2,975 lb (1,350 kg) static thrust was never reached because most units rarely delivered 2,425 lb (1,100 kg) of thrust. By the end of the war approximately forty examples of the HeS 011 had been completed, but none flew exclusively under its own power.

Before relating the history of the four-engined Do 335, we will mention three interesting Dornier projects with a direct connection to the Do 335. None of these three projects were considered for production, but they represent creative variations of a theme.

The first, the **Do P 247/6-01** of 1942, was a single-seat day fighter design powered by a Jumo 213 J (a development of the Jumo 213 A fitted with four valves per cylinder instead of three and equipped with a single-stage, three-speed supercharger delivering 2,600 hp for takeoff), mounted in the fuselage and driving a pusher propeller at the end of the cruciform tail assembly. It carried an armament of 3 x MK 108 cannon in the nose and incorporated a tricycle undercarriage. Wingspan was 41 feet (12.5 m), length was 39.5 feet (12.0 m).

The **Do P 252/3-01** was a 1943 design for a three-seat, night- and bad-weather fighter to be powered by two DB 603 LA engines (or alternatively Jumo 213 J engines) driving, by means of coaxial extension shafts, two counter-rotating propellers located in the tail. The radiator for the forward engine was located in front of the forward engine with cooling air supplied by two wing root intakes, while the rear engine radiator was mounted above the fuselage centerline, and its intake was positioned above the rear fuselage just before the cruciform tail assembly. Radar was to be located in the nose, and an exceptionally heavy armament of two 30 mm MK

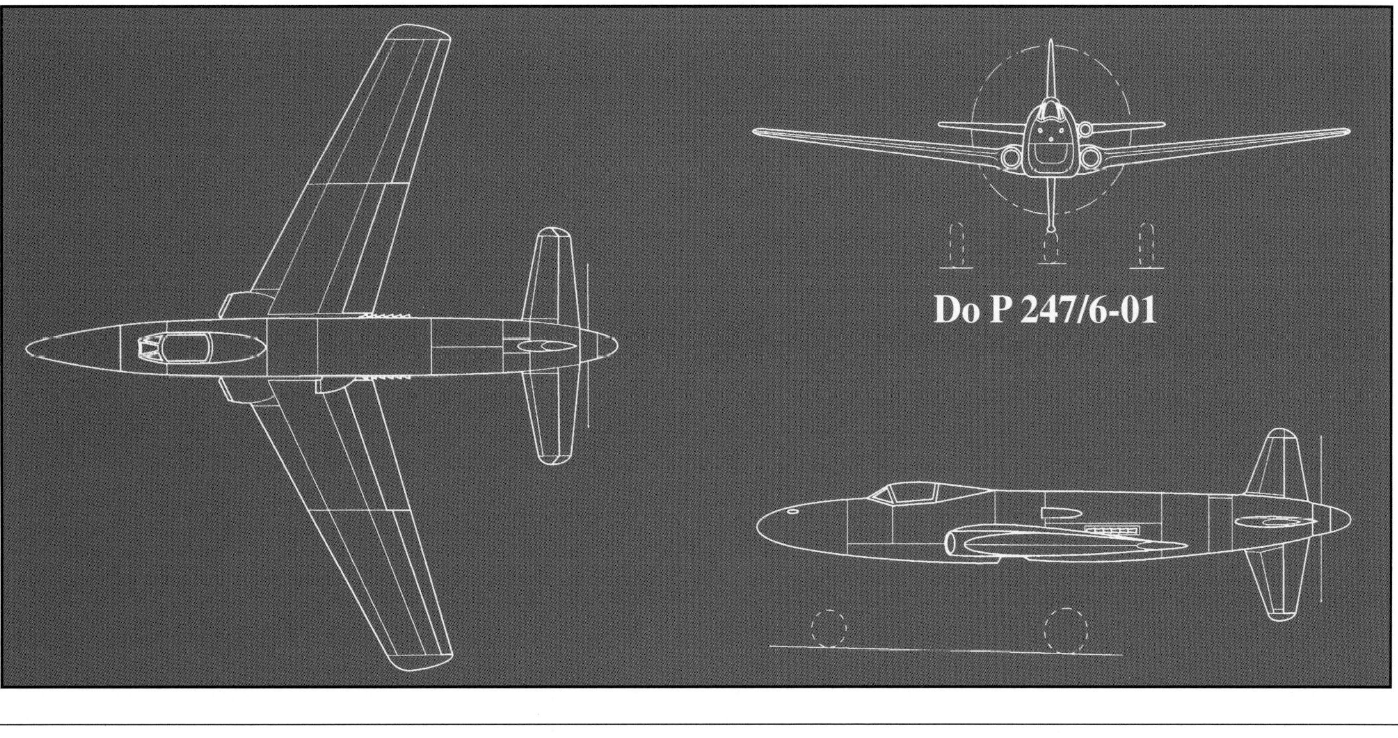

213 cannons and two 30 mm MK 108 cannons were to be positioned above and below the nose cone. In addition, two fixed MK 108s were to be mounted behind the cockpit to fire obliquely upward. Back-to-back seating for the pilot and radar operator was on the left, while the third seat, reserved for the navigator, was forward-facing and located midway between the pilot and radar operator. Dornier estimated a maximum speed of 470 mph (756 km/h) at 20,000 feet (6,096 m).

The **Do P 256/1-01** of 1944 essentially represented a jet-powered version of the Do 335. With a wingspan of 50.8 feet (5.5 m) and a length of 45 feet (13.7 m), it was comparable in size to the Do 335. Intended as a two-seat night- fighter powered by two HeS 011 turbojets mounted beneath the wings, the project was estimated to have a maximum speed of 515 mph (828 km/h) at 19,700 feet (6,005 m).

A radar dish was contained within the nose cone and a forward-firing armament of 4 x MK 108 cannons were mounted above and below the nose. Two additional obliquely-mounted 30 mm MK 108s were to be installed in the fuselage to fire upward and slightly forward. The rear-facing radar operator sat deep in the rear fuselage just aft of the wing training edge. The pilot was enclosed in a standard Do 335 cockpit complete with rearview mirrors enclosed in teardrop canopy blisters.

The crew were separated by three fuel tanks for the thirsty turbojets. The forward tank contained 343 gal (1,300 liters), the second held 436 gal (1,650 liters), while the third contained 250 gal (950 liters) for a total of 1,029 gal (3,895 liters).

Of the three projects just described, it is likely the last, the P 256, represented the way of the future. It was a straight forward proven design and appeared to lend itself to quick engine changes should the proposed HeS 011 fail to materialize. But, in the end, none of these projects advanced beyond the drawing stage before the end of the war.

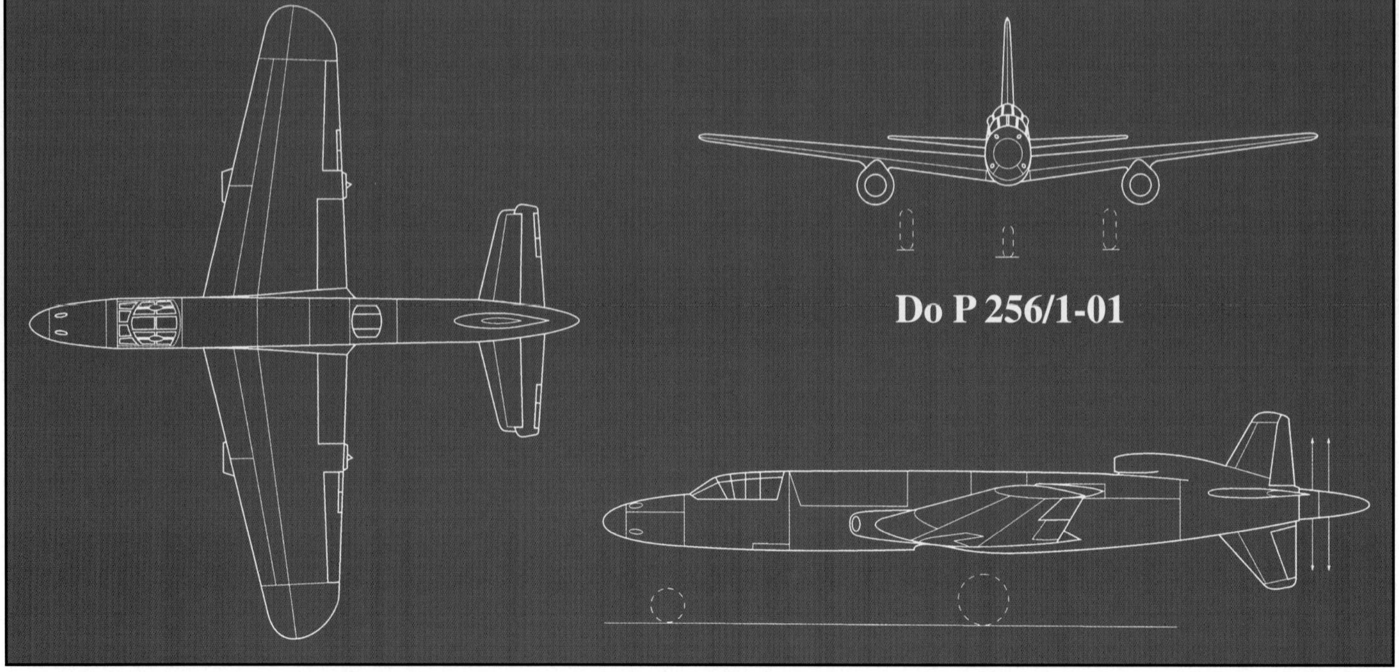

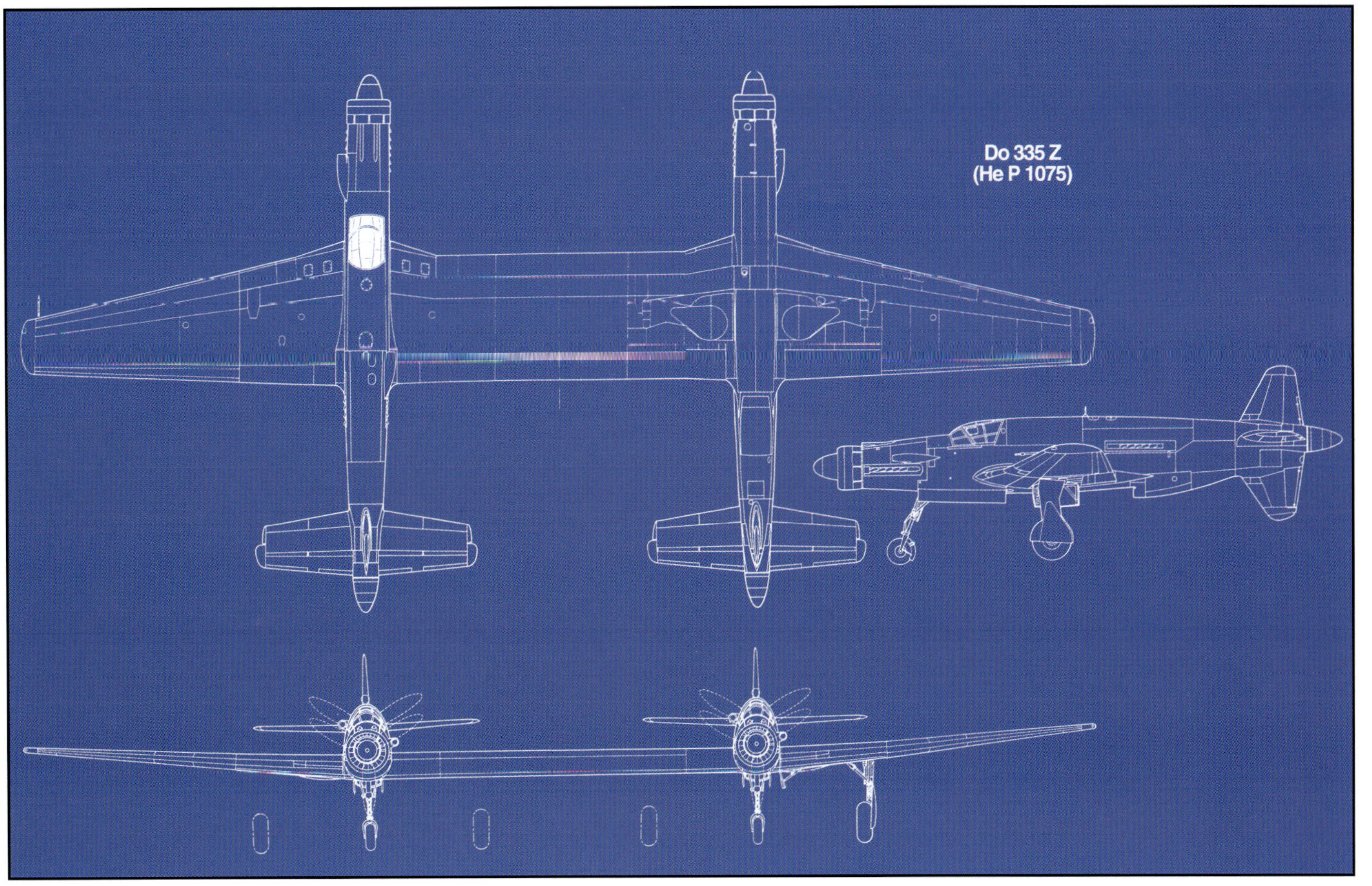

THE TWIN ARROW

The Air Ministry had always considered strategic reconnaissance an essential requirement. During the early period of its development, the Do 335 was expected to perform a reconnaissance mission. No fewer than three different versions were planned. These included the Do 335 A-4 , A-9, and B-4 series, none of which were built. But the first Do 335 to actually carry a camera was the third prototype, the Do 335 V3 (see p 56). Little was accomplished with this aircraft due in part to protracted serviceability difficulties. Late in 1943, the RLM's interest in a new, specially built, strategic photo-reconnaissance aircraft, with an operational range of at least 3,728 miles (6,000 km) built to shadow Allied shipping convoys in the North Atlantic, while operating in concert with the U-boats, was a high priority. Dornier was approached by the RLM to determine if a specialized version of the Do 335 could be created to fulfill such a mission.

One of the more radical possibilities which emerged from preliminary discussions was taking two standard Do 335s and joining them together by adding a new wing center section storing enough fuel to give the resulting twin the necessary range. Because Dornier lacked experience in building such aircraft, the proficient Heinkel firm was brought into the picture. Heinkel had the experience and ability to bring the project forward. Earlier, Heinkel had successfully joined two of their standard twin-engined bombers together with a new wing center section (plus adding a fifth engine in the new section). Although the resulting aircraft, the He 111 Z *(Zwilling* - Twin) was devised for totally different reasons, the engineering challenge was the same. Therefore, Dornier and Heinkel were the logical choice to thoroughly examine the feasibility of creating a **Do 335 Z**. Handicapped by other commitments, the project moved forward slowly until mid 1944. Heinkel had by this time completed a project feasibility study, He P 1075, which was similar to early Dornier sketches, but was characterized by the addition of Heinkel-designed longspan wings and other improvements. Other than the new wing center section, Heinkel project P 1075 utilized existing Do 335 components including the landing gear and the important camera installation.

At this juncture, it was decided that for reasons of expediency, since Heinkel was already fully occupied in the manufacture of other urgently needed aircraft, the whole project should be transferred to the Junkers firm at Dessau. Junkers had no experience with twin aircraft but did possess considerable know-how with large, multi-engined types such as the four-engined Ju 290.

The Ju 290 A *See Adler* (Sea Eagle) was popular and a dependable long-range maritime reconnaissance aircraft, but it was essentially a converted transport with all the limitations of such an aircraft. The new twin Arrow project was, therefore, a logical replacement for the *See Adler*.

The engineers at Dornier and Heinkel cooperated in preliminary design studies which were prepared for presentation to Junkers at Dessau. On October 12, 1944, key Junkers engineers, *Prof.* Heinrich Hertel, *Dipl. Ing.* Ernst Zindel and *Obering.* Bernhard Cruse attended a conference called to review the current status of the Ju 88 and Ju 388. The Do 335 Z was also high on the list of topics to be discussed. After carefully examining the proposal, the Junkers team accepted the Dornier-Heinkel project, but noted that considerable redesign would be required to accommodate the outer wing extensions and concentration of the crew in one fuselage. As a consequence, it was estimated that the first prototype would not be ready before the autumn of 1945. *Prof.* Hertel, then referred to revised drawings provided by Heinkel of P 1075.01-21/W 00304, which involved much less redesign and modification. He further offered the opinion that, based on these drawings, the first prototype could be ready by February 1945.

Two days later, on October 14, 1944, the first official project conference was held in Ernst Zindel's office attended by his key staff including: *Dr.* Hofmann, *Dr.* Backhaus, *Herr* Thorn, *Obering*, Cruse, *Herr* Roos, and Herr Schmidt-Stiebitz. During this initial meeting the engineers observed that the gap between the two fuselages and the small inefficient vertical fin would make single-engine flight difficult. They also noted that the short tailplane lever arm and the fixed stabilizer offered insufficient center of gravity movement, that the Dornier-designed undercarriage of four retractable plus two jettisonable wheels was too complicated. The Heinkel project was also tail-heavy. But, if they were to use the undercarriage from a Ju 352 B-1 as the main wheels, plus one jettisonable, combined with a lengthened fuselage fore and aft by 2½ feet (0.8 m), the planned center nacelle could then be eliminated. For fuel storage, the center wing chord could be increased to 16.4 feet (5 m) (15 percent thickness) with the gap between the fuselages reduced to 23 feet (7 m). In order to maintain the required aspect ratio, each tip was to be increased by 3.3 feet (1 m). Finally, it was concluded that because of fuel storage it was impossible to build two identical fuselages. *Herr* Roos stated the flutter characteristics were critical without consideration of stabilizer damping. *Herr* Thorn suggested 80 to 100 hours would be needed to investigate this area and that this could be handled by Prague only if work on the Ju 388 wing were deferred.

Two days later, *Major* Fischer, commander of the long-range reconnaissance and U-boat cooperation unit, FAG 5, and *Herr* Gemballa of the RLM presented their requirements to representatives from Dornier, Heinkel, and Junkers for strategic reconnaissance aircraft with a range of no less than 4,971 miles (8,000 km) and one fuselage bay for flares but at least 70 percent of the bay should be available for fuel, and with a desired monthly production rate of 1-3-3-3-4. *Herr* Uschmann received Heinkel's documents on October 21, 1944, but these were considered very sketchy. Two days later, *Herr* Riepl of Heinkel's development office in Vienna delivered further documents which were also of limited value. On October 25, *Herr* Jaksch began working on the engine and related equipment. *Dr.* Hofmann was to be responsible for cockpit equipment, and the overall project design was to be supervised by *Herr* Wessel at Oranienbaum. On October 26th, Dornier was to have the fuselage mock-up ready. They were also to dispatch one Do 335 to Dessau the next day for inspection. Over the next few days additional calculations revealed weight and drag concerns in addition to continued questions about the fuel load. In order to fulfill its mission and remain aloft for at least eight hours, a large quantity of fuel had to be carried. The center wing was therefore redesigned with a gap of 24½ feet (7.5 m) and thickness of 15.5 percent. Questions arose about the main wheels. *Herr* Thorn expressed his opinion that the standard Ju 352 B-1 gear assembly with wheel size 520 x 1440 was not satisfactory. On November 1, 1944, the fuselage mock-up was delivered.

By this time, the RLM authorized Junkers use of the GL/C number 635 for the twin Arrow, becoming the **Ju 635** with a purchase order (SS 5103) for four prototypes (Ju 635 V1 - V4) and six preproduction (Ju 635 A-0) aircraft. It was further suggested that total production should reach twenty aircraft.

Between November 3 and 18, further design work was carried out adjusting dimensions of the fuselage with respect to the position and contents of fuel and lubricants as well as some adjustment to the cockpit and crew positions. There were to be ten internal wing fuel tanks, four in the fuselage plus the possibility for two more in the fuselage bays. In addition to these, two large external drop tanks were optional, which would have brought the total fuel load to 4,631 gal (17,530 liters). Placing fuel in the two fuselage bays was initially not considered desirable, since the port bay was to contain two Rb 50/30 cameras, or one camera and one 66 gal (250 liter) tank for GM 1 power-boosting, while the starboard bay was to contain five 132 lb (60 kg) marker bombs.

Below: This Heinkel He 111 Z-3, DG+DY, was a five-engine aircraft created by joining two standard twin-engined bombers together with a new wing center section supporting the fifth engine. Designed to tow heavy troop gliders, it was surprisingly effective. The technology required to build this hybrid was put to good use in designing the Ju 635.

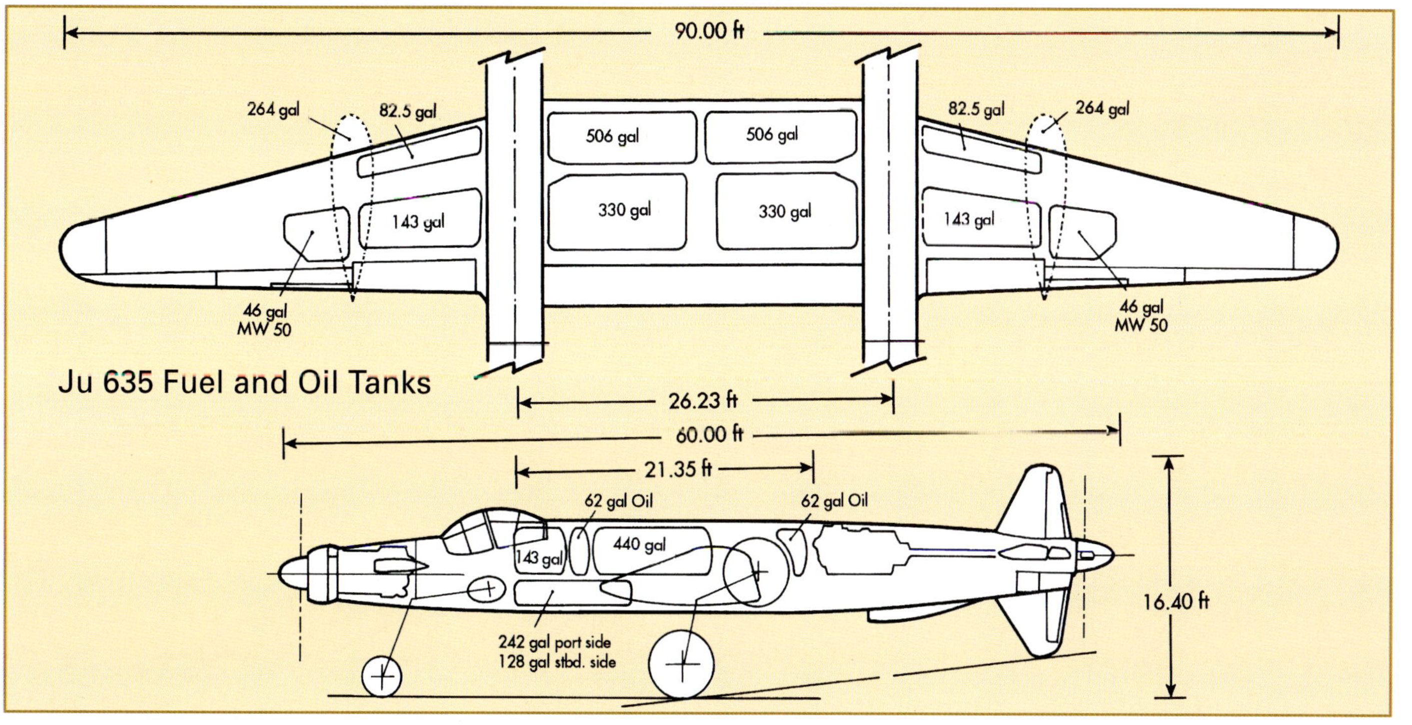

Because of the length of the mission and the vast distances to be flown, a crew of three was initially specified, a pilot and a radio operator in the port fuselage and a second pilot in the starboard fuselage, it was further suggested that the starboard fuselage could eventually hold a fourth crew member. The navigator and second pilot would have astronomical navigation equipment, and enough oxygen was to be carried for eight hours of flying time. For boarding, only one folding ladder, projecting over the aircraft center, was provided. *Herr* Thorn devised components for a new, symmetrical undercarriage (because of similar fuselages) based on the Ju 352 B-1 but with its crossbeam set higher. The anticipated elastic travel of the gear would be compensated by toe-in. Mudguards were to be fitted to the two main fuselage wheels to protect the rear radiator intakes. The 922 lb (418 kg) fifth wheel, also modified from a standard Ju 352 B-1, would have been fitted with a parachute and jettisoned upon takeoff. To further assist in the take-off, two 4,828 lb (2,190 kg) static- thrust RATO units, with recovery parachutes, would have been mounted beneath the aircraft.

On Nov. 14, 1944, a Do 335 finally arrived at Dessau for inspection. On November 27, 1944 the mock-up was inspected by *Maj.* Fischer and Oblt. Müller, who were very satisfied with the left cockpit but recommended to *Herr* Zindel that the proposed complex lubricant heating be abolished in favor of a simplified electrical heating system for both cockpits.

Between the end of November up to mid December 1944, the positioning of electronics was finalized. Radio equipment was to include FuG 10 or FuG 10 K3P with its antenna on the top left fuselage and the trailing wire to a point mid-wing of the center section. A Peil G 6 long-wave direction-finding loop was to be mounted beneath the left fuselage just ahead of the fuselage bay. A FuG 16Z or FuG 15Z vhf radio-telephone was to be mounted in the left cockpit with its antenna in the left vertical fin. Additional electronic equipment including the FuBl 2 blind approach, to be mounted in the left fuselage; the FuG 101 radio altimeter, mounted under the starboard wing; the FuG 25A IFF (identification-friend-foe); FuG 217 tail-warning radar, with horizontal antenna mounted on the vertical fin; FuG 200 *Hotentwiel* airborne-to-surface vessel radar which was to be supplemented, or replaced, with FuG 224 Berlin A target-indicating radar.

With the arrival of a Do 335 at Dessau, Junkers test pilot Siegfried Holzbaur put the aircraft through its paces and noted poor cockpit visibility to the rear and slow flap retraction. At high speeds, he noted roll and yaw momentum was insufficient showing a slight tendency to spiral. Upon landing, the aircraft's brakes were barely adequate. During this period, *Herr* Gemballa of the RLM passed on to Junkers a list of equipment demands for the Ju 635 which included a camera installation identical to the Do 335 A-4, a 10 ft (3m) rubber dinghy, a *Schwan-See* FuG 302c radio buoy, small marker bombs and the heaviest possible rear-facing armament.

During this desperate period, the German government approached the Japanese about certain advanced German military aircraft that the Japanese could use in the Pacific war. Among the aircraft designs offered to the Japanese was the Ju 635, which was shown to representatives of the Imperial Japanese Naval Air Force on December 15, 1944. The Japanese were quite interested in the project and were favorably impressed with the Ju 635's estimated capabilities.

From the middle of December up to the end of 1944, Junkers engineers continued to work out details pertaining to the landing-gear hydraulic system, the autopilot, and the latest search radar installation. The control surfaces and the landing flaps on the outer wing panels were standard Do 335 components, but the ailerons were longer than usual. As on the Ju 287 jet bomber, the wing center section is fitted with a slotted flap of 20 percent chord. An interesting feature is the placing of the landing-flap actuating mechanism in the flaps themselves so that space may be preserved for extra fuel tanks (MW 50) in the outer wings. On lowering the flaps, the center section moves first, and on retraction, it moves last. De-icing for the outer wings and tailplane is electric with current supplied by two 3,000 watt generators. Fire-extinguishing equipment consists of four tanks of liquid which can be fed

to the engines and all internal fuel tanks.

At the beginning of 1945, wind-tunnel tests with scale models fitted with freely rotating propellers disclosed wing-tip airflow separation but oddly only on one side. Additional, test reports from Rechlin's pilots flying various Do 335s noted cowl-flap problems and persistent complaints about the undercarriage and fuselage joints.

Meanwhile, additional work had finalized the cockpit interior including wall lining and canopy de-icing. *Herr* Muttray created a second plywood interior lining contoured at about 1 inch (25 mm) from the outer skin. Other details concerning propeller de-icing and the use of MW 50 powerboost were each resolved. However, by January 5, 1945, although everyone knew that there was almost no hope the Ju 635 would be built, several engineers pleaded for the project's continuation.

On January 8, 1945, Junkers received a puzzling and senseless memorandum from the RLM demanding the installation of four fixed fuselage MG 151s, firing rearward, or FDL 151Z, FDL-B, or C 151Z (remotely-controlled turrets) plus attack armament. *Herr* Zindel was incredulous, but replied on

Above: An artist impression of the unusual four-engined Ju 635 designed during 1944 as a long-range maritime reconnaissance for operations over the North Atlantic. With a wing span of 90 feet (27.45 m), it would have been an impressive aircraft. **Below:** Two views of the Ju 635 full-size wooden mock-up of the port two-man cockpit showing the precise location of controls and instruments. The third crewman was positioned in the starboard cockpit, which was essentially a standard Do 335 design with appropriate modifications.

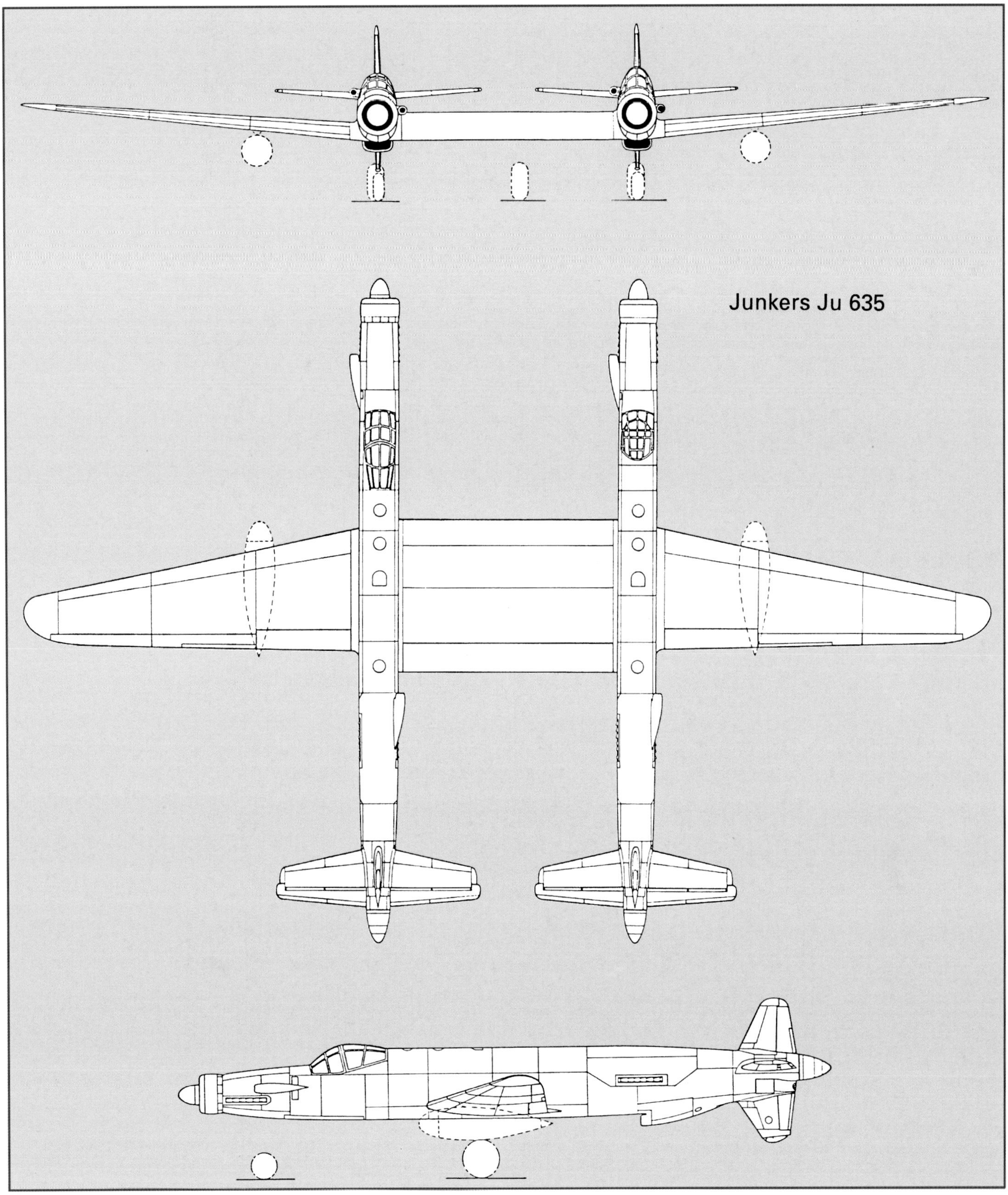

January 17 that armament of any type would be detrimental to performance and the purpose of the aircraft. He further stated that "...the Ju 635 should rely on its high speed to elude the enemy....like the British Mosquito". Zindel also proposed to increase fuel weight by using C3 fuel (96-100 octane), instead of B4 fuel (87 octane), for the four DB 603 E engines, but *Herr* Gemballa of the RLM advised that this was unrealistic since C3 was in short supply. At the same time he instructed Zindel to fit the Ju 635 with ejection seats. By January 18, 1945, data sheets and general arrangement drawings of the Ju 635 had been formally handed over to the Japanese, but by this time their interest in the aircraft had slackened. Finally, by February 5, 1945, the war situation was such that all further work on the Ju 635 was aborted. On this date *Prof.* Hertel received performance data sheet 635/4 which compared the twin-engined Hütter Hü 211 (a high-altitude long-range reconnaissance derivative of the He 219), the four-engined Ju 488 (not completed) and the Ju 635. It is not known what *Prof.* Hertel thought of the other two designs, (only the Hü 211 was actually built) but he was undoubtedly disappointed that the Ju 635 was never completed and flown.

Epilogue

By Thomas H. Hitchcock

Prof. Dornier was quoted as having said "I was always endeavoring to pursue my design principles even when I was risking the possibility that my ideas would be regarded as out-of-date." This somewhat self-effacing comment belies the fact that Dornier's design ideas were hardly dated. In truth, the opposite was the case. *Prof.* Dornier was a visionary willing to take risks. The Do 335 was a bold and logical creation devised to meet a specific stringent combat mission. It was at the same time orthodox yet radical. It was the perfect solution to the Air Ministry's specification. The fact that the Do 335 failed to attain service use, is less attributable to a lack of manufacturing capacity, than it was to changing priorities and mission demands based on immediate, short-range needs. However, in its final configuration as a single-seat, heavy fighter of mixed power, the He 535 employed technology of the day combined with that of the future. That future was the turbojet.

Meanwhile, five-thousand miles to the west, and unknown to *Prof.* Dornier, the engineers at The Ryan Aeronautical Company of San Diego, were facing a similar set of engineering challenges. Ryan's chief engineer, Benjamin T. Salmon assisted by William T. Immenschuh, were trying to develop a mixed power, twin-engined, single-seat, carrier-based, fighter powered by a conventional internal combustion engine in the nose with a turbojet in the rear fuselage.

The US Navy was skeptical the jet engine would ever become adaptable to carrier-based aircraft, primarily because of the jet's long takeoff distance. Of course, the Navy was also equally concerned about jets landing aboard carriers, since early jet engines did not have very rapid acceleration capabilities which were essential in the event of a wave-off during the landing approach. However, determined not to be left behind in the development of jet powered carrier aircraft, The Bureau of Aeronautics, supported development of Ryan's project Model 28, which incorporated a 1,425 hp Wright R-1820-72W, Cyclone, nine-cylinder, air-cooled radial engine in the nose and a 1,600 lb s.t. General Electric J31-GE-3 turbojet in the rear. A development contract was awarded to Ryan in January 1943 for the FR Fireball, as the project was now known.

On June 25, 1944, the first prototype, the XFR-1, took to the air under the power of the front Wright Cyclone only. On September 20, 1944, the second Fireball prototype, the XFR-2 flew for the first time utilizing both the Cyclone and the GE jet.

The Navy took delivery of the FR-1 in March 1945 allocating all production Fireballs to VF-66, the only squadron to operate the aircraft. With the end of the war, the Navy canceled the Fireball after approximately sixty-six were completed. The FR-1, shown left, is flying solely on its rear engine while the propeller is in the fully feathered position proving the aircraft could maintain flight with only the thrust of the jet engine.

Thus, while the Do 335 was unique in its tandem arrangement of two internal combustion engines, it was not the first to feature mixed power arranged in the tandem configuration for single-seat fighters. Although the early turbojets, were limited in their performance and reliability, it was apparent that this form of propulsion was the way of the future.

The mixed power concept was, therefore, only a stop-gap measure until the turbojet became sufficiently powerful and reliable to become the prime powerplant for all military single-seat fighters.

Appendix 1

CAMOUFLAGE, INSIGNIA & MARKINGS

By Thomas H. Hitchcock

CAMOUFLAGE

On October 28, 1943, the Do 335 V1 took to the air for the first time camouflaged in a single overall uppersurface application of Color 71 *Dunkelgrün* (Dark Green), which extended down the sides of the aircraft until it met Color 65 Hellblau (Bright Blue), the under surface color. The two metal propellers and spinners were finished in Color 70 *Schwarzgrün* (Black-Green). This scheme was essentially the one associated with twin-engined bombers and reconnaissance aircraft of the period. It involved the use of lusterless paints sprayed evenly over the airframe but lacking a hard edge where the Dark Green met the Bright Blue. The Bright Blue being sprayed on last with about a 1 inch (25mm) fade area where the two colors met. The use of a single upper surface color for an aircraft of this type was unusual inasmuch as most twin-engined bombers and reconnaissance types employed a so-called splinter pattern of two greens; Color 70 and Color 71. It is unknown why Dornier elected to use a single upper surface color for the first prototype.

By the time the third prototype, the Do 335 V3, appeared in January 1944, the aircraft had received its standard second upper surface color in a splinter pattern similar to the diagram shown on page 163. The two upper surface colors were the usual 70 and 71, but this prototype's ventral tailplane discarded the two greens for a solid application of the undersurface color, Bright Blue. Metal spinners and propellers were in the obligatory Black-Green.

Between January 1944 through June 1944, four additional Do 335 prototypes (V6,V7,V8,V9) had been completed. So far as is known, all of these aircraft were camouflaged similar to one another using colors 70,71,65. However, with the V7 (and possibly the V6), the ventral tailplane was once again camouflaged in the top surface colors.

In July 1944, the Air Ministry issued instructions to the aircraft industry that new camouflage colors were to be instituted as soon as possible. These new colors had been under test over many months and were now approved for service-wide implementation. Essentially, the new directive allowed that those aircraft which previously had flown with colors 70,71,65, were to transition to the new colors 81,82,76. The Do 335 certainly qualified for the new colors. The written description for colors 81 and 82 appears to have been omitted from initial Air Ministry directives leaving open exactly what these colors were to represent. It was stated that color cards displaying these new colors, would be forthcoming. In the meantime, aircraft manufacturers were instructed to use up all existing stocks of colors 70 and 71 before switching over exclusively to the new colors. Thus, Color 70 could be paired with Color 82 while Color 71 could be paired with Color 81 as long as stocks of the older colors were available. The new camouflage colors did not extend to the spinners and propellers. The painting of these items was unaffected by the new regulations. The color specified for under surfaces, Color 76 *Lichtblau* (Light Blue), was well known having been in use for some time as the official under surface color for day fighters.

What were colors 81 and 82 and how did they differ from the older camouflage paints? Since an official Air Ministry color card for the period has never been found, it is necessary to complete the puzzle by indirect means; working with surviving written descriptions of the new col-

Above: The Do 335 V3 was camouflaged in a splinter pattern of top surface colors 70 Black-Green and 71 Dark Green. Propellers and their spinners were also in Color 70. All undersurfaces were in Color 65 Bright Blue.

Below: The Do 335 A-1, W.Nr. 240117, was undoubtedly painted in the new late war camouflage colors of 81 and 82 with all under surfaces in Color 76.

Above: The Do 335 M15 as it was found by American troops in 1945 following the capture of Oberpfaffenhofen. Since tailplane component manufacture for the Do 335 was decentralized, parts were prepainted prior to assembly.

Below: The Do 335 A-12, W.Nr. 240119, was the forth production two-seat trainer. At the time of capture, it was almost complete but lacked camouflage and insignia.

ors in conjunction with actual paint samples recovered from aircraft of the period.

Written descriptions for Color 81 range from Olive-Brown to Dark Green to Brown-Violet depending on the source[5]. Color 82 was the lighter of the two in value. Its written description varied from Dark Green to Bright Green, again depending upon the source[6]. This ambiguity is not easily explained apart from the obvious conclusion that the aircraft manufacturers were forced to make up their own descriptions of what they perceived the new colors should represent.

Original paint samples recovered from surviving German aircraft as well as well preserved fragments from crash sites have yielded a considerable number of excellent paint samples from the period. In addition, further paint samples have been obtained from other sources including old paint cans and official company camouflage charts for other aircraft. From the weight of evidence from all available sources, it is now recognized that Color 81 was undoubtedly a form of brown and Color 82 a form of green.

The thirty-day period between early July and early August 1944 saw the completion of two additional Do 335 prototypes; the V4 and V5 concurrent with preparations to build ten preproduction aircraft. In 1972 the author made a detailed inspection of the Do 335 A-02 while it was still in its original, though very faded, wartime finish. His conclusions, published in 1973[7], indicated this aircraft, the second preproduction Do 335, completed in October 1944, was camouflaged dark green and bright green on upper surfaces while the under sides were in light blue. Presumably, Dornier interpreted the two new greens as colors 81 and 82.

With the completion of the Do 335 M13 and M14 in October and November 1944 respectively, it might be assumed that the true identity of 81 and 82 had been standardized, yet when the Dornier company published their camouflage schematic (see page 163) in November 1944, *both* uppersurface colors were curiously identified as dark green. Obviously something was lacking.

To complicate matters, another new color also appeared in 1944; Color 83. First mentioned in a directive dated August 15, 1944, it was simply identified as a dark color. In order to determine the nature of this new color, it was necessary to first establish the true identity for colors 81 and 82. By carefully examining surviving evidence, the authors are convinced that Color 81 was in fact Brown-Violet, Color 82 Bright Green and Color 83 was Dark Green [8].

When the Dornier company restored Do 335 A-02 in 1975, they choose camouflage colors which were a close approximation for Brown-Violet 81 and Bright Green 82, but which were nevertheless different from the original colors applied to this aircraft thirty-one years earlier. In addition, Dornier elected to incorrectly paint the two spinners and propellers black instead of the specified Black-Green.

NATIONAL AIRCRAFT INSIGNIA

At the time the first Do 335 appeared in late autumn 1943, the German national aircraft insignia consisted of a *Balkenkreuz* (Bar cross) and *Hakenkreuz* (Swastika). The *Balkenkreuz* was applied to six positions on the airframe; both sides of the rear fuselage and the top and bottom of both wings. The *Hakenkreuz* appeared on two surfaces; port and starboard sides of the dorsal fin. They are shown in detail on pages 46,47 and 132.

The *Balkenkreuz* displayed on the fuselage was a much simplified version of the basic *Balkenkreuz* insignia carried by German military aircraft at the beginning of the war. This simplified cross was simply the older insignia with all black areas eliminated leaving only four white arms to form the cross. The *Balkenkreuz* displayed on the top surface of the wings was a simplified cross similar to the fuselage insignia, but having proportionally narrower white arms. The *Balkenkreuz* located on the underside of the wings was the older original *Balkenkreuz* complete with black inner cross plus four white arms and four very narrow black trim arms.

The size of the *Balkenkreuz* insignia varied slightly, but essentially all Do 335 prototypes, from the V1 up to and including the M12, carried 1000 mm fuselage crosses while the remaining prototypes (M13 on) employed a slightly larger cross measuring 1250 mm. The top wing

Balkonkreuz measured 1000 mm and remained unchanged throughout Do 335 production. The underwing *Balkenkreuz* for the Do 335 prototypes measured 1525 mm, but subsequent preproduction and production aircraft standardized on a slightly smaller cross measuring 1000 mm.

The fin-positioned *Hakenkreuz,* like the fuselage cross, was merely a simplified white outlined swastika. It measured 535 mm and was applied in the same style and location throughout the entire Do 335 production, with only one exception. The photograph of the Do 335 M13 at the top of page 117 reveals a slight deviation from accepted practice. In this instance, Dornier painters first sprayed a 575 mm square on its point in a dark camouflage color, presumably Color 70, followed by the white swastika superimposed upon the square.

MARKINGS

Maintenance and safety data were stenciled on the aircraft, and are well documented in the drawings of Arthur L. Bentley (see pages 46,47,98,132). Other markings carried by the Do 335 were those associated with the aircraft's four-letter primary identification code, prototype number, and serial number which are documented in Appendix 2 and 3 (which see).

An unusual underwing marking appeared on the Do 335 M13 in the form of wing tips painted in a unknown color distinct from the light blue. It is possible yellow or red was applied to this prototype as a ground recognition feature, but confirmation has not been possible. Since no production Do 335 was ever issued to an operational *Luftwaffe* unit, the aircraft never carried insignia or other markings commonly associated with such units.

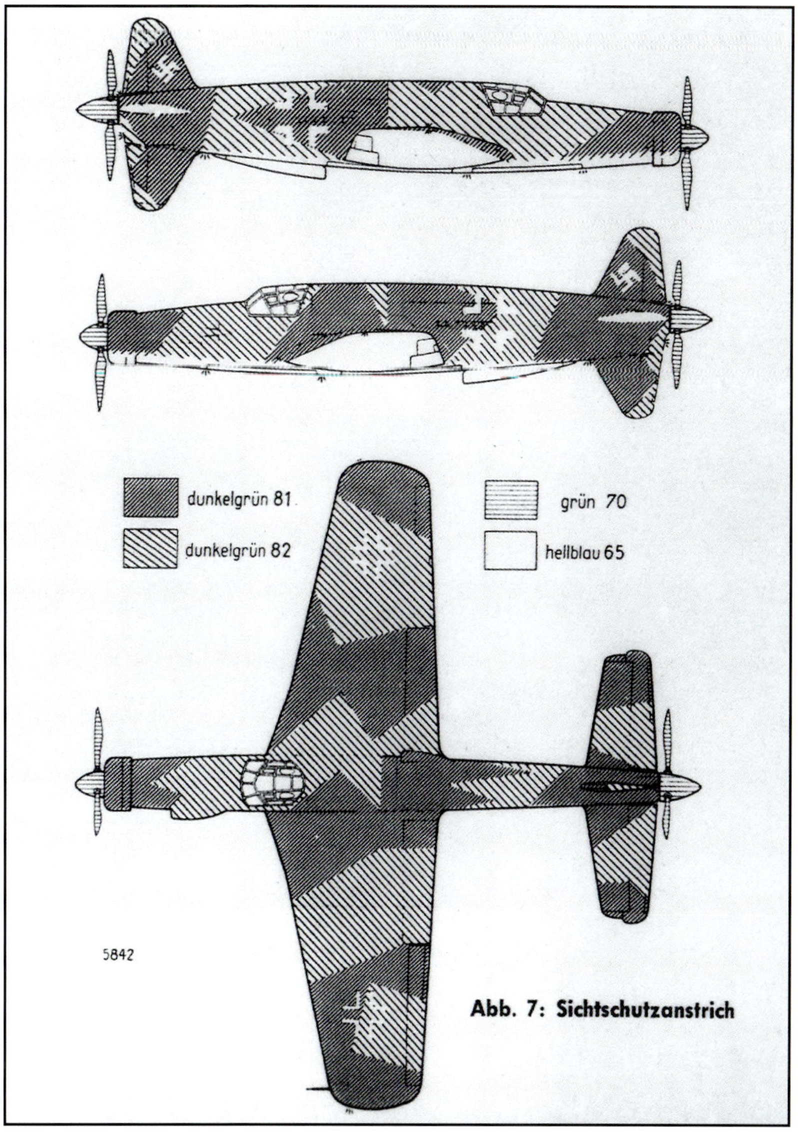

Abb. 7: Sichtschutzanstrich

5 Blohm & Voss, Dornier and Messerschmitt,respectively.

6 Dornier and Messerschmitt, respectively.

7 See Messerschmitt 'O-Nine' Gallery, Monogram, 1973, by T.H. Hitchcock.

8 See The Official Monogram German Aircraft Color Guide 1935-1945, Vol. 2, by Merrick, Smith and Hitchcock, EYP 1998.

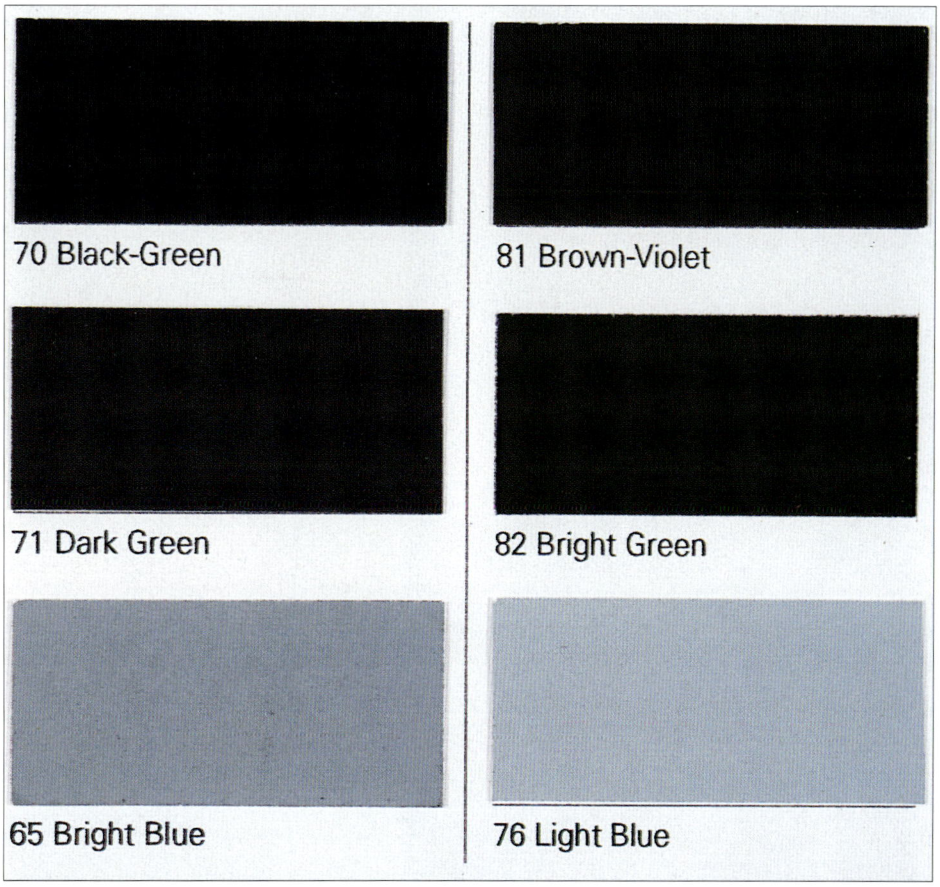

Opposite: Günter Sengfelder's precise and impressive large-scale model of the Do 335 M19 shows the aircraft in appropriate late war camouflage and markings. **Right:** A photograph of the six major exterior camouflage colors employed by the Do 335. While not as precise as genuine paint samples, the reader can nevertheless appreciate the relative intensity of each color. Readers desiring more precise samples of German wartime colors are advise to consult two excellent reference sources: THE OFFICIAL MONOGRAM PAINTING GUIDE TO GERMAN AIRCRAFT 1935-1945, Monogram, 1980, by Merrick & Hitchcock (out of stock by the publisher), THE OFFICIAL MONOGRAM GERMAN AIRCRAFT COLOR GUIDE 1935-1945, Vol. 2, Monogram, by Merrick, Smith and Hitchcock (expected in 1998).

PH

Appendix 2

WERKNUMMERN, PRIMARY & UNIT IDENTIFICATION CODES

By Thomas H. Hitchcock

SERIAL NUMBERS

Concurrent with the appearance of the first prototype of the Do 335 during the autumn of 1943, the RLM established a new standardized system of aircraft *werknummern* (serial numbers). Up to this time, the aircraft manufacturers exercised considerable latitude in the allocation of serial numbers for their aircraft. Three, four and five-digit numbers were frequently assigned to aircraft by their makers in a random fashion. However, the new RLM system called for the issuance of six-digit serial numbers by block allocation.

As a result of this new system, the first batch of Do 335 prototypes were assigned consecutive numbers in the 230000 block beginning with 230001 and extending to 230014. It must be stressed that these six-digit block allocations could be simultaneously assigned to more than one manufacturer. For example, the 230000 block was also allocated to Junkers and Messerschmitt for used by the Ju 188 and the Bf 109 respectively.

The 240000 block was also allocated to Dornier and assigned to the Do 335, and is summarized on pages 166 and 170. Note that several gaps were built into the numbering sequence within this block.

The aircraft identification plate, which recorded the serial number, was positioned on the airframe and was similar to the plate shown on page 167. This plate would usually carry at least three lines of information. The top line would carry the *Muster* (type) identification written as Do 335 A-0, or 8-335 A-0, or simply 335 A-0. The second line would list the aircraft's *Werk Nr.* (serial number) e.g. 240102 while the third line would give the three-letter code for the *Hersteller* (manufacturer).

The following four codes were used by Dornier:

hmv Dornier-Werke GmbH Flugzeugbau, Friedrichshafen (Bodensee)

hmw Norddeutsche Dornier-Werke GmbH, Flugzeugbau, Seestadt Wismar

jbo Dornier-Werke GmbH Flugzeugbau, Zweigw. Oberpfaffenhofen b/München

mch Dornier-Reparaturwerft GmbH (repair facilities) Oberpfaffenhofen b/München

Since these identification plates yielded little useful information to enemy intelligence, it was thought German security concerns could be maintained in the event an aircraft, or parts from an aircraft, were recovered by enemy forces. Without a means to decode the numbers and letters, it would not be possible to determine much about the aircraft. In this way, not only would the type be obscured, but also any real indication of its maker, their location, or how many examples had been built.

In addition to the standard identification plate, German aircraft frequently had their six-digit serial number painted prominent, in black or white digits, at some appropriate location on the fuselage or vertical tailplane. Late in the war, as a further security measure, the RLM issued instructions that only the last three digits of the aircraft's serial number, out of the six, should be painted on the airframe. With the Do 335, the first ten preproduction aircraft (A-01 to A-010) and thirteen production (A-1) machines had the last three digits (101 - 123) painted in 315 mm white numbers at the top of their vertical fins.

Above: Prototypes were identified by a white letter and number painted to the ventral fin. The eighth Do 335 prototype is shown above.

Above: The first 23 preproduction and production aircraft had the last three digits of their serial number painted in white atop the vertical fin. Do 335 A-0, W.Nr. 240104 is shown above.

Above: Fraction numbers identified B-series development aircraft. The numerator was the last two digits of the serial number. The denominator identified the *Muster* (Model). Shown above is the Do 335 M20, serial number 240316.

Dornier Do 335 Werknummern for Versuch and Muster Aircraft

Number	Stamm-kennzeichen[1]	Tailplane Nr.	Versuch	Muster	First Flown	Remarks
230001	CP+UA		V1		October 28, 1943	To Versuch-Verband O.bd.L. on Nov. 19, 1943. Damaged on 11/22/44 at Lärz. Returned to Dornier. Testbed for DB 603 E engines.
230002	CP+UB		V2		December 31, 1943	Crashed April 14/15/16, 1944 (different dates are recorded) near Buxheim.
230003	CP+UC (T9+ZH)		V3		January 20, 1944	Modified for photo reconnaissance on July 26, 1944 then delivered to 1./Aufkl.Gr. Ob.d.L. Damaged in Nov. 1944. Returned to Do.
230004	CP+UD		V4	M4	July 9, 1944	Tested as a fighter-bomber. In Jan. 1945 still with Dornier.
230005	CP+UE	5	V5	M5	August 2, 1944	To Rechlin Sept.30, 1944 with armament 2xMG 15, 1xMK Later tested two wing-mounted MK 103.With EK 335 at Mengen.
230006	CP+UF		V6	M6	March 23, 1944	Dornier test aircraft. To Junkers during May/June 1944 for tests to replace DB 603 for Jumo 213.Later returned to Dornier.
230007	CP+UG	7	V7	M7	May 19, 1944	To Dessau to test Jumo 213 installation. Returned to Dornier in January 1945.
230008	CP+UH	V8	V8	M8	May 31, 1944	Fitted with DB 603 E-1 for high altitude test flights at Mengenin Oct. 1944. Then to Rechlin for further tests up to February 1945.
230009	CP+UI	V9	V9	M9	June 29, 1944	Prototype for A-0 series. Tested MK 103 as engine-mounted cannon in July 1944.To Rechlin Aug. 7, 1944. Crash landed on 18th.
230010	CP+UK (D5+??)		V10	M10	January 24, 1945	Modified to A-6 night fighter standards at Heinkel in Vienna. Appointed to test center at Diepensee. Probably to staff I./NJG 3.
230011	CP+UL	11		M11	October 11, 1944	Prototype for A-11 series. Tested jettison of rear propeller. Damaged at Mengen during landing with undercarriage failure.
230012	RP+UO	12		M12	September , 1944	Intended for A-11 series development. Fitted with Me P 8 prop. Blown up at Friedrichshafen in April 1945.
230013	RP+UP	13		M13	October 31, 1944	Intended for B-2 series development with MK 103 wing cannon At Friedrichshafen in Dec.1944 for weapons testing.
230014	RP+UQ	14		M14	November, 1944	Intended for B-2 series development. At Mengen in Dec. 1944. Captured by French.
240311		11/15		M15	Not completed.	Probably B-1 series development aircraft. Incomplete construction.
240312		12/16		M16	Not completed.	Probably B-1 series development aircraft. Incomplete construction.
240313		13/17		M17	April 2, 1947.	For B-6 series completed by French after the war from spares.
240314		14/18		M18	Not completed.	Intended for B-3 series development.
240315		15/19		M19	Not completed.	Intended for B-3 series development.
240316		16/20		M20	Not completed.	Intended for B-3 series development.
240317		17/21		M21	Not completed.	Intended for B-6 series development.
240318		18/11		M11	Not completed	Second M11 after loss of W.Nr. 230011
240319				M22	Not completed.	Intended for B-7 series development.
240320				M23	Not completed.	Intended for B-8 series development.

1. Stammkennzeichen - Primary identication. Four-letter identifying codes, beginning with a consonant, issued to both new and acquired military aircraft by the General Aircraft Planning Board of the Air Ministry. Such codes were a permanent part of the aircraft's identification and remained with the aircraft throughout its career. They were applied to the fuselage and under wing (almost always in black) using a water base paint and were usually removed, or replaced, on the exterior of the airframe by operational units.

Above: The ninth Do 335 prototype, the Do 335 V9, is shown carrying it's factory-applied four letter *Stammkennzeichen* (primary identification) code painted in black distemper paint evenly about the white national aircraft insignia. The white V9 on the ventral fin identifies this aircraft as the ninth *Versuch* (test) prototype.

Prototype numbers were occasionally painted in white on the ventral fin, but by 1945 the Dornier firm devised a method of identifying prototypes using a slash, or so-called fraction system. It is believed this unique system sought to incorporate the *Muster* number with the last one or two digits of the aircraft's serial number. This new means of identification can be seen in the photograph of the Do 335 A-1 at the top of page 169. The tailplane number 1/3 undoubtedly indicates this aircraft was the M3 with *Werk Nr.* 240161.

PRIMARY IDENTIFICATION CODE

The *Stammkennzeichen* (primary identification) code was an additional means of aircraft identification which provided recognition down to a specific machine. It consisted of a factory-applied four-letter code, beginning with a consonant, positioned evenly to the left and right of the national aircraft insignia (cross), which were assigned to aircraft at the time of manufacture. It was usually applied in black letters at three locations; both sides of the rear fuselage and the under side of the wings (see pages 46,47). Letters were applied with water-base black distemper paint which allowed for their quick removal in the field.

Sequencing of the *Stammkennzeichen* occurred at the fourth letter. But a new batch of codes sequences did not necessarily require the letter "A" to be the beginning letter in the sequence. For example, the first Do 335 A-0, W.Nr. 240101, began the sequence with the letter "G" (VG+PG).

In theory, two German aircraft could have the same serial number, but no two could have the same *Stammkennzeichen.* In 1945, as a further security measure, the RLM issued instructions that manufacturers should omit painting the primary identification code to the outside of the airframe.

UNIT IDENTIFICATION CODES

When the Do 335 V3 was assigned for service evaluation to 1./Aufkl. Gr. Obd.L. (see pages 55,56), the aircraft painters from that unit removed the primary identification code, CP+UC, from the fuselage and under side of the wings, and replaced these with a fuselage code reading T9+ZH. This new unit identification code specified the unit (T9), the individual aircraft (Z) and the 1st Staffel (H). In keeping with regulations, the unit code was painted only one-fifth the size of the letters to the right of the cross.

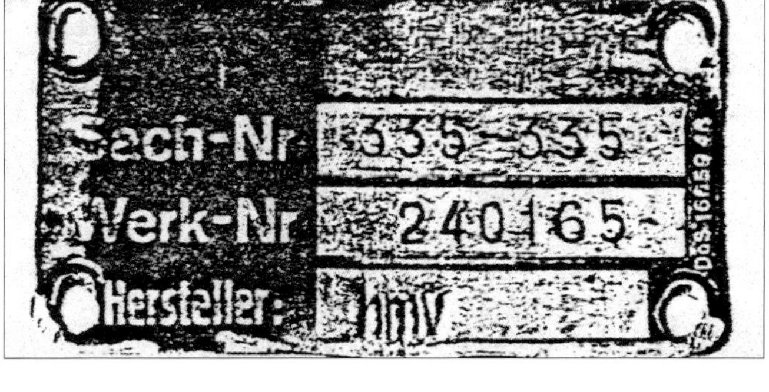

Right: A typical identification plate from the Do 335. *Sach-Nr* (Part number) gives the aircraft type (Do 335), while the first number of the second group (3) identifies the main assembly of the aircraft (tail, ailerons and flaps). The second and third numbers (3, 5) further break the part down to the individual component. *Werk-Nr* (works number) identifies the particular aircraft. *Hersteller:* identifies the manufacturer (hmv - Dornier at Friedrichshafen). Shown approximately full size.

Top: Do 335 A-02, VG+PH, shown after restoration in December 1975. **Above:** Do 335 A-07, has the last three digits to the aircraft's serial number painted in white atop the vertical fin. Apparently, only the first two preproduction aircraft (240101 and 240102) had their primary identification code painted to the outside of their airframes. The remaining eight preproduction aircraft, including 240107, deleted their codes from the airframe's exterior. It was, however, a permanent part of the aircraft's identification card carried inside the cockpit. **Left:** A close-up of the rear fuselage and tail of the Do 335 V9.

Right: Do 335 A-1, W.Nr. 240161, also known as the Do 335 M3 (which should not be confused with the Do 335 V3). This aircraft, captured by American troops at Oberpfaffenhofen, was selected for shipment to the United States. Upon arrival at Wright Field it received Foreign Equipment number FE-1012. It is believed the tailplane number (1/3), indicates the last digit of the serial number (240161) and the *Muster* (Model) number (3).

Above: An American Army Air Corps Lieutenant strikes a jaunty pose atop the tail of Do 335 A-03, W.Nr. 240103 at Oberpfaffenhofen. To the right may be seen an incomplete Do 335 A-12, W.Nr. 240123, while W.Nr. 240114, another A-12 two-seat trainer is in the background. It is interesting to note that the left aileron attached to the port wing of the aircraft in the foreground has been correctly painted in the prescribed camouflage pattern, but the wing was unpainted. **Right:** Another view of Do 335 V9. This particular Arrow served as the principal prototype for the Do 335 A-0 and A-1 series.

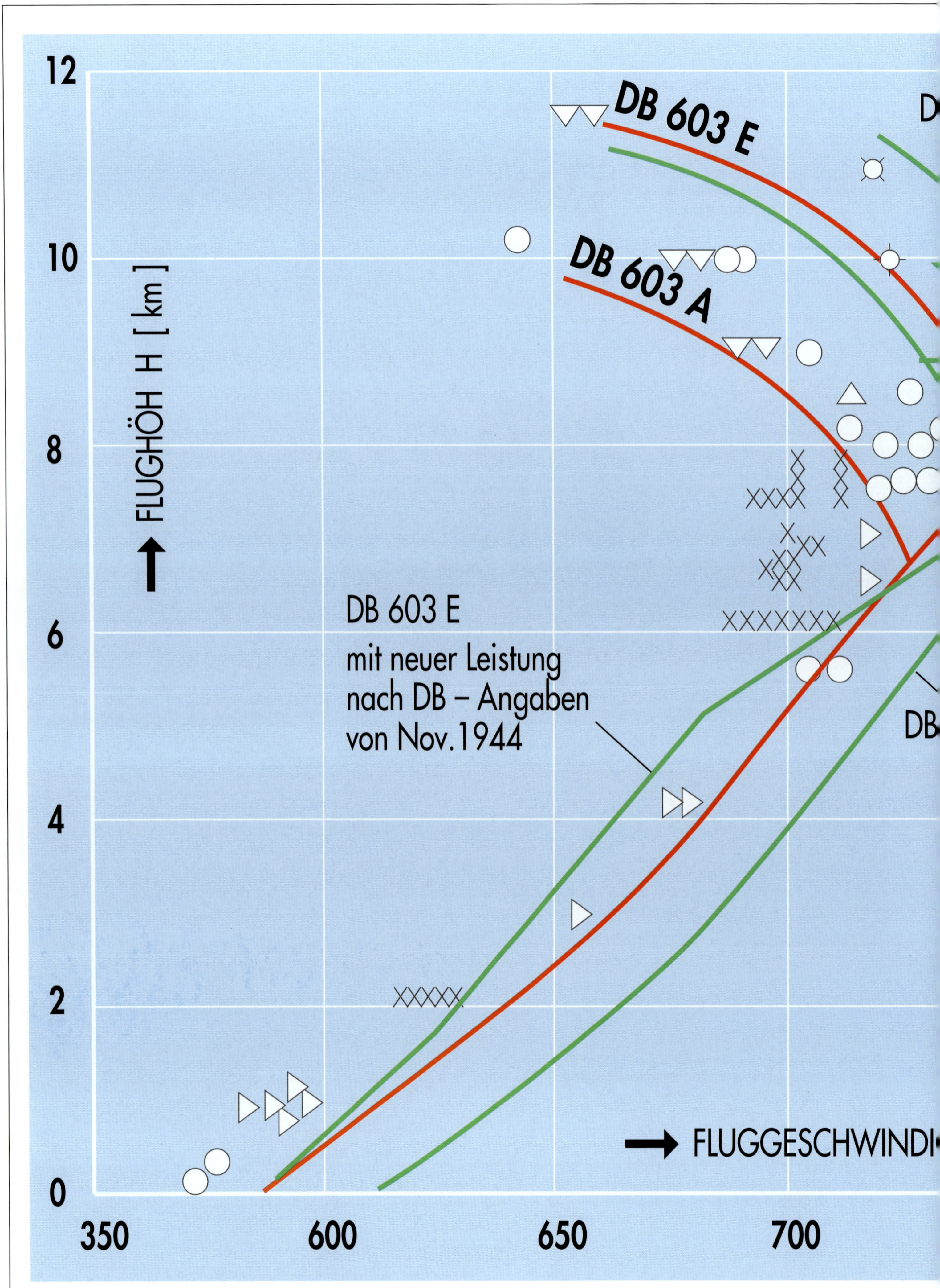

DB 603 E
DB 603 A
DB 603 E
mit neuer Leistung
nach DB – Angaben
von Nov.1944
FLUGHÖH H [km]
FLUGGESCHWINDI
12
10
8
6
4
2
0
350
600
650
700

Appendix 3

TECHNICAL DESCRIPTION, SPECIFICATIONS, PERFORMANCE & PRIZES OF WAR

By Thomas H. Hitchcock

The Do 335 represented a significant departure from previous construction techniques. This was necessitated by the unusual tandem engine layout of the aircraft. The principal features are described in the following description.

Fuselage

The fuselage was an all-metal monocoupe structure. The top of the fuselage is cut away for the cockpit canopy, the fuselage fuel tank access panel and the rear engine doors. The lower section is cut away for the nose gear doors, the fuselage bay doors and the radiator ducts. The sides of the fuselage, together with a number of heavy longerons form in effect a pair of plate web girders with strength to resist the longitudinal bending imposed by the vertical tail loads, the weight of the two engines, the fuselage fuel and lubricant tanks as well as the fuselage bay racks (for bombs, extra fuel or cameras). The sides are braced together to resist bending imposed by lateral loads, by the floor of the cabin and fuel tank bay and by a "V"bracing of tubes below the rear engine.

At any fuselage section there are four main longerons which, together with the skin forming the sides of the fuselage, resist vertical bending. There were also a number of heavy longitudinal stringers which support the skin. The two lower main longerons are continuous from the front bulkhead to the center section spar and from the spar to the tail, but the function of the upper longerons was shared between different pairs along the length of the fuselage.

The center section spar is of similar design to the spars in the wings except that the rear plate web is replaced by a bracing of 2 x $1\frac{1}{2}$ x 1/8 inch "T" section members. Two $4\frac{1}{2}$ x $1\frac{1}{2}$ x 0.1 inch hat sections run spanwise along the inside of the upper side of the box and one along the lower. These are riveted over the tapered legs of the steel angles which carry the attachment bolts for the wings. A plate rib was located outside the fuselage skin proper over the section of the wing root.

The fuselage skin is 0.07 inch thick from the forward firewall to the forward firewall of the rear engine, and 0.05 inch thick from the front firewall of the rear engine aft to the frame located at the rear radiator. From the frame at the rear radiator to the rear propeller, the skin thickness was 0.04 inch.

Wing

The wings were of a trapezoidal plan form with a thirteen degree sweepback on leading edge and blunt wing tips. The wings are detachable and

Do 335 M1/DB 603 A, ASbzw E

▷ DW – Test (DB 603A)

△ Test unit of the OKL (DB 603 As)

▽ E.Stelle Rechlin (DB 603 E)
E. Nr. 2014/TB 2310/Nr. 4

Test condition as of December 1944
with aircraft flying weight of 8.3 tons

Do 335 M3/DB 603 E

○ Test report Octbober BB Nr.324/44

60 gr GM 1

120 gr GM 1

Do335 M8/DB 603 A
XDW test flight

DORNIER 335 A-0, A-1, B-SERIES AIRCRAFT				
Number	Stamm-kennzeichen	Tailplane Nr.	Series	Remarks
240101	VG+PG	101	A-0	Preproduction aircraft A-01. Probably destroyed in bombing.
240102	VG+PH	102	A-0	Preproduction aircraft A-02. Captured and brought to USA. Became Bu Aer No. 121447.
240103	VG+PI	103	A-0	Preproduction aircraft A-03. Captured intact at Oberpfaffenhofen but not airworthy.
240104	VG+PK	104	A-0	Preproduction aircraft A-04. Flown to Rechlin via Dessau Dec. 5-22, 1944.
240105	VG+PL	105	A-0	Preproduction aircraft A-05. Flown to Rechlin then returned to Dornier at Mengen.
240106	VG+PM	106	A-0	Preproduction aircraft A-06. Probably destroyed by bombing.
240107	VG+PN	107	A-0	Preproduction aircraft A-07. Under test in September 1944.
240108	VG+PO	108	A-0	Preproduction aircraft A-08. Crashed at Donefeld Dec.24, 1944.
240109	VG+PP	109	A-0	Preproduction aircraft A-09. Fuselage broken January 15, 1945. Crashed on icy runway.
240110	VG+PQ	110	A-0	Preproduction aircraft A-010. Probably destroyed in bombing.
240111	RP+UA	111	A-1/A-12	Modified as 2-seat trainer. Also listed as A-11 in several reports.
240112	RP+UB	112	A-1/A-12	Modified as 2-seat trainer. Captured at Oberpfaffenhofen. Shipped to England after war.
240113	RP+UC	113	A-1	Captured in damaged condition at Bindlach near Nürnberg .
240114	RP+UD	114	A-1/A-12	Modified as 2-seat trainer. Captured at Oberpfaffenhofen but not airworthy.
240115	RP+UE	115	A-1	No details known.
240116	RP+UF	116	A-1	No details known.
240117	RP+UG	117	A-1	Flown at Rechlin by *Oblt.* Joachim Eisermann on October 12, 1944.
240118	RP+UH	118	A-1	No details known.
240119	RP+UI	119	A-1/A-12	Modified as 2-seat trainer. Captured at Oberpfaffenhofen. Not airworthy.
240120	RP+UK	120	A-1/A-12	Modified as 2-seat trainer. Modifications incomplete.
240121	RP+UL	121	A-1/A-12	Modified as 2-seat trainer. Modifications incomplete.
240122	RP+UM	122	A-1/A-12	Modified as 2-seat trainer. Modifications incomplete.
240123	RP+UN	123	A-1/A-12	Modified as 2-seat trainer. Modifications incomplete.
240161		1/3	A-1	Believed to be the M3. Captured and brought to USA. Became FE-1012
240162		2/1	A-1	Believed to be the M1. Captured at Oberpfaffenhofen. Not airworthy.
240163		3/7	A-1	Believed to be the M7. Captured at Oberpfaffenhofen. Not airworthy.
240164			A-1	} Assembled at Friedrichshafen . No further details known.
240165			A-1	
240241			B-?	} Incomplete airframes found at Friedrichshafen. Probably B-1,B-2 or B-3 aircraft.
240242			B-?	
240243			B-?	
240244			B-?	
240245			B-?	
240246			B-?	
240247			B-?	
240248			B-?	
240249			B-?	

Note: *Stammkennzeichen* (Primary identification) codes ending in the letter 'J' (e.g. VG+PJ and RP+UJ) were not favored and not used by Dornier for the Do 335. However, many other German military aircraft did freely use the letter 'J' as the fourth letter.

are of all-metal stressed-skin structure built around a single box spar. Variable chamber flaps are located inboard of the ailerons and the deicing of the leading edge is provided.

The box spar had its center at 33 percent of the chord from the leading edge of the root. The spar is of dural with steel root fittings. The spar is reduced in width, depth and the sections of its components until 42 inches from the wing tip. The spar was attached to the fuselage at the root by thirty-three 9/16 inch diameter bolts at 2¾ inch pitch passing through the short legs of steel 1½ x 5 x 3/8 inch angles whose outer legs are tapered in thickness and riveted to the flanges and webs of the box. Forward of the spar, the upper skin was 0.06 inch thick. Over a span of 36 inches outboard from the root, the wing had an airfoil section of the sharp nose form designed to control the prop wash over the tailplane to improve low speed maneuverability and to diffuse stall characteristics by minimizing buffeting. The nose of this section is made up from welded steel plate 0.045 inch thick. The detachable wing tip consisted of 0.035 inch skin stiffened by two "Z" section ribs with a 1 x ¾ x 0.085 inch angle round the inboard edge. It was attached to the wing by bolts. The wing root was enclosed by a fairing secured by a cable passing through hooks on the fuselage.

Flaps

The flaps were all-metal of one piece and of the camber-changing type. Each flap had a metal skin of 0.02 inch thickness attached to plate ribs at eight-inch pitch. The spar was a plate 0.04 inch thick with its edges turned over and riveted to the skin and was placed 25 percent of the chord from the leading edge. The flap was mounted on three hinges on brackets attached to the ribs and was actuated by a hydraulic jack located inside the wing.

Ailerons

The ailerons were of similar construction as the flaps and were mounted on three brackets. The ailerons were operated by a system of 1½ inch diameter dural push-pull tubes and bell cranks. An additional link connected with the flap was introduced so that the ailerons were dropped when the flaps were lowered. The metal trim tab was operated by a system of shafts and universal joints from the lateral trim control in the cockpit.

Tail

The tail assembly was all-metal stressed skin construction except for the leading edge of the dorsal fin which was wood housing the radio antenna. Deicing was provided to the leading edges of the horizontal stabilizers. Rudders and elevators were both aerodynamically and mass-balanced.

Each side of the tailplane was based on two spars. There were three ribs each and the skin was 0.035 inch thick and was in three pieces, the "D" nose and the upper and lower

Continued on p. 176

DORNIER 335 PROPOSED AND PRODUCTION SERIES

Series	Primary Mission	Front Engine	Rear Engine	Remarks
A-0	Single-Seat Day Fighter	DB 603 A-2	DB 603 QA-2	Ten preproduction aircraft completed.
A-1	Single-Seat Day Fighter	DB 603 E-1	DB 603 QE-1	Approximately ten aircraft completed.
A-2	Single-Seat Bomber	DB 603 G	DB 603 G	None completed.
A-3	Single-Seat Zerstörer	DB 603 G	DB 603 G	None completed.
A-4	Single-Seat Reconnaissance	DB 603 E	DB 603 E	None completed.
A-5	Single-Seat Day Fighter	Jumo 213	Jumo 213	None completed.
A-6	Two-Seat Night Fighter	DB 603 E-1	DB 603 QE-1	One prototype (V10/M10) completed. No production.
A-7	Single-Seat Bomber	Jumo 213	Jumo 213	None completed.
A-8	Single-Seat Zerstörer	Jumo 213	Jumo 213	Two prototypes (V6, V7) Burnt out prior to capture of Mengen.
A-9	Single-Seat Reconnaissance	Jumo 213	Jumo 213	None completed.
A-10	Two-Seat Trainer	Jumo 213	Jumo 213	None completed.
A-11	Two-Seat Trainer	DB 603 A-2	DB 603 A-2	Two prototypes (M11, M12) completed.
A-12	Two-Seat Trainer	DB 603 E-1	DB 603 E-1	Eight aircraft completed or under construction.
B-1	Single-Seat Day Fighter	DB 603 E-1	DB 603 QE-1	Two prototypes (M15, M16) under construction.
B-2	Single-Seat Zerstörer	DB 603 E-1	DB 603 QE-1	Two prototypes (M13, M14) completed. Others incomplete.
B-3	Single-Seat Zerstörer	DB 603 LA	DB 603 LA	Three prototypes (M18, M19,M20) under construction.
B-4	Single-Seat Reconnaissance	DB 603 LA	DB 603 LA	None completed. To use the Heinkel long-span wing.
B-5	Two-Seat Trainer	DB 603 E-1	DB 603 E-1	None completed. Second M11 possibly planned prototype.
B-6	Two-Seat Night Fighter	DB 603 E-1	DB 603 E-1	Two prototypes (M17, M21) assigned. M17 completed by French.
B-7	Two-Seat High Altitude Night Fighter	DB 603 LA	DB 603 LA	One prototype (M22) assigned. To use laminar flow wing.
B-8	Two-Seat High Altitude Night Fighter	DB 603 LA	DB 603 LA	One prototype (M23) incomplete with Heinkel long-span.

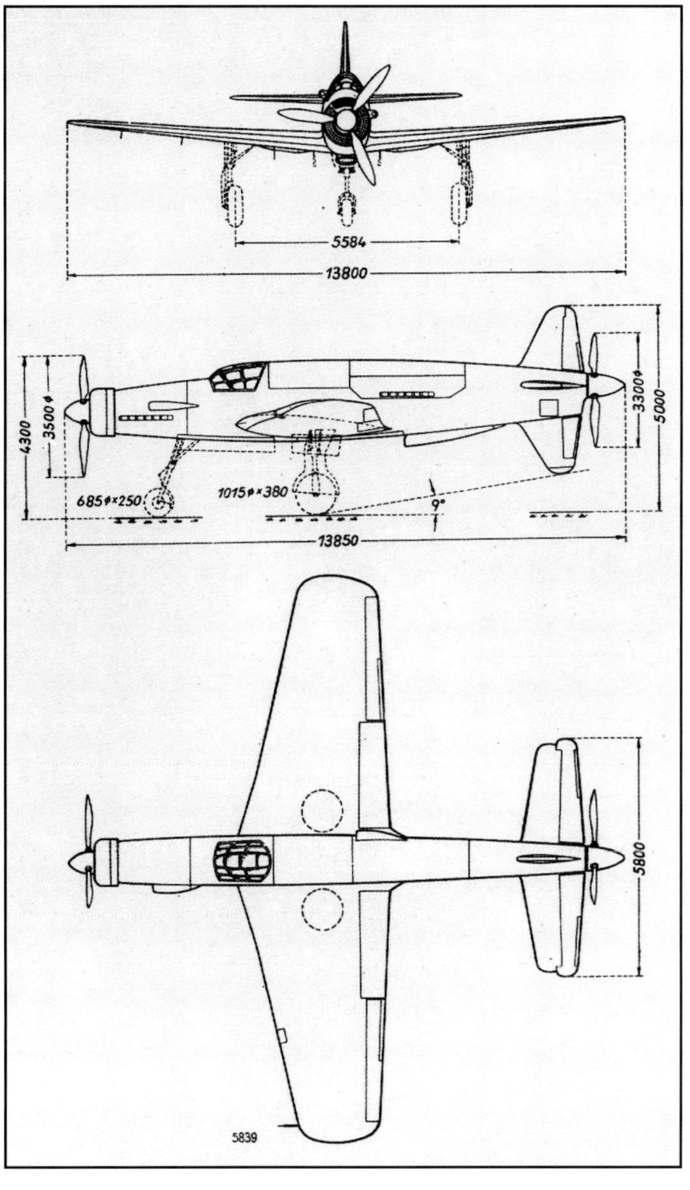

Below: Close-up of the pilot's ejection seat of the Do 335 M13 showing a number of changes from earlier versions of the Arrow.

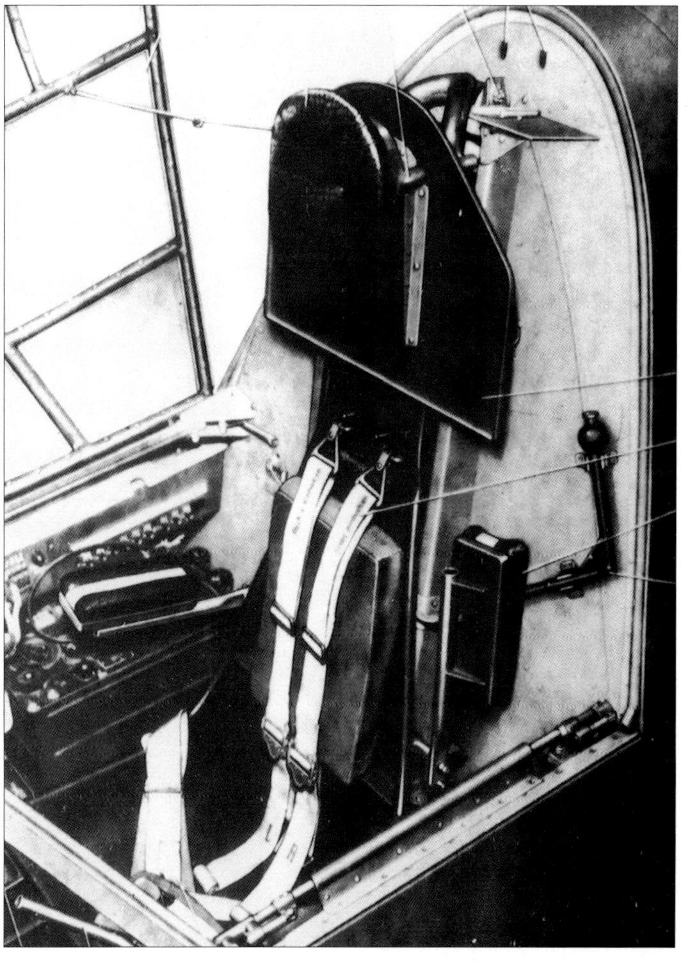

Above Left: A close-up of the nose gear from the Do 335 V9 showing the 685 x 250 wheel with mud guard. **Above Right:** Another close-up of the same prototype showing the main gear assembly and the large 1015 x 380 main wheel. **Below:** Various detail views of the extended and retracted undercarriage system for the Do 335.

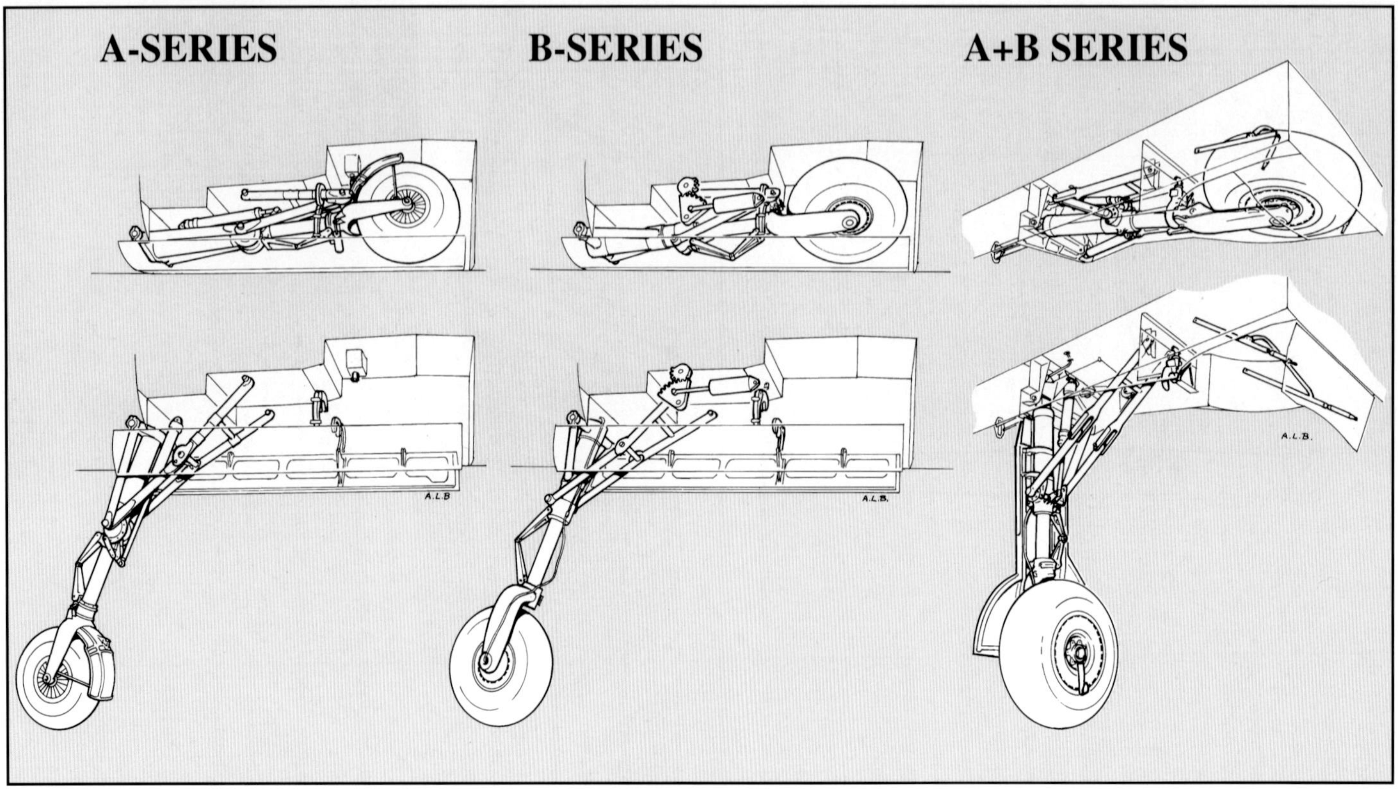

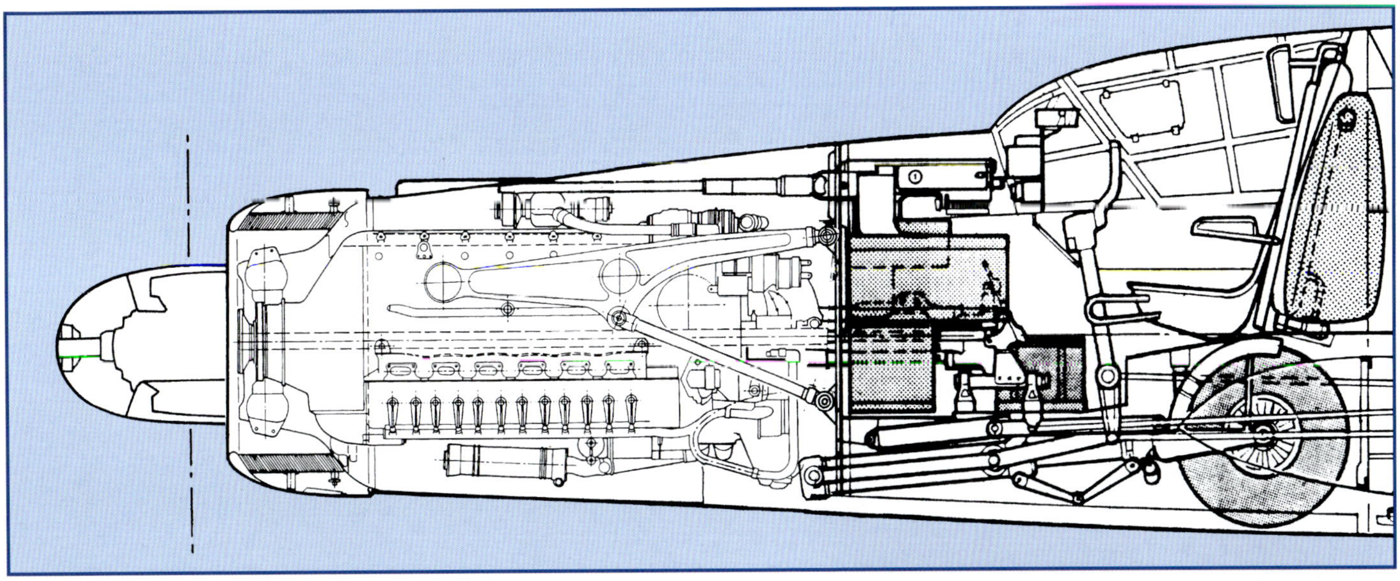

Above: A sectional view showing how the Junkers Jumo 213 A would have been installed in the Do 335. One prototype, the Do 335 V7, and possibly the V6, was sent to Junkers at Dessau during the summer of 1944 to switch their nose-mounted DB 603s for the Jumo 213. It is unclear if Junkers had also planned to test the Jumo 213 in the rear position. However, the five A-series versions (A-5, A-7, A-8, A-9 and A-10) earmarked for the Jumo 213...which were never built...would have carried this engine in both locations. **Right:** A close-up of the tail section to the Do 335 V7 taken at Mengen airfield after the war. **Below:** The open cowl of the Do 335 V9 showing the compact nature of the engine compartment behind the large annular nose radiator. In this view of the port side, the supercharger opening is shown just below the engine bearer arm.

Continued from p. 172

panels between the spars. Each is attached by rivets to the spar flanges. The inside was accessible before the root and tip ribs were fitted. The tip is separate and is attached by screws to the tip rib. The inboard end of each spar carries steel fittings for two bolts by which it is attached to the fuselage. The forward attachment bolts have slots and serrated plates so that the tailplane incidence can be adjusted on the ground. The tailplane root is enclosed by a fairing secured by screws. The dorsal and ventral fins are of similar construction apart from the wooden leading edge of the upper unit. The tip of the lower unit is strengthened and hinged to the bottom of an oleo strut located inside the fin designed to act as a safety skid.

The rudder had a single spar consisting of a plate with edges flanged and riveted to the skin placed at 20 percent of the chord from the leading edge. Plate ribs with dished lightening holes are spaced at 6 inch pitch and the metal skin is 0.02 inch thick. The elevators are of similar construction to the rudders. The dorsal and ventral rudders and both elevators cannot be directly connected because of the rear propeller drive shaft. Instead, they are linked to welded steel cranks on counter shafts controlled from the cockpit via 1¼ inch diameter push-pull dural tubes.

PRIZES OF WAR

When American forces captured the main Dornier factory at Friedrichshafen in May 1945, no complete Do 335s were found. Instead, only burnt-out wrecks were left behind in compliance with German orders to destroy aircraft likely to fall into Allied hands. However, when American troops arrived at Dornier's Oberpfaffenhofen facility, they discovered a number of complete Do 335s in addition to many additional aircraft under construction or repair. As mentioned elsewhere in this book, because of increasing Allied bombing it was decided to transfer preproduction, and initial series production of the Do 335 to Oberpfaffenhofen. It is unclear if orders were received to destroy these aircraft prior to capture, or if they were received, they were simply ignored. In any case, the Americans were delighted to find the facilities and aircraft more-or-less intact, especially since the Do 335 was high on the Allies' priority list.

After a thorough inventory had been completed, American officers determined to take the two best Dornier Do 335s back to the States. In addition to these airworthy examples, a number of spare parts were also secured for transfer.

The Americans, led by Col. Harold E. Watson, had selected a Do 335 A-1 and Do 335 A-02 for shipment to the United States. These aircraft were serviced and repainted with provisional American insignia for the ferry flight to the French port of Cherbourg. At Cherbourg, the British aircraft carrier, HMS Reaper, was waiting to take a number of captured German aircraft to the States. Owing to the tight schedule, dictated by the sailing date of the British carrier, and limited staff, Col. Watson decided that one of the American Do 335s (Do 335 A-1) had to be flown by

Below: Dornier employees install a reconditioned DB 603 QE-1 into the rear engine bay of a Do 335 A-1, during the American occupation of the Oberpfaffenhofen facility. Thanks to the efficient engine support structure, engine changes were accomplished without great difficulty.

Above: Photographed in France prior to the aircraft being placed aboard the British carrier, HMS Reaper, is Do 335 A-1, W.Nr. 240161. This aircraft had been flown to France by German test pilot, Hans Pedell in the company of an American pilot flying Do 335 A-02. Interestingly, the aircraft is juxtaposed to the remains of four German jets including no less than three He 162s and an Me 262.

a former German test pilot, *Hauptman* Hans Padell, who had been stationed at Rechlin. The other Do 335 (Do 335 A-02) was to be piloted by an American. Because of the distance, the ferry flight was to leave Oberpfaffenhofen, fly to Neubiberg near Munich for refueling, then fly on to Roth *bei* Nürnberg for another refueling for the final leg to Cherbourg.

Upon arrival at Cherbourg on June 17, 1945, the two Dorniers were assigned aircraft numbers 8 and 35 (for Do 335 A-1 and A-02 respectively), and became part of the forty German aircraft shipped to the United States aboard HMS Reaper on July 20, 1945. In the meantime, the British became interested in acquiring airworthy examples of the Do 335. Under the terms of reciprocal arrangements, British intelligence officers visited the US Zone of Occupation and selected two flyable Do 335s for transfer to Britain.

After an eight-day voyage, HMS Reaper docked at the port of Newark, New Jersey. One of the Do 335s off-loaded was to be given to the US Navy (aircraft 35) while the other (aircraft 8) was made ready for a test flight preparatory to being flown directly to Freeman Field, Indiana. Jack Woolams, Chief test pilot for Bell Aircraft, took the Do 335 A-1 up for a test spin but, he quickly returned when the rear engine over-heated ... a problem that had plagued the Do 335 from the beginning. With this incident, it was decided to transport the Do 335 to Freeman Field by truck. The Navy assigned USN Bureau of Aeronautics number BuAer 121447 to their Do 335 and transported this aircraft to the Navy's Tactical Test Division at NAS Patuxent River where it was formally received in December 1945.

Meanwhile, the Army's Do 335 A-1 had arrived at Freeman Field where it received Foreign Equipment number FE-1012. By May 17, 1946, restoration was 75-percent complete but three months later it was still not ready for flight tests because its Daimler-Benz engines were delayed in overhaul.

On March 31, 1947, the US Navy had stricken their Do 335 off the Tactical Test Division's roster because of its continued unserviciability. It was later transferred to NAS Norfolk where it remained parked in outside storage until 1961 when it was offered to the Smithsonian Institution. In the meantime, the Air Corps' Do 335 had been retired due to a lack of funding and interest. Its final disposition is not fully known, but interestingly the wings of this aircraft mysteriously found their way to the National Air and Space Museum's storage and restoration facility at Silver Hill, Maryland where they were placed alongside the fuselage of Do 335 A-02.

In May 1974, the Director of the Deutsches Museum in Munich, Germany, made a formal request for temporary loan of a German aircraft to coincide with the opening of the museum's new extension. The aircraft selected was the Do 335. Because the NASM could not undertake the restoration at this time, it was fortunate that the aircraft's maker was not only still in existence, but were willing to undertake full restoration of the aircraft under the sponsorship of the Deutsches Museum. By agreement, the Dornier was to remain in Germany on display for several years before returning to the United States. On October 7, 1974 the Dornier was loaded onto a flatbed trailer for its journey to JF Kennedy Airport where it was cautiously stowed within a Lufthansa Boeing 747F cargo carrier for a direct flight to Frankfurt on October 10, 1974.

The final leg of the flight to Oberpfaffenhofen was carried out using a Lockheed C-130. By July 1975, the Dornier Arrow had been completely disassembled so that preservation and restoration could finally begin. Late in September 1975, the aircraft was reassembled and ready for painting. The cockpit had 31 missing instruments which

had to be acquired from several sources and, in addition, a number of rotted wooden components were replaced by newly fabricated aluminum parts. Finally, in December 1975, restoration was complete and the aircraft was ready for exhibition. After many years in Germany, in the early 1990s the Dornier Arrow was finally returned to the United States for permanent display by the NASM.

The French *Armée de l'Air* first became interested in the Do 335 in a report from the 5th *Bureau* dated February 10, 1945 authored by Lieutenant-Colonel Badré to the 3rd and 4th *Bureau* of the EMGAA headquartered in Paris. But, it was not until April 27, 1945 when elements of the *Division Blindéc* of the *1er Armée* moved in and occupied the Dornier airfield at Mengen. The French discovered three Do 335s at this location which included the burnt remains of the Do 335 V7, the Do 335 M14 in maintenance, and the Do 335 M17 in final construction. The French lost little time is dispatching *Capitain* Mirles and his MIST (*Mission d' Information Scientifique et Technique*) to Mengen early in May 1945. The Do 335 M14 was dismantled for transport to France where it was reassembled at the *Centre d'Essais en Vol* (CEV) at Bretigny on August 5, 1945. In the afternoon of August 7, 1945, two ground taxiing tests were carried out by *Col.* Badré without incident. In the morning the next day, *Col.* Badré took the M14 aloft after a take-off run of 3,280 feet (1000 m) and climbed uneventfully to an altitude of 3,280 feet (1000 m). After testing the aircraft for some minutes Badré was lining up for his landing approach when the aircraft began violently vibrating with smoke filling the cockpit. Shutting down the rear engine had no effect so pilot Badré closed the front engine and deadsticked the aircraft heavily onto the runway bursting the right tire. With no hydraulics and no brakes, the aircraft left the runway and collided with a parked B-26. Inspecting the damage, Badré noted that the front engine had to be changed and repairs to the wing had to be carried out and the right undercarriage and ventral fin had to be replaced. In mid September 1945, the M14 was transferred to the SNCASO factory at Surennes near Paris by *Sectear de l'Air No 3 - Team Nord.* Following repairs, the M14 was delivered to the CEV on June 3, 1946. Over the next 7 months numerous ground tests were conducted. In February 1947 the three MK 103s were installed with ballast in place of ammunition. But, on February 24, 1947, the M14 experienced a brake and tire fire and several weeks later problems with the rear propeller arose. However, on March 13, 1947 with *Capitaine* Receveau at the controls, the M14 was again airborne. Over the next year a total of nine hours of flying time was accumulated before, on March 5, 1948, the test program was canceled. Two additional flights were conducted in May and June 1948 by which time the M14 had flown for a total of 11 hours 25 minutes.

Above: The Do 335 M14, still in its original German insignia, photographed during July 1945 at Lyon Bron awaiting delivery the French engineers at Arsenal in Villeurbanne.

Meanwhile, after 25 months of work by French and German teams, the Do 335 M17 was completed in Mengen and flown for the first time by *Capitaine* Receveau on May 29, 1947. The aircraft was flown directly to the CEV by Receveau but with the back seat occupied by a deer which had been shot that morning! The transfer flight was flown at 14,763 feet (4500 m) at an average speed of 435 mph (700 km/h) without incident. By November 27, 1948 the two-seat M17 had logged 6 hours 30 minutes, but on this day a hydraulic problem caused the right undercarriage to prematurely retract during taxiing. It was decided not to repair the M17, but to use the aircraft to test the ejection seat and the explosive charges to jettison the rear propeller together with the dorsal fin and rudder. These tests were less than successful and the Do 335 M17 was eventually scrapped in March 1949.

As recounted earlier, the British were also interested in testing the Do 335 and, like the Americans, they selected two examples of the Arrow for shipment to Britain. The first aircraft, Do 335 A-12, W.Nr. 240112, was captured intact at Oberpfaffenhofen. It was subsequently flown to Neubiberg where it

Above and Below: HMS Reaper aircraft 35 (top) and 8 (below), respectively Do 335 A-02 and A-1, are hoisted aboard the carrier for their journey to the States.

was handed over to the British Intelligence organization receiving Air Ministry number AM223. On September 7, 1945, it was flown by Squadron Leader McCarthy from Neubiberg to Strasbourg and Reims. On September 8, 1945, it flew the last leg of its journey to RAE Farnborough by way of RAF Manston. A routine test flight occurred on October 1, 1945 but then sat on the ground until January 15, 1946 when it made another test flight. Three days later, on January 18, 1946 it made its third and final test flight with Group Captain Alan F. Hards, the CO of Experimental Flying at Farnborough, at the controls. Not long after take-off the rear engine over heated causing a rear fuselage fire which burned through the control cables causing the ensuing fatal crash. The second Arrow acquired by the British was Do 335 A-1, W.Nr. 240 16?, which was obtained from the Americans at Neubiberg receiving Air Ministry number AM 225. Flight Lieutenant Taylor took off for Reims on September 7, 1945. But, at Reims it developed a service problem, which forced the Dornier to stay over for almost three months. Finally, on December 13, 1945 it took off for Merville, but coming in to land, the pilot was unable to extend the nose gear. Although the resulting crash landing caused only superficial damage, it was not repaired owing to a lack of spares and the aircraft was scrapped.

Do 335 A-1, W.Nr. 240161, 1/3
HMS Reaper Aircraft 8
USAAF test number: FE-1012

Brought to the United States and retained by the USAAF for test and evaluation at Wright Field. It received Foreign Equipment number FE-1012 (later replaced by T2-1012). Due to a lack of funding and interest, it was not flown at Wright Field. The aircraft's wings eventually went to the National Air and Space Museum at Silver Hill, MD, where they were paired with the fuselage from A-02. The remainder of the aircraft was apparently scrapped.

Do 335 A-02, W.Nr. 240102, VG+PH
HMS Reaper Aircraft 35
USN Bu Aer 121447

Brought to the United States and assigned to the US Navy. It was delivered to the Technical Test Division at NAS Patuxent River. Due to a lack of spares, funding and interest, no flight tests were undertaken. It was stricken off the roster at the end of March 1947, but remained in prolonged outside storage until it was given to the National Air and Space Museum in 1961. Currently restored and in storage at Silver Hill, MD awaiting permanent display by the NASM.

Do 335 A-12, W.Nr. 240112
British Air Ministry number AM223

This aircraft was the second production two-seat trainer completed by Dornier at Oberpfaffenhofen and given to the British by the Americans. It was taken to England and test flown a number of times before being destroyed in a crash following a rear engine fire which claimed the life of Group Captain Alan F. Hards in January 1946.

Do 335 A-1, W.Nr. 24016?
British Air Ministry number AM225

A standard production aircraft captured intact and reconditioned by the Americans at Oberpfaffenhofen before being handed over to the British for transfer to England. However, the aircraft had experienced mechanical difficulties on one occasion and a landing accident on another while in France. Because repairs were difficult owing to a lack of spares and interest slowly evaporated, the aircraft was eventually scrapped without ever leaving France.

Do 335 M14, W.Nr. 230014, RP+UQ
French Aircraft No. 1

This development aircraft was the second example of the B-2 *Zerstörer* class, which was captured intact by French forces when the occupied Dornier's Mengen facility at the end of April 1945. Taken to France by road and thoroughly recondition, it was test flown a number of times. It had sustained a crash and several serviceability problems before the test program was canceled in 1948. It was scrapped in March 1949.

Do 335 M17, W.Nr. 240313
French Aircraft No. 2

Captured in an incomplete state by French troops at Dornier's Mengen facility in late April 1945. This development aircraft was the first two-seat night fighter of the B-6 series. Together with German personnel, the French were able to finish the aircraft and transfer it to France for testing. It was flown a number of times, but late in November it crashed during taxiing trials and was not repaired owing to the extensive damage and a lack of spares. It was finally scrapped in March 1949.

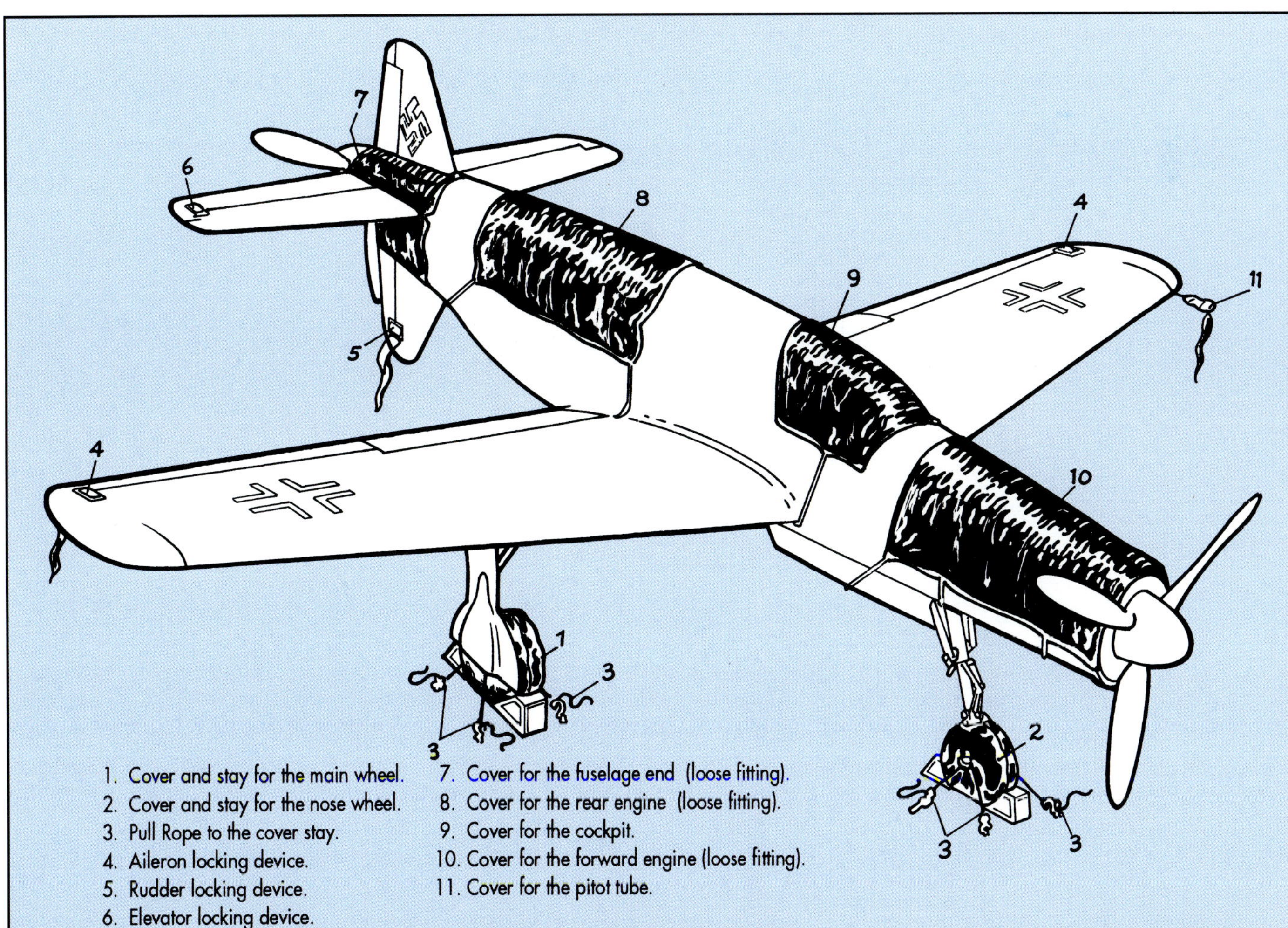

WEIGHTS, SPECIFICATION AND PERFORMANCE STATISTICS

Type		Do 335 A-0	Do 335 A-6
Role		Preproduction fighter	Night fighter
Sealing		1	2
Wing span	m (ft-in)	13.80 (45 - 3¹/₄)	13.80 (45 - 3¹/₄)
Wing area	m² (ft²)	38.5 (414.4)	38.5 (414.4)
Length	m (ft-in)	13.85 (45 - 4¹/₄)	13.85 (45 - 4¹/₄)
Height	m (ft-in)	5.00 (16 - 4³/₄)	5.00 (16 - 4³/₄)
Engines	fore (aft)	2 x DB 603 A-2 (DB 603 QA-2)	2 x DB 603 E-1 (DB 603 QE-1)
Takeoff HP ea.	PS (hp)	1,750	1,800
Propellers	fore (aft)	VDM Ø 3.5m (VDM Ø 3.3m)	VDM/Me P 6 (VDM Ø 3.3m)
Fuel		B4 (87 octane)	C3 (96 octane)
MW powerboost	Ltr (US gal)		2 x 75 (2 x 19.8)
Electronics		Fu 25a, FuG 125, FuG 16ZY	FuG 15, Ei V 15, FuG 25a, FuG, FuG 120, FuG 220 (later 218), FuG 350, FuG 101A
Empty weight	kg (lb)		6,830 (15, 101)
Equipped weight	kg (lb)	6,530 (14,396)	7,830 (17,262)
Internal fuel	Ltr (US gal)	1,850 (489)	1,720 (454)
Loaded weight	kg (lb)	9,510 (20,966)	10,100 (22,266)
Maximum Speed at sea level	km/h (mph)	580 (360)	622 (386)
Maximum speed at	km/h-km (mph-ft)	763 at 6.4 (477 at 21,000)	692 at 5.4 (430 at 17,717)
Economical cruising at	km/h-km (mph-ft)	472 at 6.0 (293 at 19,685)	415 at 5 (258 at 19,685)
Landing speed	km.h (mph)	175 (109)	190 (118)
Normal range	km (mi)	1,380 (857)	1,330 (826)
Maximum range	km (mi)	2,150 (1,336)	2,540 (1,578)
Climb to 6 km (19,685 ft)	min	10.0	11.8
Service ceiling	m (ft)	9,500 (31,168)	10,800 (35,433)
Armament		1 x MK 103 (70 rounds) engine 2 x MG 151 (200 rpg) cowl	1 x MK 103 (70 rounds) engine 2 x MG 151 (200 rpg) cowl
Rüstsätze (aux. apparatus)			1 x Schloss 502 A01 2 x 300 Ltr drop tanks

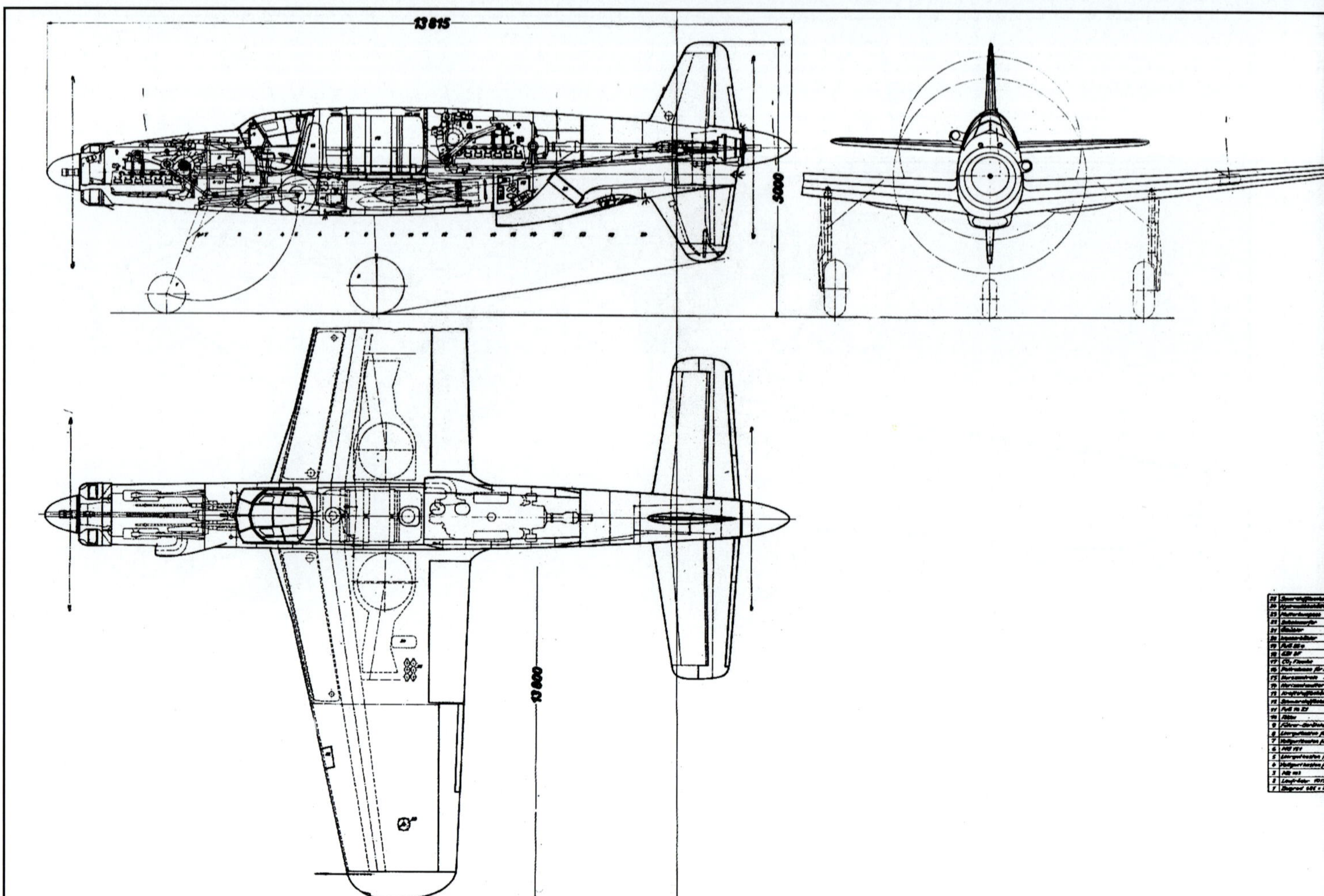

Do 335 B-2 Zerstörer 1 13.80 (45 - 3¹/₄) 38.5 (414.4) 13.85 (45 - 4¹/₄) 5.00 (16 - 4³/₄)	Do 435 C-1 Night fighter 2 13.80 (45 - 3¹/₄) 38.5 (414.4) 13.85 (45 - 4¹/₄) 5.60 (18 - 4³/₄)	He 535 A-1 Night fighter 2 13.80 (45 - 3¹/₄) 38.5 (414.4) 13.85 (43 - 11¹/₂) 5.60 (18 - 4³/₄)	Ju 635 A-0 Reconnaissance 3 27.45 (90 - 0¹/₄) 80.5 (866.5) 18.50 (60 - 8¹/₄) 5.00 (16 - 4³/₄)
2 x DB 603 E-1 (DB 603 QE-1) 1,800 VDM Ø 3.5m (VDM Ø 3.3m) C3 (96 octane)	2 x Jumo 222 A/B 2,500 VS Ø 3.5m (VS Ø 3.3m) B4 (87 octane)	2 x DB 603 LA (HeS 011A) 2,100 (1300 kp - 2,866 lb) VDM Ø 3.5m (VDM Ø 3.3m) B4 (87 octane)	4 x DB 603 E-1 (DB 603 QE-1) 1,800 VDM Ø 3.5m (VDM Ø 3.3m) C3 (96 octane)
2 x 75 (2 x 19.8)			2 x 209 (2 x 55.2)
FuG 15, Ei V 15, FuG 25a,	FuG 15, Ei V 15, FuG 25a, FuG 101A, FuG 120 FuG 220	FuG 15, Ei V 15, FuG 25a FuG 101A, FuG 120 FuG 218, FuG 350	FuG 10 GP or FuG 10P, FuG 16 Z or FuG 15 Z, FuB1 2, FuG 101, FuG 25a, FuG 217, FuG 200 (later 224)
	11,793 (26,000)		17,464 (38,500) 16,634 (4,394) 33,000 (72,751)
			539 (335) 720 at 6.5 (447 at 21,120)
			7,450 (4,629) 7,982 (4,960) 11,000 (36,089)
1 x MK 103 (70 rounds) engine 2 x MG 151 (200 rpg) cowl 2 x MK 103 (70 rounds) wings	1 x MK 103 (70 rounds) engine 2 x MG 151 (200 rpg) cowl	1 x MK 103 (70 rounds) engine 2 x MG 151 (200 rpg) cowl 2 x MG 108 oblique mounted	none
			2 x 300 kg marker bombs 2 x 1200 Ltr drop tanks

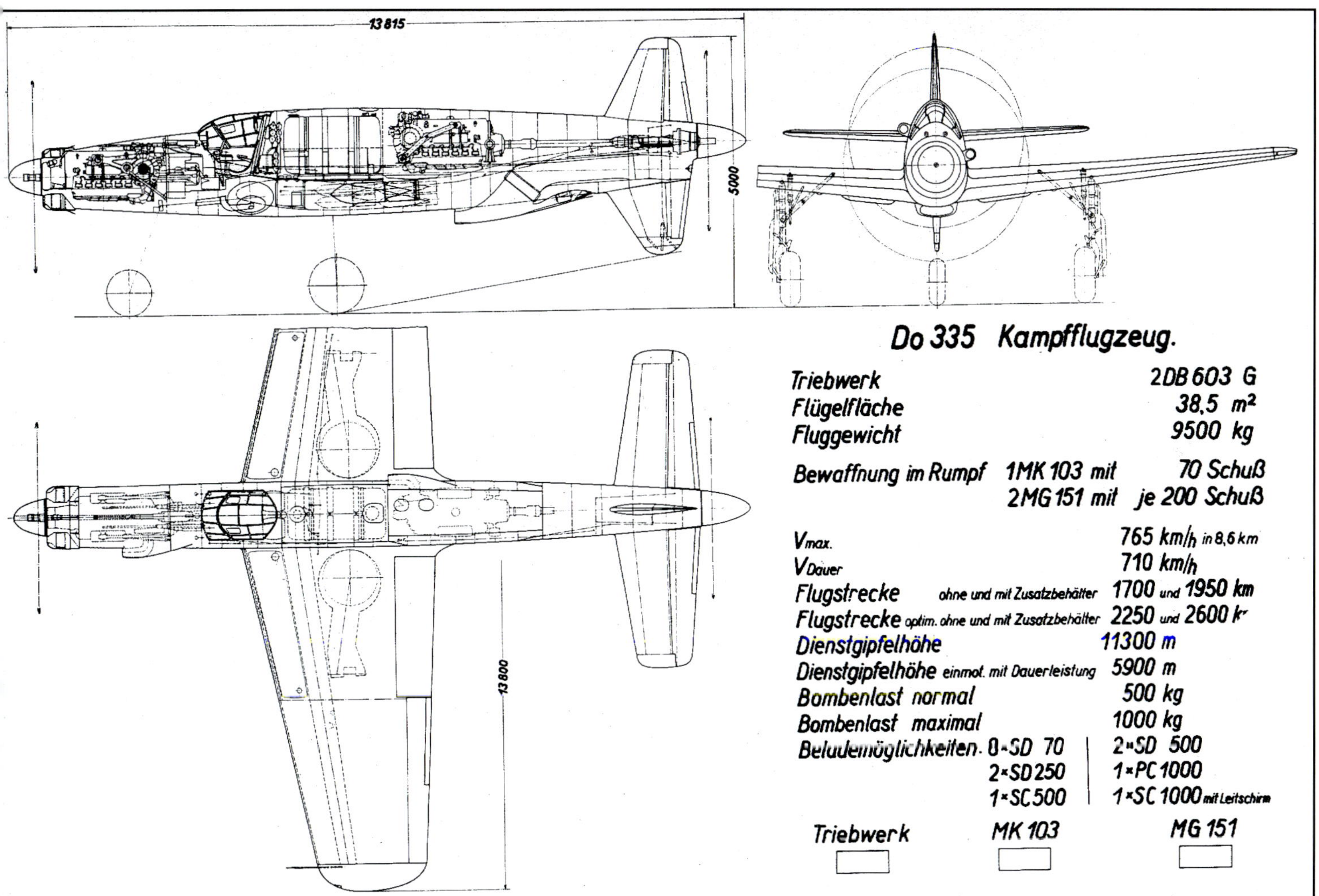

INDEX

PERSONALITIES

AIRCRAFT PHOTOGRAPHS

Dornier

Göppingen

Heinkel

Junkers

Ryan

AIRCRAFT ILLUSTRATIONS

CREDITS

PHOTOGRAPHIC – AGENCY

Animals-Animals: 105T; Candid-Aero Files: 10; Dornier AG: 6, 14, 20, 24B, 26B, 28T, 31, 32, 34, 53, 55B, 56, 61B, 69T, 70, 71T, 74, 75, 79, 89T, 89BR, 91T, 93, 110B, 158-159, 164-165, 168T, 168M; National Air and Space Museum: 100T, 179; The Picture Cube: 8; Public Record Office: 55T, 58M, 104B, 117T, 118T, 141M, 169B; Society of Experimental Test Pilots: 12; Teledyne-Ryan Aeronautical: 156-157; United States Air Force: 72B, 73T, 110T, 116T, 118B, 119, 140, 177; United States Army: 97T.

PHOTOGRAPHIC – INDIVIDUAL

Hideya Ando: 16B, 17, 18B, 19T; Paul Badré: 122B, 123, 124, 175M, 178; Adrian P. Bishop: 141T; Philippe Couderchon: 126, 127, 128, 129ML, 129MR, 129B, 130, 136M, 137M, 137B, 181; Peter W. Cohausz: 85, 86T, 87, 88, 90, 91BL, 91MR, 91BR, 92B; Eddie J. Creek: 38, 39, 45, 50, 52, 59, 110B; James V. Crow: 60T, 95T, 96B, 97B, 105B, 106M, 106B, 108T, 111TL, 111B, 112, 113, 122T, 169M, 170MB; Jeffrey L. Ethell (†): 134T; Edgar Deigan: 180T, 180MT; Kenneth Francella: 108M; Manfred Griehl: 106T; Udo E. Hafner: 44B; Thomas H. Hitchcock: 16T, 18T, 18M, 19B, 21, 22, 23, 25, 26T, 27B, 28B, 29, 30B, 33T, 44M, 62, 63T, 64, 65T, 71B, 95B, 100BL, 109T, 141B, 144, 163; John H. Kuehnert: 63B, 66, 67, 68; Theo Lederer: 92T; Hans-Werner Lerche: 78; F. Louvat: 58T, 125, 136T, 137T, 138; Richard P. Lutz, Jr.: 36, 48, 51, 54, 57, 65B, 86B, 89BL, 94B, 100BR, 101, 104T, 111TR, 167, 173, 174, 175B; J. Mutin: 180B; Heinz J. Nowarra (†): 24T, 27T, 30T, 152, 169T; Merle C. Olmsted: 94T, 107, 108B; R. Receveau: 129T; Hans Redemann (†): 69B, 80-82; Jürgen Rosenstock: 77; Günter Sengfelder: 162; Steven Sheflin: 60B, 76, 176; William L. Swisher: 61T, 72T, 96T, 109B; Richard Tyson: 109M; Maj.Gen. Harold E. Watson (†): 73B.

DRAWING AND ILLUSTRATION

John Amendola: Jacket, 114; Arthur L. Bentley: 46,47,98, 99,113, 119, 120-121, 132, 133, 174; Dornier AG: 53, 84, 107, 139T, 145B, 163, 173, 182, 183; Thomas H. Hitchcock: 44, 101, 155; Steve Hussey: 11, 38, 79, 102B, 136B, 145T, 145M, 153, 166, 170-171, 175, 181; David Pentland: 144, 148T; Sonny Schug: 35, 42, 43, 102T, 154, 160, 161; Thomas A. Tullis: 39, 40, 41, 83, 127, 143, 146, 147B, 148B, 149, 150, 151; Keith Wookcock: 29, 32, 33, 135, 142, 147T.

Key: B = Bottom; M = Middle; L = Left; R = Right; T = Top

LITERARY

Hans-Werner Lerche, 76-79, English translation of magazine article appearing in Flug-Revue, May 1976.

PRODUCTION

Copy Editing: Cecilia E. Thurlow, Barbara W. Hitchcock; Layout Design Assistant: Mark Abair; Formatting: Steve Hussey. Jacket mechanicals: MBI Graphics.